HOME DESIGN IDEAS

HOME DESIGN IDEAS
HOW TO PLAN AND DECORATE A BEAUTIFUL HOME

Caroline Clifton-Mogg   Joanna Simmons   Rebecca Tanqueray

RYLAND
PETERS
& SMALL

LONDON NEW YORK

A CIP record from this book is available from the British Library.

Library of Congress Cataloging-in-Publication Data

Clifton-Mogg, Caroline.
  Home design ideas : how to plan and decorate a beautiful home / Caroline Clifton-Mogg, Joanna Simmons, Rebecca Tanqueray.
    p. cm.
  Includes index.
  ISBN 978-1-84597-750-4 -- ISBN 978-1-84597-751-1
  1. Interior decoration. I. Simmons, Joanna. II. Tanqueray, Rebecca. III. Title.
  NK2115.C735 2008
  747--dc22

2008021895

Designer   Paul Tilby
Senior editor   Clare Double
Picture research   Emily Westlake
Production manager   Patricia Harrington
Art director   Leslie Harrington
Publishing director   Alison Starling
Text by Caroline Clifton-Mogg, Joanna Simmons and Rebecca Tanqueray.

First published in the UK in 2008
by Ryland Peters & Small
20–21 Jockey's Fields
London WC1R 4BW

and in the US by Ryland Peters & Small, Inc.
519 Broadway, 5th Floor
New York, NY 10012
www.rylandpeters.com
10 9 8 7 6 5 4 3 2 1

UK ISBN: 978 1 84597 751 1
US ISBN: 978 1 84597 750 4

Printed and bound in China.

The publishers cannot accept liability for any injury, damage or loss to person or property, direct or inconsequential, arising from suggestions made in this book. The publishers recommend that any structural, electrical or plumbing work is carried out by a qualified professional.

contents

INTRODUCTION	6
KITCHENS by Caroline Clifton-Mogg	8
LIVING ROOMS by Caroline Clifton-Mogg	50
BEDROOMS by Joanna Simmons	90
BATHROOMS by Rebecca Tanqueray	122
CHILDREN'S ROOMS by Joanna Simmons	154
HOME OFFICES by Rebecca Tanqueray	188
OPEN-PLAN LIVING by Rebecca Tanqueray	210
OUTDOOR LIVING by Joanna Simmons	224
Stockists	240
Credits	244
Index	252

introduction

The way your home looks and feels is important. If you don't feel comfortable at home, you don't feel truly yourself, so reinventing your space to suit the way you want to live can have a profound impact.

This book will help you with interior design challenges large and small, from big decisions like colours and flooring materials to the little details that make a house your home. This could mean always having a strong light to read a book by, enough work space in the kitchen to enjoy cooking, and plenty of room for your shoe collection, among other things – and whether you are planning a major decorating blitz or just want to organize your space more efficiently, *Home Design Ideas* is here to help.

Every area of your home, including the outside space, is covered here. Initial planning and thinking about what you want in each room is often the key to decorating success, so every chapter begins with thoughts on design, decoration and planning, and guides you through thinking about how you want to live in each room – for example how to accommodate all the family's needs. Practical issues such as flooring and lighting are then discussed, including a section of helpful key points. At the end of each chapter you'll find a selection of styles for that room, offering an inspirational picture gallery and plenty of expert advice on how to achieve each look.

The book is designed so that each article is a complete resource. If you just want kitchen flooring, for example, you don't need to read the whole Kitchens chapter but go straight to the relevant page. Whether you are decorating your first home or you're a serial renovator, have fun putting your home together with *Home Design Ideas*.

kitchens

ABOVE LEFT Simple and functional, this small kitchen with pure white walls has striking white-glazed ceramics as decorative punctuation.

ABOVE RIGHT A country kitchen, complete with range, is decorated in a manner that is true to its origins, including still life paintings, decorated crockery and even an oversized wicker hamper.

OPPOSITE Careful thought has achieved the successful integration of a kitchen into part of a flamboyantly decorated larger room. Colour is the key, and the bright colours of the furnishings and accessories in the living area are reflected in the palette of reds and violets used on the kitchen doors and drawers, as well as key accessories.

design & decoration

The design and decoration of what is often the most important, and certainly the hardest-working, room in the house is a matter to be carefully pondered; forethought is the answer.

The kitchen has long outgrown its original role as merely the place where food is prepared and cooked. These days it is a room for leisure and pleasure as well as the place where most entertaining is done, all of which means that its design and decoration are crucial. The kitchen is also a very personal room, in which you can spend a lot of time, so when you are there you should feel at ease.

The actual design of your kitchen – the style of kitchen, units and appliances – will, to a certain extent, inform the decoration of the room, so it is sensible to

think of these aspects at the same time, rather than superimposing one style upon another at a later date.

Many kitchens today are a smallish part of a greater whole. If that is the case, the design of the kitchen area must work with the overall design, and feel, of the larger room; a work area of metallic, minimalist design would look out of place in a room that was otherwise decorated with old pine furniture, for example. Even if the kitchen is a separate room, there should still be a stylistic link between it and the next room, to ensure continuity of design.

planning

Planning is the keystone of successful interior design and nowhere more so than in the kitchen, where an efficient working system of some sort, no matter how loosely defined, is absolutely essential.

Getting the kitchen right, whether it is large or small, is so important. Whether you are buying the complete kitchen from one company, or incorporating pieces from different places, a kitchen is expensive to buy and install, and as you spend a great deal of time there it not only warrants, but really requires, effort during the early stages. There are professional kitchen planners, of course, but even the best of them needs help from the most important person in the equation – you – for no one understands how to plan a kitchen better than he or she who will use it.

When thinking about how to plan for what you want, if it seems hard to decide exactly what you need, start from the other end of the scale and make a list of what you positively don't want, need or like; everyone has strong views on kitchens – not enough work space, fridge in the wrong place and so on – but you don't always remember such minus points when making your own plans.

Although it is often-repeated advice, the first step is to look at photos of kitchens in magazines, supplements and, of course, in books. It is here that you will find not

ABOVE LEFT A freestanding kitchen of traditional mien, with a retro-style cooker, a butcher's block on castors, and the most traditional touch of all – linen curtains below the work surfaces, which hide utensils and equipment.

ABOVE RIGHT Neutral colours make a kitchen look not only large but workmanlike. This is a classically designed space with simple cupboards, open shelves, and as much worktop as anyone could ask, stretching around the room.

OPPOSITE A well-planned kitchen is not necessarily a complicated one. At one end of this Danish kitchen is an oversized antique table, in the centre is the cooking island with storage beneath, and against the far wall are the sink and dishwasher. Work surfaces abound, and storage is arranged on simple shelves and in low-level cupboards.

only the overview, but also the cunning solutions and clever details – the sort of innovative ideas, particularly in storage and arrangement of space, that have been thought through by professionals and described in detail on the page. These are the things you might not think of yourself, but once you know, many of them can be incorporated, even in modified form, into your design.

Another obvious but really useful idea is to look at friends' kitchens. Ask them why they like – or don't like – their own efforts and what they would change or never replace. Finally, if you can, get to some kitchen showrooms to look at display layouts – you may pick up many useful ideas, not least in the area of finish and colour. The more of this research that you do, the clearer will be the picture in your own mind of what you want, and there's no better place to start than that.

adapting an existing kitchen

Not everyone has the luxury of being able to design a kitchen from scratch, but the kitchen you've got doesn't necessarily have to stay as you found it.

First identify precisely which elements of the kitchen don't work for you. They may be major disadvantages – poor siting of major or plumbed appliances – or relatively minor (ugly cupboard fronts). Make a note of everything you don't like, then assess what the solutions might be. Major upheavals, such as moving units, should be carefully costed first to see whether they are worth the bother and expense, or if it would be better to start from scratch.

Cosmetic changes are worth doing, if only to alter your attitude to the room. First consider paint: all wooden doors can be painted in tough, good-looking finishes. New cupboard fronts, ready- or custom-made, come in materials from laminate and vinyl to painted MDF and solid wood, and in many designs; so do worktops and splashbacks. For an easy transformation, fit new handles.

ABOVE **The virtues of paint are well demonstrated here: in an old-fashioned but charming kitchen, the original wooden units and cupboards and the walls have been brought together with a subtle and considered scheme of neutral, soft colours.**

ABOVE RIGHT **A narrow kitchen has been given a soignée look with understated cupboard and drawer fronts that unite the whole.**

OPPOSITE **One of the most effective ways of transforming an existing kitchen is to install** new work surfaces. Surfaces made of wood are always good-looking and the choice in finishes is wide; some companies make wooden upstands that fit into the space behind and between the worktop and the wall, adding a neat finish to the installation.

fitted versus unfitted

ABOVE LEFT A fitted kitchen in a classic design that combines wood, paint, a small table and an abundance of decorative accessories, to create a style that is timeless.

ABOVE RIGHT Unfitted with a fitted touch: freestanding appliances and a full-sized table are united by a run of fitted units – albeit in an antique pine finish.

RIGHT As sleek and up to date as you could wish, this L-shaped kitchen of white laminated units, intersected by a section of black lacquer, epitomizes the fitted kitchen at its monochrome best.

OPPOSITE An intriguing, and successful, combination of the very rustic – sealed stone walls, ancient cupboard doors and garden table and chairs – mixed with contemporary brushed-steel appliances.

For many, the initial choice of kitchen is between the fitted – a structured arrangement of units – or the unfitted, a freestanding, less structured arrangement.

The kitchen usually has to be designed to fit the space allocated for it, rather than vice versa, so in many cases a fitted kitchen is the only practicable answer. In a larger space, however, a design of freestanding pieces – or one encompassing fitted and freestanding – may be preferred, particularly if the kitchen is to be part of a living space.

Which direction you choose may depend on the ease with which you can combine the functions of a kitchen – preparation, cooking and cleaning – into a sensible 'work triangle', the phrase used to describe the arranging of the separate kitchen elements into a manageable, efficient layout that flows between the different workstations.

Fitted kitchens might be the narrow galley kitchen, or a larger, rectangular version; they might be L- or U-shaped, often with an island or peninsular unit, which can add an unfitted flexibility to the design. Unfitted kitchens, because of their more fluid perimeters, are often more successful as part of a larger space, where their blend of styles works with a more eclectic mix of design and decoration.

THIS PAGE **A tiny corner of an open-plan apartment has been converted into an ultra-efficient kitchen, complete with breakfast bar. The cooking features are sited on one side, while the plumbing is concealed against the other.**

galleys & small spaces

In converted flats or houses, in particular, there is often only a small space in which a kitchen can be installed, and it is here that the galley kitchen comes into its own.

ABOVE LEFT AND RIGHT A minute L-shaped kitchen, cunningly designed into a mezzanine space and abutting onto a window, conceals all necessary appliances, from refrigerator to dishwasher, behind brushed-steel doors. This compact kitchen is a more than perfect solution for a hitherto unused space.

RIGHT The space leading to an entrance is often ignored; a discreet galley kitchen can add another function to an otherwise underused area.

CENTRE RIGHT Integrated into a larger space, this corner kitchen is designed so that everything functional can be hidden behind cupboard doors that are part of the greater stylistic scheme.

FAR RIGHT The dead space beneath a staircase is always a good area in which to install a small and practical kitchen-in-a-cupboard.

At its most confined, the galley kitchen can be one wall with all appliances, plumbing and storage along it; at the next remove, there may be a further area or opposite wall in which some elements can find a home. Often created out of a corridor, the galley kitchen may seem small, but some of the most efficient and easiest kitchens designed are galleys – everything is conveniently within reach.

In such a confined space, it is important to use every inch of height and depth to create enough storage. If your kitchen is situated in a corridor, or an almost-corridor, extend shelves and cupboards up towards the ceiling, to store what could be called the fish kettle collection – those utensils you don't use every day, but are essential sometimes. And in a small area, remember that good ventilation is vital. Spend money on an efficient cooker hood and other feats of smell-reducing technology.

large kitchens

A large kitchen might seem an unbelievable luxury, and in truth it is, but just as in a small kitchen, much care is needed to work out how best to use the space.

ABOVE LEFT **In a period house, a large kitchen that is part old, part new: the cooking area, which houses a contemporary hob and oven surrounded by decorative antique crockery and pans, is separated from the rest of the room by an antique shop counter that abuts a wooden column.**

ABOVE RIGHT **In a large period apartment, the cooking area is housed against the far wall, balanced by a wall of storage as well as a good-sized dining table and a comfortable sofa.**

RIGHT **A large kitchen, whose size is emphasized by the use of commanding furniture such as the antique armoire.**

OPPOSITE **An old-fashioned, large kitchen in the best sense. The luxury of space is used to display and store everything in useful order.**

However large the kitchen, it is still important to keep the actual work area relatively compact and efficient; there is little point in having the cooking zone yards from the preparation area. Instead, use the space for worktop features – a granite surface for pastry- and bread-making; endgrain maple for chopping; a small, inset sink for preparing vegetables; or a specialist hob. A larger room means that you can have bigger equipment as well – an oversized fridge-freezer, a wine cooler or a walk-in larder.

An island unit is a good idea here, as it breaks up the space in a practical and aesthetic manner, creating a demarcation line between the functional and hospitable activities of the same room. The unit can have stools against it facing the preparation area, and might even house a hob and sink so the cook can face the room.

LEFT This is a busy kitchen; on one side of the island unit – which runs the length of the units on the outside wall – all is concerned with cooking and eating. On the other side, from the bar stools lined up against the countertop to the comfortable chairs around the extendable table, the room has been designed for sociable family life.

RIGHT This is a kitchen which can expand when required; a refectory table, benches and stools are ready for work or play, and large glass double doors, which bring extra light into the existing space, lead out into a new living area outside, which, when required, increases the available living area enormously.

fitting in the family

It has been interesting to see, over the last few years, the extent to which so many kitchens have become family rooms, rather than merely rooms for preparing food.

The ideal family kitchen is one in which other activities can take place alongside the traditional kitchen tasks of food preparation and cooking. It is somewhere all members of the family want to spend time comfortably – whether chatting, sharing a drink, reading or even doing homework. Where there is the space, the kitchen can be a real family centre.

If the kitchen is a large one, then it is a question of dividing its functions in a way that is both practical and aesthetically pleasing, perhaps using an island unit to demarcate the different areas. If, however, the kitchen is relatively small, then – where it is feasible – think of bringing an adjoining room into play, either by removing an internal wall to make one large room or, less drastically, to enlarge the existing doorway between the two, and then visually linking the two areas with wall colour and co-ordinated flooring.

The best family kitchens have comfortable seating – an armchair, sofa or upholstered bench – with adequate lighting so books may be read without strain. Above all, they need lots of clever storage; if you want children to do their homework, or play, at the kitchen table, then they should be able to get at equipment they need easily and without fuss.

LEFT In a Manhattan apartment, one end of the room is taken up with a well-designed cooking area, with an island unit that holds a second sink; there are two seating areas – bar stools in front of the island and, at right angles, a full-length table which seats the family in comfort.

BELOW LEFT The simplest of all country kitchens, with functional elements around the sides of the room and an unadorned table that dominates the central space.

BELOW RIGHT The decorative aspects of this kitchen are the first priority. A striking table and an oversized country cupboard are more important than the almost peripheral kitchen elements.

OPPOSITE A prime example of combining the eating and cooking elements of the room in perfect harmony. The cheerful polka-dot rug adds a touch of welcoming comfort.

dining areas within kitchens

With the gradual disappearance of the dining room, more and more kitchens do double duty as places where food is not only cooked but also enjoyed.

The idea of eating in the kitchen can only be welcomed, bringing as it does traditional hospitality into the heart of the home. There may not be room in a very small kitchen for a full, or even half-sized dining table, but a little lateral thinking will often provide ideas for somewhere to sit and eat in comfort. This might be a round table in a corner, which is also used to display bowls of fruit, decorative objects and flowers; or perhaps a banquette seat, with storage beneath, built into an alcove, and used with a narrow table that is pushed into the wall when not in use.

The closer the dining area is to the kitchen proper, the more important it is that the style of the kitchen should work with that of the dining space: cupboard fronts that smudge the line between function and decoration, and, behind the units, upstands in glass or wood rather than tiles or metal; open as well as closed storage so that utensils and artefacts can be on decorative display. Dining tables and chairs should also work with the kitchen. Finally, choose a dishwasher that is quiet!

If you are buying a large appliance such as a cooker or fridge, decide exactly what your budget is at the start, for this is an area where the cost can vary dramatically.

large appliances

Widely available on the market are simple and functional appliances at very reasonable cost; also easy to find are designs which cost more, but have additional design and function details and are often better made. Finally, there are what one might term the supermodels – designs that incorporate sophisticated technological advances with aesthetic subtlety: wine coolers with separate thermostatic controls for white and red wines; giant freezer-fridges; and freestanding freezer columns, with pillar-like freezer, fridge and wine cooler units that can be sited separately around the kitchen.

Cooking options range from a freestanding cooker combining a hob and one or two ovens, to individual hobs made in every size and every material from steel to ceramic, and individual ovens with an infinite variety of features, and powered by electricity or gas. Range cookers go from the traditional oil- or gas-fired designs to advanced electric cookers disguised within an antique façade.

OPPOSITE A powerful range-style cooker that makes no apologies for its presence; its combination of old and new means that it fits in well within a kitchen designed on contemporary country lines.

ABOVE RIGHT Sleek and modern stainless-steel appliances, and units finished in a complementary material, mean that the wall has a unified, simple look that belies the ample size of the cooker and fridge.

BELOW RIGHT On a wall of storage units, an unobtrusive wall-hung conventional oven and microwave have been fitted at exactly the right height for easy access.

BELOW For many people, nothing will ever replace the charm of the traditional British Aga, first produced in the Twenties. Its constant heat and comfortable lines, as well as its ability to provide hot water, make it still a necessity for many families, particularly in the country.

■ The internet really comes into its own when comparing prices and styles of large kitchen appliances. Research takes time, but the benefit of all this choice is that there really is a combination of appliances out there to suit every kitchen and every pocket.

■ Induction hobs can only be used with ferrous-based pans. If a magnet sticks to the base, they will work.

■ Among the modular hob options now available are barbecues, woks, deep-fat fryers and steamers.

■ Make sure that any glass-doored, built-in ovens are installed at a high enough level so that you can both see and move the contents with ease.

■ Take precise measurements of the space available before you order a new appliance. Many of the new designs are super-sized and too big for a conventional fitted kitchen.

■ In addition to a conventional fridge, a fridge drawer, which can be used to store everyday foods at a reasonable chilled temperature, can be an useful extra.

■ Traditionally, most sinks faced a window on an outside wall – both for the view and the drainage – but now it is possible to site a sink or sinks almost anywhere you need them.

■ In a small kitchen, instead of making room for a traditional dishwasher look at dishwasher drawers, which are literally that: housed in drawers, compact dishwashers that can be operated individually.

■ When thinking about where to install the dishwasher, consider situating it at eye level, rather than on the floor, particularly if you include in the design a crockery cupboard above for everyday china and glass.

■ If you choose a tap/faucet with a movable spout, make sure the spout is long enough to reach into the centre of the sink.

■ Teak worktops around the sink should be kept nourished and water-resistant with oil.

■ Double sinks work well as long as each sink is of a practical size.

■ A movable over-sink vegetable drainer or colander is a useful accessory.

■ A tap/faucet that dispenses boiling water is handy and more energy-efficient than boiling water in a kettle. You could also look at a filtered drinking water tap/faucet.

ABOVE In this unit, two pull-out dishwasher drawers are stacked one on top of the other, the advantage being that you can use one drawer on its own. The drawers are easy to stack and empty, too.

BELOW For many kitchen owners, a deep white enamel butler's, or Belfast, sink is the only possible solution in a country kitchen – deep enough for washing the largest home-grown produce.

OPPOSITE, ABOVE Deep double sinks in stainless steel with a stainless-steel surround are serviced with a single tap/faucet with swivelling spout. The streamlined design makes this sink easy to keep clean.

OPPOSITE, BELOW LEFT The most efficient design of tap/faucet is one like this, which has a control that can be pushed with the flat of the hand. The worktop and drainer are black granite.

OPPOSITE, BELOW RIGHT Copper sinks are striking, although they do require particular maintenance. A matching metallic mixer tap/faucet and toning wooden worktop complete the picture.

Plumbing. The very word makes people sigh, but it is particularly important to get it right in the kitchen, where so much depends on where and how water is used.

water ways

The first thing to remember about any plumbing is that, once it is in place, it is difficult and expensive to alter, so think carefully about what you want before you begin any work.

Every kitchen needs at least one sink; where it is positioned, and its size, is of vital importance to the layout. Choose as large and deep a sink as possible: so many items, from delicate china to roasting pans, can only be washed by hand. Plenty of draining room – preferably either side – is also a good idea. The best sink shape is based on the circular or the rectangular, depending on the configuration of the kitchen, and possible materials range from stainless steel to enamel (as in butler's sinks) or a composite.

A tap/faucet of fairly classical design, with a single mixer spout, works well at a kitchen sink, particularly if it has a movable spout. Finally, a dishwasher is energy-efficient, cleans well and holds plenty of dirty crocks. This is not a luxury; this is a necessity!

■ Technological advances mean that toughened glass can now be used as a finish in the kitchen, perhaps as a screen near the hob, on a counter, or used over a laminated surface.

■ Steel-fronted units give a professional finish and look best in a contemporary kitchen. Choose between matt brushed steel and more reflective stainless steel.

■ Most kitchens look best with a combination of materials or, in the case of an all-wood kitchen, with different varieties and cuts of wood used in contrast.

■ If you are linking a kitchen or cooking area with a dining area, rather than making one the mirror image of the other, just carry through one or two elements.

BELOW LEFT Tongue and groove wood, painted white, is the perfect backdrop for a country kitchen where simple white dishes are stored.

BELOW RIGHT A clean, modern combination of white laminated units with reflective toughened-glass worktops.

BOTTOM LEFT A kitchen with work surfaces and drawers all in brushed steel looks softer than one of stainless steel.

BOTTOM RIGHT A mix of hard-working, traditional materials – enamel sink, wooden base units and marble worktop.

RIGHT The suspended metal shelves make this kitchen both light and bright.

OPPOSITE A kitchen of warm wood might be overpowering were it not for the contrast of the brushed-steel appliances.

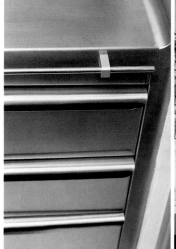

The choice of materials for the kitchen is as much to do with the kitchen's style as whether you prefer wood or metal.

materials

The materials that you choose for the units and worktops will depend, to a certain extent, on your preferred style or design, for the options are endless. For many, wood is the preferred material for base units – either in its solid form, with many varieties to choose from such as oak, cherry and beech to maple, iroko and walnut, or as a veneered finish on a composite core. Wood can also be painted, laminated and lacquered. There is a wide choice of other materials to combine with wood, used on countertops and working surfaces perhaps, but also as inset panels, upstands, screens and door fronts. Composite materials such as Corian are endlessly versatile, as are hard materials such as marble, slate and granite, which are useful next to a hob for hot pans as well as inset where a cool surface is required for bread- or pastry-making.

■ Using dimmers on more than one lighting circuit can be very useful in the kitchen, allowing you to vary the mood and intensity of light throughout the room.

■ If you have decorative displays of glass in the kitchen, consider back-lighting the whole unit.

■ Remember that even a room which receives enough natural light during the day will need specific task lighting in the evening, as well as ambient light.

■ Lighting today is both a science and an art; experts can design ambient lighting schemes that can simulate natural light at different times of day.

■ If you have a table in the kitchen, consider installing overhead pendant lights that can be raised or lowered as necessary.

LEFT A kitchen that combines different, contrasting light sources: inset downlighters over the working area and dramatic, steel-shaded pendant lights over the dining table.

OPPOSITE A large traditional kitchen with wall-hung wooden cupboards, which absorb rather than reflect light, requires strong lighting, and plenty of it, to illuminate the different areas. A row of metal-shaded lamps hung from a central beam gives overall light, while discreet downlighters (just seen top right) illuminate the island unit in the centre of the room.

BELOW Neat, classic swan-necked wall lights set above an open shelf illuminate the sink and draining area below.

The ideal kitchen has light streaming through a large window, with every surface lit to best advantage. But in the real world most kitchens require some degree of help. Getting the lighting right in the kitchen must be a priority, to be considered from the first, as part of the design.

lighting

Like the other rooms in the house, a combination of task and ambient lighting is best, from under-shelf strip lighting to illuminate the work surface below to adjustable swan-necked over-cabinet lighting. Task lighting should target specific close-working areas, with the light placed or directed in front of your body so that you are not working in your own shadow. Look at all the possible areas where it might be used: directed onto the cooker perhaps, the worktops and towards the fridge; strip lighting beneath wall units is useful, as is track lighting, to be positioned where needed. Press available natural light into service (make sure blinds/shades or curtains are washable – even with an extractor, grease will coat them). If your kitchen has little or no natural light, use light-reflecting colours and surfaces to maximize what you have and use back- and uplighters to create pools of light.

THIS PAGE **A terrazzo floor in a mottled finish brings a soft contrast to a kitchen area of severe lines, dominated by wooden units.**

OPPOSITE, LEFT **In a traditionally designed kitchen that leads into an airy dining room, the warm wooden floor is made of large planks, polished and sealed.**

OPPOSITE, RIGHT **Large stone tiles in pearl grey are in strong contrast to the dark, distressed blue of the island unit. The pale tones of the floor reflect light back into what would otherwise be a shady room.**

Flooring is an important element in the kitchen, so consider it in conjunction with the other decorative options.

flooring

The kitchen floor must work with the materials chosen for the units and appliances; it must also be comfortable to walk on, easy to clean and hardwearing, because kitchens are very high-traffic areas.

Wood is warm to look at and touch; it can be new or old, light or dark; it can be left in its natural state (but well sealed and finished) or stained or painted (this option requires particularly tough sealing).

Stone and marble, granite and slate look wonderful and last for ever, but can be cold underfoot and over a large area; underfloor heating might be a necessity. Ceramic tiles can also be cold. Terracotta, which works well in a country or traditional kitchen, looks and feels warmer than stone, is hard- and long-wearing and comes in machine- and handmade versions. The latter is more interesting in appearance, while the former often emulates an antique look.

Other natural flooring options include linoleum, cork and rubber, while synthetic floorings such as vinyl can now emulate almost any other material from wood to marble.

■ Decide early on the flooring material. The best time to lay any floor is when the room has been stripped out and the plastering and electrical work completed.

■ If you are combining a dining area with a kitchen, a sisal or seagrass square, rather than a more elaborate wool rug, would separate visually the eating area from the working one, without breaking up the space.

■ There is no need to limit the flooring options in the kitchen to one material; very often in the immediate vicinity of cooker and sink, for example, a harder-working finish is needed than elsewhere in the room. Options

might include linoleum combined with tiles, stone with wood or rubber with terracotta.

■ Rubber flooring can be bought on a roll and is a good-looking, inexpensive option.

■ The range of colours available in linoleum is wide. This natural material can also be precision cut and inlaid to create simple or complex designs, which could range from a geometric overall pattern to a design with a central motif and border.

■ Poured, polished concrete that has been coloured is a relatively inexpensive hard floor finish and can look extremely striking.

Everyone needs storage, and everyone needs storage in a kitchen most of all; the application of logic is often the solution.

storage

There is nothing more frustrating in a kitchen than not having a place for everything and everything in its place. Kitchen storage encompasses a variety of elements – there is food, fresh and dried or tinned; cooking equipment and utensils; and china and glass.

Much of this can be accommodated in conventional cupboards, both floor-standing and wall-hung. In truth, good kitchen storage is as much about logic as cupboard space. Group different functions and store them closest to that point. Saucepans should be close to the hob and oven, everyday china and glass close to the sink and dishwasher (a cupboard above the latter, perhaps), and perishable food should be ranged in a fridge and cupboards close to the preparation area. Large utensils not in use every day, and china and glass used for entertaining, can live in less accessible cupboards.

■ Many hobs are situated on their own separately from the oven, and there is therefore often room beneath for one or two deep drawers in which to store saucepans and casseroles without stacking them.

■ Rather than being kept in the fridge, root vegetables are best stored in a dark place in cane or wicker baskets, where air can circulate around them.

■ A wide shallow drawer close to the hob, with permanent or movable divisions inside, is perfect for unwieldy but essential utensils like spatulas, ladles and slotted spoons, and saves the worktop space a canister takes.

■ Make sure you install enough power points to keep kettles and toasters neatly in a corner of the work surface and ready for action.

THIS PAGE **A wall of storage, teamed with drawers at waist level, means that nothing need be on view in this kitchen until required. In one corner, a cupboard front slides up to reveal electrical equipment neatly tucked away.**

OPPOSITE, ABOVE LEFT **Simple hanging rails and shelves and a magnetic knife rack keep necessities close to hand.**

OPPOSITE, ABOVE RIGHT **Almost a storeroom, this wall of open storage holds everyday items at eye level and less-used crocks high and low.**

OPPOSITE, BELOW LEFT **A butcher's rail and hooks keep heavy pans and equipment close to hand above the sink.**

OPPOSITE, BELOW RIGHT **Decorative and practical, china is in easy reach in a glass-fronted cupboard.**

■ Finishing touches need not be tangible objects; bright accents of colour, like unit door panels painted in lime-green, yellow and orange, can personalize a working area.

■ If you eat in the kitchen, consider a shelf or space for books – reference books, in particular. They not only look friendly, they also serve a purpose, as questions of the who-what-when variety invariably come up over leisurely meals.

■ If you hanker after an iconic bit of kitchen equipment – such as a Dualit toaster or a state-of-the-art coffee machine – bite the bullet and buy it. It will last for years, and give you pleasure every time you look at it, and that is really the best sort of finishing touch.

■ Flowers in the kitchen are one of the most pleasing things, informally arranged and placed wherever there is room, whether on a shelf or a work surface.

ABOVE **Paint is used as a very personal finishing touch, as well as dramatically defining this narrow kitchen space; lateral bands of colour on the walls highlight the deliberate use of oranges for specific pieces of equipment and together immediately make the area both larger and brighter.**

LEFT **Whether it's the thought that having an Aga is as much fun as being at the beach, or a reminder of sunny days when there is no need to huddle round the range, the golden letters are both striking and funny.**

OPPOSITE **The traditional wooden Welsh dresser is the ultimate finishing touch, the friendly comforting piece of furniture for every bit of decorative detail that you care about and want on show. And, as an ever-changing seasonal display, it neatly combines the decorative with the functional.**

Finishing touches to the kitchen are those which make it individual, and set it aside from the showroom model; decorative and design extras that make a room stand out.

finishing touches

Finishing touches in this space are all a question of detail. They are the thought-out personal additions that mark the room as your own. Design details lift something standard to a different level; they are the carefully considered mouldings round an open storage unit, the bull-nose edging on a marble countertop, the metal rods for hot pans set into a wooden work surface next to a hob, the standard wine rack cut down to go into a dead space in a corner. Ideas like these can be found in kitchen showrooms, magazines and – yes! – books, and are often worth incorporating at comparatively little cost.

Then there are the decorative details. Here is where it pays to be bold. Consider using unusual paint colours, or objects and pictures that you arrange with care around the room in unexpected corners; these are striking and unusual additions that not only mark the room as yours but which add an air of hospitality and welcome to others.

The country kitchen could almost be called a state of mind. Espousing the traditional and the comfortable, it is as at home in the inner city as down a country lane.

country kitchens

■ A country kitchen is the ideal place to incorporate old pieces of wooden furniture; a pine chest of drawers for pans and linens, or an antique armoire for just about everything from china and glass to food storage.

■ Combine storage and display in open wooden shelving, with cup hooks for cloths, cups and utensils – a cheap and effective way to get the look.

■ For paint, go for either light clear colours or shades taken from one of the many widely available ranges of historical colours.

■ Collect odd and interesting bits to use as decoration – old kitchen utensils can be found in junk and antique shops, as can small, quirky pictures and eccentric prints.

■ Rather than being hidden away, food is often out on display in the country kitchen, as are china, glass and equipment – a traditional dresser is the perfect display case for them.

When people say they want a country kitchen, what exactly do they mean? First of all, the materials used are important – in most people's minds, a country kitchen does not glitter with stainless steel and Perspex (although state-of-the-art gadgets are definitely not banned; they are usually concealed behind cupboard doors). The materials of country choice are traditional – predominantly wood, used everywhere from floor to units and sometimes on the walls, as well as for many of the utensils. Stone in all its guises, from slate to York, is also employed for many of the hard surfaces, as are earthenware and enamelling. A country kitchen is not a Luddite kitchen, however. There may be a silent dishwasher as well as a large refrigerator (which will often, if there is enough space, be kept in a pantry alcove or room). Although there may be a contemporary hob, for many people the country kitchen is tied up with the idea of a cooking range, with all its warm and welcoming associations. Traditionally heated by wood, solid fuel, or oil, ranges are now more often fired by electricity or gas, and many incorporate modern innovations (although all such are usually enclosed in a traditional outer case).

What there will also nearly always be in this country kitchen is colour, on the woodwork and on the walls. It will probably not be very strong colour, even almost imperceptible colour, and if it is on the wood it may well be distressed either naturally or with the help of a little elbow grease. But it will be there and it will be accentuated by the colours of the objects that country kitchen owners, as a breed, like to collect – they will be both decorative and also useful, ranging from pictures to pails, and sometimes old, and sometimes new, but always with a traditional feel or appearance.

Above all, country kitchens exude warmth – there really is no such thing as a cold country kitchen. When people wish for the style, they are saying that they want a kitchen that is friendly and hospitable, that exudes an air of comfort and, even more importantly, of warmth.

Creating a retro kitchen gives you the chance to indulge a taste for mid-century modern style, combined with the best of today's kitchen technology.

retro-style kitchens

When applied to interior decoration, the term 'retro style' is pretty open-ended. To some it means anything designed in the mid-20th century; to others it is the style between the Thirties and Seventies; to yet others, it is very specifically the Fifties and Sixties. But although there may be confusion about the actual dates, aficionados agree that retro style in general describes the period when 'modern' design was in the ascendant, with its characteristic clean lines, bold colour and pattern, and use of exciting new materials like plastic.

Today, unless you want to recreate in its totality a slice of 20th-century domestic life, your retro-style kitchen will probably be a room that shows off some of the best of 20th-century design combined with 21st-century technology. In design terms, it will be fitted, obviously – this was the period when the only kitchen to have was a fitted one – and rectangular of line. Somewhere there will be refreshingly bold colour and a few semi-iconic pieces of furniture, such as a chrome-legged bar stool or moulded plastic chair. These pieces, very much of their time, remind one how powerful the design movement of the mid-20th century was.

Accessories might include some fabulous glass and ceramics of the period, or bright melamine kitchen pieces. In a retro-style kitchen, as background to the furniture and accessories, you could recreate what were known as feature walls: one wall covered in a large-scale, dramatic wallpaper, or an eye-catching paint colour – lime-green, bright orange or chocolate brown. You could feature ceramics and plastic in a specific display or mix them in with more contemporary pieces.

■ The cheapest way to get a sense of a retro-style scheme is with paint colour; bright walls (think bowls of citrus fruits) and white units. Mix the colours up and temper them with brilliant white – no subtle off-key colours here!

■ This could be the moment and the place for a lava lamp – the instantly recognizable rocket cone of glass filled with moving swirling patterns. First designed in 1963, they are still made by the original company, Mathmos.

■ Retro-style accessories can be found in abundance in specialist shops, second-hand at auction and of course on the internet. Look out for original ceramics, glass, textiles and lighting to add finishing touches.

■ Twentieth-century design was liberating and fun, so the most important thing in your retro-style kitchen should be that the finished result not only looks fun, but is fun – both for you and your friends.

As its name implies, stainless steel is a most durable material, and it is associated with the professional chef. He who chooses such a style is often an accomplished cook. Perhaps because of its finish, the material implies a sense of order, and is particularly effective used in a large open area, where it becomes part of the architecture of the place, blending in a way that other materials do not.

The stainless-steel kitchen is not cosy – it is the antithesis of the country kitchen – and is not a repository for nostalgic artefacts. It makes a statement, is chic and sophisticated, and is a space for the contemporary purist who wishes for cleanliness and uncluttered surfaces.

For some, an all-stainless-steel kitchen, gleaming in its shining, reflective glory, can be a bit too much of a good thing, and many designers prefer the finish and texture of brushed steel as a less reflective and a softer look.

Because stainless steel is such a dominant material, many designers temper it with other elements – in particular, wood – mixing base and wall-hung units, or using steel appliances cased in wood, a felicitous combination that is both contemporary and easy to live with. Warm, mid-toned woods such as beech and maple work best, as their golden tones are reflected in the steel's mirror surface. It is this reflective quality that makes stainless steel a good material to have in a dark kitchen, as the finish will bounce back any available natural light.

A kitchen reflects how you wish, in culinary terms, to be seen by the world. The stainless-steel kitchen is very much the preferred style of the serious cook.

stainless-steel kitchens

■ Looking after a stainless-steel kitchen is not difficult; the surfaces need to be washed down with soapy water or diluted white vinegar. With time, the material develops a patina and therefore a resistance to fingerprints and grease marks.

■ Remember that chopping boards are necessities on stainless-steel worktops.

■ If you are unsure about committing to the entire steel experience, try out the look first with just a touch – a row of saucepans on a shelf or a small steel-finished appliance such as a food processor or a kettle.

■ Although not all of them have a polished finish, industrial fittings in steel can make interesting and bargain additions to an unfitted kitchen. Look online for companies that make freestanding pieces for restaurant kitchens and hospitals, such as catering sinks, tables, worktops and workbenches.

When the first fitted kitchens were introduced, they came – rather like Henry Ford's first cars – in one colour only, but unlike the famous black cars, these early kitchens were white. White was the colour of modernity and of progress; it represented cleanliness, efficiency and hygiene.

With time came choice and change, and kitchens, fitted or unfitted, began to be produced in many other colours and finishes; but, for many people and in many settings, the white kitchen still reigns supreme.

The thing about white is that it is a style, not a colour; far from being fashionable, and therefore in or out, white is beyond fashion, and its very versatility gives it the edge over many other styles and designs.

White is right for a super-contemporary, high-lacquered, technological dream kitchen, and it is just as right for a classic, functional practical room. It works admirably in a comfortable country kitchen that is part living room and part cooking zone, and it is the perfect way to unite the disparate elements of an unfitted kitchen, where you may have some freestanding pieces of furniture mixed with more conventional fitted units.

White has an easy ability to blend in to the background when required, and for that reason works very well as part of a larger open-plan living space where it will not vie for attention with stronger architectural elements.

It also, conversely, is often the colour of choice for a small kitchen, where it opens up the space and makes it appear larger. And, for the same reasons, white is the ideal colour for a dark kitchen; white's light-reflecting qualities mean that it collects all available natural light and throws it back into the room. A glossy reflective finish will obviously bounce back more light than a matt texture, and a light-toned floor will take the process further.

If you are updating an old or tired kitchen, one of the simplest and often cheapest tricks is to buy replacement doors for base and wall-hung units; if they are painted white wood, the improvement will be tangible.

White is infinitely adaptable. It works with small kitchens and works with large. White works with old kitchens and, yes, it also works with new!

the white stuff

■ If you are installing a new kitchen on a tight budget, a simple white kitchen will make the most of your money as well as look good. Go for plain units without excess decoration, keep details such as handles and taps/faucets as simple as possible and choose a warm wooden work surface.

■ Make sure that any dining table and chairs work with the style of the white kitchen; polished wood is a perfect foil for an otherwise white background.

■ There are cool whites and there are warm whites, with many variations in each group. Your choice of palette might well be influenced by how much sun your kitchen gets each day.

■ If the kitchen leads into a dining area, continue the white palette through but use different, richer tones within the same palette. You can also add textural interest with fabrics and furnishings, to mark the contrasting functions of the spaces.

■ Enough storage for non-cooking equipment is important in a family-friendly kitchen – drawers where paper, pens and pencils can be kept, shelves where books and magazines can rest undisturbed.

■ Adaptable, portable storage is useful when a room has several different functions and uses: deep baskets are a good idea, where toys and other necessities can easily be stored when the function of the room changes at different times of day.

■ The right lighting is important – adjustable, specific task lights, but also enough ambient lighting to change the mood from that of function to that of leisure.

■ Make sure there is easy access to everyday glasses, cups and mugs that does not necessitate general upheaval in the food preparation area.

■ The family-friendly kitchen is always a place for pictures and photographs, whether they are hung on walls or propped on shelves.

The kitchen as the hearth of the family home is not new. From medieval Great Halls to farmhouse kitchens, for centuries family life centred here.

family-friendly kitchens

It was the rapid growth of cities in the 19th century that saw the kitchen relocated to somewhere below stairs in the new, narrow houses built in long terraces in every town. Now, two centuries later, new living patterns and a generally more informal way of life mean that once again the kitchen is being seen as a room that should play a central role in the everyday life of the family.

It makes sense, in so many ways, for the kitchen, particularly a larger kitchen, to be the centre of the domestic web. Few of us want separate dining rooms, so moving a table into, or just beyond, the kitchen makes sense. Once there is a table, what better place to do homework, read the paper or sit and chat? In a kitchen that cannot fit in a conventional table, an island unit or bar with stools at one side facing into the cooking area plays much the same role, connecting the functional and social aspects of the room – both a vital part of family life.

A family-friendly kitchen should not be too clinical in design; colour and decoration make it a welcoming place. If there is enough space, some of the accoutrements of the traditional living room could be included – not to replace the living room, but to extend it – such as a comfortable armchair or, even better, a small sofa and shelves for books. All these things bring people together, and that surely is what being family-friendly is all about.

living rooms

THIS PAGE **A room designed for Sunday afternoons, furnished with comfortable sofa and chairs, log basket fully stacked, and board games and books at the ready.**

design & decoration

Ideally, the living room is the place where all the family comes together. It is neutral territory – somewhere all can spend time, together or alone, and its design, decoration and arrangement should reflect its multi-faceted nature.

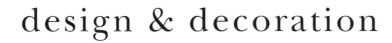

The design of this central room is very important, for the living room, for better or worse, makes the strongest impression on others. Gimlet-eyed visitors will notice the colours that you have chosen, the pieces of furniture you have bought, and the way that you have arranged them. They will look at where you have put your pictures, books and music. In short, they will check out how you live.

To make matters more complicated, it is vital that the design of the living room represents, as well as the views of others, the likes and dislikes of the people who use it most. It should accommodate the daily needs of all its occupants, and be somewhere both peaceful and convivial pleasures can be enjoyed, from reading to giving a party. It may also double as a study and eating area, all of which is a great deal of work for one room.

The essence of good design lies in careful planning, which we explore over the page, but in general terms both the design and decoration of a living room should be neither too dramatic nor too specific, interesting of course, but above all both comfortable and welcoming.

TOP LEFT In a bay of windows a comfortable daybed is arranged facing the landscape, next to a table for books and refreshment.

ABOVE LEFT An architecturally ordinary living room is transformed into a quirky and comfortable space by the introduction of a kaleidoscope of print and pattern covering the large comfortable sofas, the cushions and even the chimneybreast.

ABOVE RIGHT The essence of comfort in this corner of a living room, with two low-backed comfortable armchairs, covered in a practical check with two warm, matching throws – ready for immediate use.

LEFT A large, luxurious living room in Paris has been created from what were originally two small rooms and a corridor that ran down one side. Great attention has been taken to make sure that the overall proportions of the new room, particularly the doors and windows, are to scale. There are two focal points: one facing the fireplace, the other a group of sofa and chairs.

BELOW A traditional 19th-century living room with high ceilings and tall windows is arranged and furnished to show the classical proportions and design at their best.

OPPOSITE This pretty sitting room has been planned with the fireplace as the focal point, and all the seating arranged around it. The fireplace and chimneybreast are balanced by the imposing doors at the other end of the room, which lead to the kitchen and eating area.

planning

Before you immerse yourself in choosing the colours and materials, furniture and furnishings for your new living room, the first and possibly most essential task is to plan the room, both in the broadest of terms, as well as, if possible, the finest of details.

Whether your living room is pint-sized or oversized, getting the proportions and scale right are all-important. This means choosing correctly scaled furniture for the room, and arranging both the large and the small pieces in the most pleasing and practical way. Decide on what functions you want the room to have. What sort of furniture will you need? What seating? What tables? What storage and what decoration? Everything in the room should balance; there should be equal densities, equal masses of weight.

Every room needs a focal point – possibly two if the room is large. The fireplace is a traditional and natural focal point, and still works well. Be wary of designating the TV a focus – rather, use a round central table with one or two chairs, or a sofa and armchairs around a lower table. Other areas should be linked to the focal point, both visually and practically – you must be able to walk through the room without bumping into anything.

If you are of a practical nature, make a floor plan showing any built-in features, then use approximate shapes to plot the best positions for furniture. It's easy to do and gives a visual sense of the room in a way that is difficult to achieve by writing things on a list.

OPPOSITE A clever use of the often dead space found beneath a flight of stairs. In the angle of the stairs is a comfortable, built-in, cushioned seat, with useful cupboards beneath, and running along the wall into the space is a set of open display and bookshelves that serves to extend the room's length.

RIGHT A room that could appear both long and narrow is transformed by the use of substantial pieces of antique furniture that add an immediate air of comfort and ease by breaking up the space, thus visually altering its proportions.

BELOW A cottage living room dominated by the old fireplace and stove has been made appealing through simplicity: importantly, comfortable chairs and sofas draped with throws, coupled with white-painted shutters and a chest used as a table.

adapting an existing living room

When an existing, not-quite-perfect living room has to be adapted to suit different demands and needs, lateral design thinking is often required.

How nice it would be if every living room were exactly the right size, the right proportions, with a place for everything and ready for instant occupation – but that is rarely the case.

The first thing to do is to evaluate what cannot be changed, whether for reasons of finance or structure; these will usually be architectural features such as windows, doors and load-bearing walls. Although you may not be able to change them, you may well be able to disguise, hide or adapt, and this is where the lateral thinking comes in. Doors, for instance, that lead nowhere or are too numerous can be permanently closed, and hung with pictures or hidden with a piece of furniture in front; windows can appear smaller or taller with the clever use of blinds/shades, or curtains that are hung beyond or within the area of glass. Difficult corners and angles can be made into shelved areas or cupboards, which can be built to correct ungainly proportions. Furniture changes the visual proportions of a long thin room; for example, if pieces are arranged across the width of the space, rather than down its length. Lastly, do not underestimate the importance of an unbiased eye: a friend, whose taste you rate, will often point out a way of dealing with a problem.

fitting in the family

Family life means family compromise and a willingness to be adaptable – virtues that are necessary, not only in personal relations, but also, more prosaically, in practical living terms.

It is likely that this room must encompass the varying interests of several family members – which can seem difficult. But with a bit of thought most rooms can work very successfully in more than one way. This doesn't mean a corner for each person like a giant game of forfeits, but planning the room around everyone's preferences.

Flexibility of furniture and the arrangement of space is part of the answer; tables that are the right height to work at, modular seating units that can be reconfigured to suit the occasion, and low upholstered units that can work as stools or low tables are some of the possible options.

Furniture solutions should be coupled with the right storage, which can be as simple as boxes and baskets, or as complicated as custom-designed show pieces. Open units that are deep enough to hold books, DVDs and CDs, perhaps with adjustable shelves, are relatively simple to find. Another idea is to group similar elements

together – toys, for instance, are best kept in one place where they can easily be found and put away. Such small things bring continuity to a space and mean that the room works as one whole rather than several disparate parts.

ABOVE CENTRE **A football table cannot easily be hidden; better by far to make it an integral – and fun – part of living-room life, merely distancing it partly from the rest of the room behind a freestanding bookcase.**

BELOW **Both music lovers and readers like to have their collections close to hand and ranged in order; adjustable shelving built along a fireplace wall is an effective solution.**

ABOVE LEFT **The ultimate combination-of-interests living room. At one side of the wooden-floored room, which also has comfortable chairs for reading, a net has been attached to the wall for shooting practice, and a tub holds other sports equipment.**

ABOVE RIGHT **Wooden floors, along which furniture, equipment and playthings can be moved, are much easier in a multi-purpose room than wall-to-wall carpet. A simple combination of shelving and deep cupboards at floor level, which also provide an extra display surface, make this a room that can easily switch from one mode to another.**

THIS PAGE **For all this room's evident sophistication and urbanity, it is in fact adaptable to a degree; no piece of furniture is built in, and the sweeping sofa is a combination of units that can be used in different ways. Rugs can be rolled up, stools and tables shifted – the whole space can be reconfigured.**

technology

There is no escaping technology in the 21st-century home. The only question is how to house it and use it.

The good thing about what one might call leisure technology today is that the designs themselves are so much better-looking than they once were: television screens are flatter, thinner and less obtrusive; CD and DVD players are neater and smaller. The bad thing is that there is far more of it about and many of us want our living rooms to be the home for the screen, DVD player and games console as well as some sort of music centre.

The decision, which ideally should be made when you are planning the room so that all necessary cables can be discreetly hidden, is whether to reveal or conceal and, if so, how? Concealing a television screen is simple – install it in a cupboard, either especially made or an old piece converted, or – a decorator's trick – by installing a hinged or sliding mechanism that suspends a painting in front of the screen and pivots or slides to reveal the screen.

The other (easier) option is simply to install it unapologetically, on a wall, set into a storage unit or sat on a surface of the right height. Ensure that wherever and however you place it, it is easily accessed and watched. No one wants to move furniture to get to the television.

OPPOSITE **Simple, unapologetic and effective. A built-in wall of storage that incorporates the screen in an open alcove, with a cupboard beneath that houses all the necessary technological extras from remote controls to discs.**

RIGHT **Revealed and concealed: the screen has been installed on the wall but in an unobtrusive position, with all wires hidden and partly hidden by old beams; modern it might be, but its simplicity is perfectly in keeping with both the furniture and decoration of this period house.**

ABOVE LEFT **One of the most successful ways to incorporate a television set into a living room is to find a home for it among the books. On a wall of shelves, this screen is easily accessible and yet does not dominate, competing for attention as it does with a library of volumes.**

ABOVE RIGHT **No attempt at concealment here; a handsome, freestanding set lives on a purpose-designed unit with castors, which means that set and stand can be easily moved.**

furniture

All living rooms need furniture, but that does not mean that any old thing will do. Some unfortunate examples, instead of appearing welcoming and comfortable havens, seem on first glance more like burial grounds for unwanted and unloved pieces.

Of course it is essential to have furniture, but it is also essential to have the right pieces of furniture – from the seating and occasional tables to lamps and objects – and all must be chosen with due regard to their place in this most important of rooms.

Seating comes first, naturally, and what works best here is usually a combination of styles and designs, to accommodate different situations and people. Personal preference should be taken into account – people can have very decided opinions about what sort of seating they like. Many people like to sink into an upholstered and cushioned easy chair or sofa to read or chat, but there are others who are only comfortable in an upright upholstered chair, so there should always be a choice available. Chairs that can stand against the wall and be brought into play when they are needed are useful, as are low stools that can be sat on or drawn up to a chair, as well as doubling as a table for drinks and books. Whatever you choose, remember the overall design plan that you conceived for the room, and into which the separate pieces must fit. Scale and proportion should especially be taken into account; sofas in particular should be large enough for the space that they are going to occupy, for nothing looks more uncomfortable than a small sofa in a large room.

Where there are chairs, there should be tables – or other flat surfaces. If you are using tables, remember that you will need more than you think to hold drinks, lamps, books. They must be within easy reach of the chairs and sofas, but avoid the Victorian parlour look; choose pieces of different heights and shapes, mixing side tables with chests, low tables and even small cupboards to stand against the wall, beside a sofa perhaps.

TOP **A practical and stylish solution to the seating problem is to have seating units that can be used to fill corners and small spaces and can also be broken up to be placed elsewhere in the room.**

ABOVE **A classic piece of furniture design – the timeless Barcelona daybed designed by Mies van der Rohe in 1930 is at the same time a sofa, a daybed or a general seat. Immensely adaptable, it can be used in many situations and decorative schemes.**

RIGHT **More classic design – the red and black leather chairs designed by Le Corbusier in 1929 work seamlessly with the other pieces of furniture here, as the scale and proportions are of equal value.**

FAR RIGHT **A quirky metal-legged antique garden table is the perfect height for a low-armed antique sofa.**

THIS PAGE Around a long glass and metal table, a combination of upholstered sofas, chairs and stools, all of different styles and finishes, works well because the colour palette used is one of soft neutrals that unifies the separate pieces.

INSET In this living room, which combines a work space as well as a seating area, the chairs, sofas and floor lamp are all pieces from the mid-20th century; the very low central table acts almost as a mini-library with its carefully arranged stacks of books.

collections & display

One of the pleasures of building a collection is enjoying it on a daily basis, and where better to display a collection than the living room? Not just a place to sit and relax, it is also a room with interesting and pretty things to look at.

As the principal reception room, the living room is the perfect place to display and arrange pictures as well as other collections of objects and pieces. A collection can be amassed over the years, and an important part of your daily life, or it can simply be a group of things that you are fond of and which are connected to each other in some way – through design, perhaps, or theme, or material. The important thing, no matter what the basis of your collection, is that they be grouped and displayed together in a way that shows them in the best possible light.

Good display does not have to be intricate, elaborate or expensive; all it needs is care and thought about how to best show off what you have. Some objects look their best in open display cases or shelves; others are best set out on low surfaces. Almost every collection that numbers more than two looks better in a close-knit arrangement, whether on a surface or the wall. Judicious lighting can be helpful, but most effective groups rely just on pleasing arrangements, balancing height and shape to best effect.

The hanging of pictures and photographs together is not difficult, but can require practice to achieve a pleasing result. You may find it helpful to see the group on the floor first, moving pieces and seeing what works best together, before committing to hammer and picture hooks.

OPPOSITE, ABOVE The owners of this Manhattan apartment like to use art as a movable display, grouping pieces closely on a designated wall.

OPPOSITE, BELOW LEFT Carefully arranged objects, linked by shape and texture, are displayed over a fireplace.

OPPOSITE, BELOW RIGHT Open units that also act as room dividers display sculpture and objects in a striking way.

TOP LEFT One of the best ways to hang a large group of similar prints is to group them in blocks very close together.

ABOVE LEFT As this canine collection consists of pictures and plaques of different sizes and shapes, it was important to find a pleasing, asymmetric grouping before hanging.

ABOVE RIGHT Open boxes hung on their sides on the wall make perfect display cabinets.

OPPOSITE An inviting and calm room, achieved with a palette of almost neutral, but warm, tones – pale caramels and soft creams on walls, floor and furnishings. All-important contrast has been achieved with small touches of a brighter, sharper yellow-green.

RIGHT This room could feel cold with its grey-painted, wood-lined walls and its uncompromising wooden floor, but it looks warm and welcoming, the result of upholstering the daybed in a soft grape shade and adding patterned cushions in warm tones of brown, grey and blue.

living room palettes

A successful palette of colours for a living room has to be just that – a colour scheme easy to live with in all situations and at all times.

As the most important room in the home, or certainly the room that has to work the hardest in many different ways, the colours and textures used in the living room are all-important. They should make the room a pleasant place to be: somewhere to sit and read, watch television, listen to music or talk; a place also, perhaps, in which to work or to eat. The room should exude not only an air of pleasant comfort and relaxation,

but also a sense of purposefulness. All these different and sometimes conflicting aspects can be encouraged by the choice of colour – and also texture – throughout the room.

The colour palette should suit all those who use it, so in a family home should not be over-feminine or unduly masculine, as well as being easy to live with and welcoming to guests, easy to dress down, as well as up. It sounds a tall order, but look to outside factors, the most important being quality of light, to inform your choice and find the right shades. Which way does the room face, how much natural light does it get, is it naturally warm or cold? A north-facing room will benefit from warm colours; a south-facing, many-windowed room can take cooler tones.

FAR LEFT A sophisticated scheme of horizontal stripes and a rather severe palette of greys, black and silver works in this room because of the accents of red in the cushions, vase and even the picture. All of these are really important in an uncompromising scheme.

LEFT Sometimes less is more, and sometimes – as here – more is more. Pink on pink is not the easiest of schemes to pull off. This works because of the differences in both scale and pattern. A bold wallpaper and pink chairs are highlighted by more flowers in the painting and on the cushions.

Individuality can be easily expressed in a living room with clever choice of soft furnishings, and the right material can add colour and pattern in an instant.

soft furnishings

LEFT Bright on bright; a gros-point cushion highlights and softens the bright pattern of the upholstery fabric.

BELOW LEFT An antique settee is upholstered in a design that is sympathetic to its style and which highlights the gilded and carved surround.

OPPOSITE, ABOVE LEFT What appears to be a choice of mismatching fabrics used to cover this sofa are in fact carefully linked and matched into a harmonious design.

OPPOSITE, BELOW LEFT A story of texture – leather, fur and oversized fluffy sequins; inviting and comfortable.

OPPOSITE, RIGHT, TOP TO BOTTOM A painted period design covered in a printed two-tone fabric, edged with double piping/cording; Small cushions in unusual textures – one knitted with appliqué flowers, another a patchwork of patterns; A trio of toning cushions in French ticking.

Next to the colours of the papers and paints that you choose for the walls, the quickest, most effective and often cheapest way to bring personality and comfort into a room is with the soft furnishings. Old pieces of furniture can be transformed, new pieces made unique, for fabrics are the icing on every decorative cake. The price and design ranges are so huge, the patterns so numerous, the colour spectrum so wide that choosing the upholstery fabric on the sofas and chairs is one of the most enjoyable aspects of designing any room.

As far as the design of the fabric is concerned, the scale of the pattern in relation to the size of the piece to be covered is a factor to take into account; a large-scale pattern will look wholly out of proportion on a very small chair seat. Think also of the other colours in the room, such as the walls and windows; it is important that soft furnishings work with these, although a decorative scheme is always more successful if there is harmony rather than an identical match. If you prefer to keep the colours of the larger pieces of furniture subtle in tone, stack them with contrasting cushions in new and old fabrics to add interest.

■ Where soft furnishings are concerned, cheapest is really not always best: on a single chair, for example, a really fabulous, beautiful design that costs a little more per metre will transform a chair into a showstopper and give you pleasure for years, long after you have forgotten the extra cost.

■ Trimmings – from elaborate passementerie to simple braid, piping/cording and ribbon – can do wonders for a plain upholstered or loose/slipcovered chair or sofa.

■ Old textiles can be used to great effect as soft furnishings. If you do not have enough to cover a whole chair, consider just covering the seat, or even using a piece as a central panel running the length of back and seat.

■ In the same way that cheap clothes look better when simple, if you are opting for less expensive furnishing fabrics, look for simple colour combinations – two or three tones at most – and simple patterns, such as stripes or checks, which always look better than an elaborate, over-coloured design.

■ Like a different lampshade, a new and unusual cushion cover can rejuvenate a room in an instant.

OPPOSITE **In this classically proportioned living room, where everything is in a palette of cool neutrals, the tall, gracious windows require no elaborate arrangements, simply generous, full curtains, with deep headings and in the same colour tones that sweep to the floor and preserve the aspect beyond.**

ABOVE RIGHT **A feature in their own right, these shutters are, unusually, fixed at either side of the window instead of within the window, stored in the reveal. They are split horizontally into two, close to the top, so that the lower section can be closed while still allowing daylight to enter.**

BELOW RIGHT **A wide window is made even wider by using a semi-opaque Roman blind/ shade across its width, giving the impression that the whole wall is daylit.**

BELOW **A wide bay window with seating beneath it responds to blinds/shades made in a bold strong design. The blinds/shades echo the touches of bold colour seen in the seat cushions and throws.**

The living room needs as much natural light as can be collected. It also needs to be warm and comfortable; how you dress the window is the key.

window treatments

Once windows were wrapped with layer upon layer of curtains of different weight; today's windows are carefree in comparison. Simplicity is the answer: gone are heavy pelmets, swags and drapes; now curtains are hung from poles or subtle, near-invisible fixtures. Blinds/shades, narrow and wide, are in evidence and in many period houses shutters are being restored and used again.

The key to successful window treatments is making sure that all is balanced and kept in proportion. If you are buying curtains, for example, make sure that their dimensions neither overpower the window by being too long or wide, nor appear mean, by skimping on material, or being hung too short.

Blinds/shades give a clean, pared-down look. The best styles are the roller blind/shade and the flat, pleated Roman blind/shade. Roman blinds/shades look better where there is enough width to show off the design, and the pleats; rollers work well on smaller windows or where there are several windows of differing sizes.

■ Shutters can be used either on their own or in conjunction with curtains; if the latter, the curtain pole will then need to be set at a reasonable distance beyond the window so as not to impair the shutter workings.

■ The choice of curtain poles is wide indeed, and ranges from antique reeded brass poles with elaborate finials to simple polished wooden rods. Many wooden poles can be painted to work with the rest of the décor.

■ If you choose to curtain tall windows, ensure that the curtain headings are deep enough to look in proportion.

■ If you have tall windows, and even in a room that is otherwise subtly decorated, do not automatically reject the idea of curtains or blinds/shades in a bold, large-scale design. (Small-scale designs will not work well in a large room.) The contrast that a bold design adds can lift the entire scheme.

■ As a general rule, the cheaper the curtain fabric, the more metres you should use – a full curtain appears a generous one and makes the room feel warm and welcoming.

Using a living room well is about using it to its fullest extent and lighting is the key to achieving that. Lighting should be individual and personal and, of course, effective.

lighting

ABOVE **From this ornate moulded ceiling rose might once have hung a serious crystal chandelier; this fanciful, ethereal confection fits the bill just as well.**

RIGHT **Eclectic is the right word here to illustrate the variety of styles and lighting designs in this living room. The mix works, particularly against the old stone wall.**

BELOW LEFT **Ceiling lights can be difficult. The answer is to make an oversized statement, hung as low as possible – here over an even lower table.**

BELOW RIGHT **A freestanding lamp that is both super-practical and attractive; like some fast-growing plant, its arms face in different directions, beaming light to specific areas.**

As in every other room in the house, a combination of lighting is what works best, and the best way to work out what might be needed is to write down exactly what activities might be taking place in the room. There will need to be task lighting – a bald way of saying specific lights for reading, writing and so on. These can be a mixture; some table lamps, some floor, some directional. Old lights as well as new, floor lights as well as table – it is the combination of styles and designs that gives a room character.

Then there should always be ambient or mood lighting to create the atmosphere that you want at different times – a mixture of options that could be suitable both for cheery parties and cosy evenings. Don't forget that many lamps and lights are objects of beauty in their own right; there are both contemporary and traditional shapes that should be appreciated in their full and bright glory, so do not hesitate to include pieces that you really like, even if they do not do much for the practical aspects of lighting the room.

- If you use table lamps, make sure that they are of different heights, so there are varied pools of light through the room.

- Pairs of lights set with geometric regularity are monotonous; if you do have some pairs, break them up around the room, so that it is not immediately obvious.

- Do not despise the humble uplighter, which ranges from a simple cylinder to a statement piece. Hidden in dark corners, they can add depth to a room as well as subtly increasing its size.

- Dimmers are not difficult to install and are absolutely essential for living-room lighting, allowing you to vary the mood for different times of day at the turn of a switch.

- Chandeliers, in every shape and size, are once again in fashion and fun to have floating overhead; make sure, however, that they are part of an integral lighting scheme and not used as the principal source.

- Include beautiful or statement lamps. Their presence will be much appreciated and will give individuality to any living room.

THIS PAGE When is lighting just lighting and when is it art? Here, every piece has been picked for its own sake; together they are harmonious.

ABOVE LEFT A classic, contemporary design solution is polished floorboards set off with a rug made from natural fibres – sisal or seagrass.

ABOVE RIGHT Bold and original, a carpet whose abstract design is a central part of the room's design. The colour and design of the chair acknowledge this, becoming part of the overall scheme.

OPPOSITE, ABOVE LEFT
A composition of texture and colour in this apartment; the strong lines of the seating unit and the painting are grounded by a textured soft pink carpet.

OPPOSITE, CENTRE LEFT
A hard floor surface such as terracotta, however warm in appearance, benefits from one or two rugs in strategic spots.

OPPOSITE, BELOW LEFT
Poured, textured concrete is the flooring in this Parisian studio. The depth of colour gives it unexpected warmth.

OPPOSITE, ABOVE RIGHT
A dramatic way to use carpet is to pick an unusual colour – here, black – to lift the floor out of the ordinary.

OPPOSITE, BELOW RIGHT
In this pearly white apartment, the wooden floor complements the textural whites above it. Reflective and glowing, it makes the furniture appear to be sailing on a moonlit pool.

The floor is the canvas on which you paint the room. If it is right, it may go unremarked; if it is wrong, it will be noticed by all.

flooring

The right flooring for a living room is a question both of personal preference and practical issues. The main questions are whether the floor should be hard or soft, and what options are available. If you live in an apartment, does the lease require that you have a soft floor, rather than wood or tiles? Is warmth an issue? Or small children?

For many people a wooden floor is the only floor, and indeed its virtues are many. It is warm to the touch, the range of available woods is large – from deep mahogany to pale pine – and if chosen with care, it will last a lifetime. Existing wooden floors can be refurbished if necessary, painted, stained and embellished.

But wood is not suitable for everyone. Many decorators prefer, particularly where laying or repairing a whole floor would be costly and disruptive, to choose either a natural floor covering such as sisal or seagrass, or a flatweave, looped wool carpet that simulates the natural look. Both make very good backgrounds for rugs.

If you have free rein, the many other options range from rubber, linoleum or cork to polished concrete, stone and terracotta.

■ Remember that if the existing floor is uneven, you may well need hardboard laid before installing either a natural floor covering or carpet.

■ Sisal, seagrass and other natural coverings should be coated with a stain-protective covering before being laid, as they are difficult to spot-clean.

■ For lovers of traditional floors, reclaimed floorboards and parquet flooring can sometimes be found. Search the internet and architectural salvage companies. You can also find reproduction floorboards, carefully distressed to look just like old.

■ If your existing wooden floors are in reasonable condition, they can be sanded, although this is something that is best done before moving in. Old boards can also be stained, or painted, which is a quick and easy way of updating a room; the range of oil-based floor paint colours available is now as wide as that for the walls.

■ If a new floor has to be laid, investigate the possibilities of underfloor heating, which renders previously hard, cold floors warm and welcoming.

- That all-purpose and attractive piece of furniture, the French armoire, either painted or in a wooden finish, comes into its own in a country-style living room. Adaptable and commodious, within its cavernous depths it can store anything from books to bottles.

- Books really do furnish a room, and the living room is the ideal place both to store and display your books. Decorative as well as essential, try to fit shelves with adjustable fittings so that volumes of all sizes can be accommodated.

- Built-in furniture usually looks best painted the same colour as the rest of the woodwork in the room, but consider picking out any mouldings or decorative features in a slightly deeper shade or shades.

- Good-looking baskets can be the ultimate quick storage fix, either ranged in sets on open shelves, or strategically positioned in corners and under windows for magazines, papers and general junk.

- Freestanding options include a cupboard or chest of drawers; instead of a low table, try an ottoman or chest for last-minute clear-ups.

OPPOSITE **Built-in storage should tie in with the rest of the room and ideally should look as if it was always there, an effect that can usually be achieved with paint colour. This unit cleverly combines mesh-covered bookshelves with radiators hidden behind a wooden slatted panel; simple and more contemporary than the decorative metal variety.**

ABOVE RIGHT **In this cosy room, a combination of closed and open storage means that almost everything can be found a home, some things on display, others out of sight.**

CENTRE RIGHT **One of the most important rules when decorating a small room is to scale up rather than down. Here, ceiling-high cupboards frame a fireplace that is strengthened with the addition of an equally tall mirror.**

BELOW RIGHT **This set of bookshelves has been hung above the floor so that it seems almost free-floating; perversely, the books have been ranged back to front, adding a slightly surreal air to the whole picture.**

A living room without storage would actually be a room in which no one could easily live. Consider what you will need in order to enjoy this space, where many diverse activities might take place.

storage

Storage is a word that can imply things set apart, hidden away until they are finally needed. But living room storage is not like that – it means finding the best way to look after the things you need in this most companionable and personal of rooms. Yes, there can be discreet storage here – cupboards that hide a multitude of things – but there can also be storage that serves a dual purpose, such as an open unit that divides the room as well as housing essentials. A combination of built-in and freestanding pieces may work best, and the freestanding might be old or new, or a mix of both; this could be the place for a fine bookcase or old dresser or sideboard. Built-in storage looks best when designed as part of an overall concept. Should you have them, the obvious sites for built-in storage are the alcoves beside the chimneybreast. The conventional design is one of open shelves above a cupboard, but consider extending the cupboard depth into the room, to allow a more generous storage space, as well as creating an extra surface for lamps and objects.

The finishing touches to a room are the fun bits – the decorative additions that give a room an extra layer of interest.

finishing touches

Every room needs finishing touches. They are the things that distinguish a loved and lived-in room from a property developer's show apartment or a hotel room, so it is worth thinking how to show the things you like around the room to best effect. A room's finishing touches are not necessarily what the auction houses call 'important' pieces, but they are the decorative details, the things you like and which give a room personality – your personality.

Decorative details might range from pictures to old plates or bits of material; cushions are finishing touches, as are mirrors, pictures and flowers and plants. Objects, old and new, finish a room, as do books and pieces of china, glass and wood, photographs (framed and unframed), table lamps and candlesticks and candelabra.

The late David Hicks probably invented the concept, and name, of 'tablescapes', clever groupings of objects that draw the eye to points of interest throughout the room. Arranging disparate objects, combining them harmoniously, is a pleasing one, and it is also a very satisfying pastime – instant interior decoration, in effect.

■ Mix pieces together from different worlds and different periods – old and new, tied together by colour or shape.

■ Use a flat surface – a table or the top of dado-height cupboards – to form a horizontal composition, mixing vases and bowls of flowers with interesting pieces of decorative glass and a picture or two hung low, or propped against the wall.

■ On a close-up table group, go for textural contrast – rough and smooth, metal and glass.

■ Lighting is important; use either a striking lamp or candles to add depth to a group.

■ Never underestimate the power of the unexpected – a visual jolt, like a flash of colour in an otherwise neutral colour scheme, always adds interest.

■ The secret of a good decorative grouping is proportion and scale. A group of objects all of the same dimensions and height will not work. The eye must be drawn vertically upwards as well as horizontally in order to achieve visual harmony.

■ Anything and everything that gives you visual pleasure can be added to the living room as a finishing touch.

OPPOSITE, ABOVE In a country hall, the eye is immediately drawn to the contrast between the sophisticated, neo-classically inspired gilded mirror, and the simple, painted old washstand. The contrast is emphasized by the pair of gold-framed pictures and the arrangements of dried flowers and twigs.

OPPOSITE, BELOW An example of less is more: pale painted walls and woodwork, with a similarly painted table that holds a single flowering bulb in a glass pot, a glass candlestick and dish beneath an oval glass in a contrasting, dark wooden frame.

THIS PAGE Here, the opposite view has been taken and more is certainly more. But it is so carefully composed that the eye delights in this interesting grouping of objects, from the architectural relief artworks hung low on the wall, to the flowers and greenery scattered liberally along the length of the table – many of them in a collection of green-glazed pots – and the metal and glass objects scattered, as it were, amongst the greenery.

It would not be an exaggeration to say that there is a new feeling to the country-inspired living room. The uncluttered and (generally) spider-free modern country style is a contemporary take on the traditional rural genre, an easy, relaxed look that works not only in its spiritual home, the countryside, but in many city spaces as well.

Although the variants are as many as the locations are numerous, modern country style has a certain number of givens – points that are relevant to all those who espouse to a contemporary country look. First of all there is always a simplicity; simplicity of setting and style, simplicity of textiles and pattern, and simplicity of colour and material.

Rather than having fitted upholstery covers on all the seating, choose a mixture of some fitted seats and others dressed with loose, unfitted covers that are not too closely tailored; the effect that you are aiming for is the look of loose, barely fitted old country-house slipcovers – often originally made in chintz or cretonne or natural linen – that protected the grander fitted covers when the room was not in use. Modern loose/slipcovers can be very pretty made in light, clear-coloured plain fabrics that can be easily washed – another reason for going for the relaxed, baggy look, which gives more leeway should there be any shrinkage or distorting of shape.

Throws, now a classic decorating staple, come into their own in modern country style. From new cashmere to old Paisley shawls, tartan rugs to windowpane-check Welsh blankets, old and new, they add a peck of colour and pattern as they cover sofa backs and seats as well as chilly feet and shoulders. The colour schemes that work best are usually soft and harmonious; flat and eggshell finishes usually work better than high gloss.

Although this is not an expensive look to get right, it requires at least as much care – if not more – than a more extravagant style. On the floor, for instance, no covering may be needed, except perhaps a rug in front of the fire, but the floor that is there, be it wooden or tiled, must be in as good condition as its age and your handiwork allow.

Modern country style combines old favourites and new thinking. Relaxed and simple, yet stylish and comfy, it works as well in town as on the village green.

modern country

■ Curtains are not a necessity where modern country style is concerned, even at French windows, and particularly in a setting of natural charm, but windows that have been well draught-proofed certainly are.

■ Do not overplay the decorative accessories; the country living room is no place for sophisticated and overly stylized works of art. Concentrate on the natural and the appropriate, which enhance rather than contrast.

■ Mix old and new furniture together; although simply made and simply styled furniture works well in a country setting, so does the odd contrasting piece – an elaborate or fancifully decorated chair, desk or table, say.

■ Make sure that the room is warm. The simple life is one thing; the frost-bitten life quite another. Make full use of existing fires and stoves, and consider installing underfloor heating or chunky, old-fashioned radiators.

The living room is the ideal place, in decorative terms, for old to meet new, get tipped into the decorative blender, and emerge as something original and fresh.

vintage-inspired style

The term 'vintage' is sometimes rather bandied about in books and magazines, often seeming to be a synonym for the slightly less glamorous term 'second-hand' and often seeming to mean, in some contexts, almost anything that is not absolutely straight-from-the-box new.

But for most interior decorators the term translates into something slightly more precise – those patterns and designs that are not yet antique (in the auction house definition of being over 100 years old) but are not band-box new either, with particular reference to the designs of the mid- to late 20th century.

Like any period of decoration there is both good and bad to be found here, but the 20th century was a period in which some furniture and textile designers produced highly original and brilliant work, much of which is not only highly collectable today, but also has much influence on much modern design. Many of the fabric and paper designs, in particular, have an exuberance and an originality that makes them stand out, and it is these pieces that can add a huge amount to an otherwise contemporary living room.

The trick, as with all attempts at mixing styles and periods, is first, obviously, to pick the right designs, and second to use them with considered care – not to create a pastiche, but to inject some of the unusual colours and patterns of previous decades into the rest of the existing scheme, adding bold, contrasting shots that throw the other elements into relief, and add an individuality and sense of novelty into the room.

The preferred colours of the 20th century were often bold and deep, and often veered towards the sharp – all of which is great in relatively small doses, but does not work quite so well when used over every possible surface. Instead of covering every wall in a vintage colour, consider painting just one wall of your living room – a device very popular 50 years ago – or even using the contrast colour for the doors and windows.

■ Less is definitely more when introducing unusual elements into a room; it is the surprise of the contrast that works, rather than the overall blanket effect.

■ Many of the most innovative 20th-century designs were created in glass and ceramics and a collection can still be formed relatively easily, albeit not quite as cheaply as 10 or 20 years ago. The angular, exuberant glass vases and figurines in reds, oranges and yellows have great decorative charm and look wonderful grouped together on a surface or against a window.

■ The best 20th-century furniture designs, of chairs in particular, often had a sculptural quality and will therefore benefit from being displayed in comparative isolation – in a corner or beneath a window – where they may be clearly seen and appreciated.

To the relief of many observers of the interior scene, we seem to have moved – in contemporary decorative and design terms – from the rigorous and often taxing minimalism of ten years ago, where hard, often uncompromising elements were used in abundance with statement-making glee, to a look that, although it is still edited, pared-down and unfussy, also includes a palpable degree of comfort and warmth. Is this a description of the perfect living room, perhaps? It is certainly one that many will comfortably identify with.

There is an elegance in this style of room, but it is not a fussy, nor contrived effect. It is an elegance that is easy, a style that comes through the careful selection and even more careful editing of pieces put together after time spent judging how the look will work.

Everything, from sofas and chairs to pictures and decorative objects in the simple, elegant living room will be chosen because they work on their own as well as with the other elements, which means that the way that objects and decorative accessories are displayed is important.

Texture is also important, both in furnishings and on the floor; the cleaner the lines of the furniture, the more inviting should be the texture of the covers. Floors – with wood or natural finishes – are often uncovered, or finished with one or two simple rugs, which are rarely bright in colour, or highly patterned.

As well as texture, the choice of colour is also relevant. A calm atmosphere is a vital part of the simple, elegant living room and there is something about pale colours in a neutral palette that soothes the eye; the trick is to choose a neutral spectrum – colours with a grey, pink or yellow cast, perhaps – and to combine various different shades together within that group, adding just a little contrast, either in an area of sharper colour or an unexpected object.

Above all, this living room is one where order reigns; there is nothing at all simple about mess, and unnecessary or unwanted pieces should be kept out of sight in cupboards or, in extremis, a large basket or box.

Simplicity is something we all desire in our lives, and nowhere more so than in our homes. Yet simplicity does not have to mean scruffy, and the simple, elegant living room is a case in point.

simply elegant

■ Hang only those pictures that have a definite part in the overall scheme. This is not a look where every wall should be densely covered with art.

■ Alternative loose/slipcovers that can be easily replaced are a good solution to the inevitable wear and tear of elegant, pale-coloured furnishings.

■ Lighting is very important in this style of room: use table lamps of different heights and styles as well as ambient background lighting that can be adjusted to alter the mood, depending on the occasion. Natural light also is important and should be emphasized; curtains should not be heavy and light-excluding.

■ Flowers, simply arranged, are always welcome in this room, adding the right note of decorative welcome.

■ The decorators' favourite, all-purpose white is not the blinding 'brilliant white', with its detergent-like optical brighteners, but a soft white that has been mixed with a hint of yellow to give a warm hue. Look for it in paint colour cards labelled 'historical' or 'heritage'.

■ A white-toned room is a very good background for contemporary furniture – the clean lines of materials like laminates, glass, polished wood and plastic will all stand out against a cool, neutral background.

■ White is also a perfect background against which to display objects or pictures; simple white shelves become an almost professional setting.

■ That said, the successful white room is a room where the decorative accessories have been carefully selected. Start with an empty room and then add things one by one, gauging the effect after each addition.

White is the subtlest of options for a living room; cool or warm, it is adaptable, flexible to your needs and can be as sophisticated or as simple as you wish.

white and light

An all-white living room sounds wonderful, and is wonderful, but achieving the perfect white room requires thought and application. The most effective way of achieving a pleasant room is to create one that is white in feeling rather than in actual colour, with a mixture of white-based shades and tones subtly combined.

White is not a single colour, nor a single tone; every paint card tells you that. There are cool whites – like pearl and alabaster – and warm whites, such as buttermilk and ivory. It is important to decide, early on, which particular palette suits your style and, having done that, to broaden your palette, to include two, three or even more shades of white within the final scheme. The finishes should be varied too, with matt, eggshell and even a couple of points of high gloss used in the same room. Most white rooms look better when highlighted with small accents of colour – no sharp contrasts, rather subtle pointers, used in cushions, curtains or even flowers.

White is of course light, and its reflective qualities mean that it bounces back any available natural light – a good thing in principle, but in southern countries, where the natural light is far brighter than it is in the north, white needs to be subdued, used with caution, with soft tones prevailing. Artificial lighting in a white room is therefore perhaps even more important than in other colour schemes. A variety of different light fittings can temper and direct the light in a white room, giving it areas of warmth and comfort.

White living rooms respond to textural subtleties – architectural finishes in a variety of materials, and textiles in a variety of interesting finishes – so think about what floor surface and upholstery will look best. In a white room, the furniture is very important, as it must be neither overpowering nor invisible, particularly if you are using tones of white for covers. Painted furniture works well in a white living room and brings a new element into the mix.

It goes without saying that a white living room should look tidy. Clutter does not equate with the atmosphere of cool and calm that should emanate from a white room.

The living room need not look geared towards family or female taste; many successful schemes are based on a simpler, more assertive look – masculine, in fact.

masculine monochrome

■ Lighting should be ubiquitous and varied, with enough task lighting to allow many different activities.

■ A wooden floor, which is warm both to look at and to walk upon, is often a perfect solution for a room that combines different activities and pastimes, as it unifies the room and extends the feeling of cubic space.

■ A simple, well-designed space is the very place to include one or two pieces of furniture that are modern

classics – sculptural, contemporary designs of chairs and lighting that have been tried and tested over the last 50 years or so and found to be very fit for their purpose.

■ When adding colour to a masculine scheme, consider an autumnal palette – the deep tones of autumn fruit and the rich colours of changing leaves – rather than one inspired by spring or summer.

Perhaps it is a hangover from the glory days of gentlemen's clubs and the idea of the out-of-bounds inner sanctum or study, but there is something in the idea of a living room geared towards masculine taste that still touches a chord with the most metro of modern men.

Stereotypes apart, the main difference between a living room that is geared to the taste of a man and that which appeals to more feminine desires is probably the absence of soft decoration – not too much patterned chintz, and a distinct lack of ruffled, floor-flowing curtains – combined with clean lines, no mess and everything in its place. Add to this a relatively sober palette – though not a boring one – and sharp definition in pattern, design and textures, and you have the perfect masculine room, one in which others might also wish to spend time.

The ideal contemporary, masculine look focuses on a space that is well defined: one that has clarity of purpose as its overriding theme, in which every object looks as if it belongs. So thoughtful planning is essential, with enough storage for everything that needs to be there as well as maximum space for any necessary gadgets, and the wherewithal to use said gadgets – enough flexible power points and fixtures to allow all technological pieces of equipment to function.

The design of this type of room is not just enhanced, but completed by the right selection of furniture: there must be somewhere pleasant to read and sit, such as sofas and chairs with deep enough seats and tall enough backs. Wall and upholstery colours should be rich and deep or cool and sharp, but never bland and boring, and whatever is on the floor should act to unify the whole room. In a setting that relies on design and colour rather than on decorative accessories, a focal point is always a good idea – the fireplace if there is one, or perhaps a grouping of sofas and chairs around a low table.

Combine these elements and it will be evident that all is united by one factor: utter comfort. In the end, it is that which defines the perfect masculine living room.

bedrooms

design & decoration

Bedrooms often get overlooked when it comes to designing a home. Unlike the public rooms in a house – the living space and kitchen – they are less likely to be scrutinized by others, and can consequently fall to the bottom of the 'to do' list.

ABOVE **A comfy, cottagey style suits this room, with its low ceiling and exposed timbers. Pattern is kept to the curtains and bedding to prevent the space from feeling too crowded. Rich yellow walls add a sunny feel.**

OPPOSITE, ABOVE LEFT **Bedrooms often look very symmetrical: bed in the middle, tables either side, pictures above. Here, the left and right sides are mirror images of each other, creating a neat, sophisticated look.**

OPPOSITE, ABOVE RIGHT **A bedroom that opens onto a bathroom is luxurious. This subtle brown scheme gives extra sophistication.**

OPPOSITE, BELOW **Positioning the bed across a corner gives this room an informal look.**

Yet we all love the treat of staying in a boutique hotel, or harbour nostalgic memories of being snuggled under a floral eiderdown in granny's cosy spare room, so it's worth taking time over the bedroom, to maximize its potential for comfort and sensuality.

Each of us spends a great deal of time in the bedroom, but most of it asleep; by the age of 50 we will have spent more than 16 years asleep. However, the bedroom is still the first and last thing we see each day, and a well-designed space can do much to ease us into the day and soothe us to sleep each night. When carefully thought out, it can also be much more than a place to sleep and store clothes, becoming a relaxed haven, somewhere to read, potter, work, or just gaze out of the window.

The private nature of bedrooms also offers great decorating opportunities. This is the one room of the house that can be really personal, giving you a chance to experiment. Why not try that dramatic wallpaper or deep-pile carpet, or play with materials, textures and colours that would not work as well in any other room.

planning

It's easy to assume that a bedroom requires less planning than a kitchen or bathroom. But careful consideration of how it will be used and a creative approach to storage can turn a basic sleep space into a brilliantly functioning, beautiful room.

ABOVE LEFT A wall of built-in cupboards looks smart and provides ample clothes storage. The long wooden handles give vertical emphasis to the room and break up the bank of white.

TOP RIGHT A clutter-free bedroom with clear surfaces and tidy floors creates an atmosphere of calm and serenity. It also helps any room feel bigger. Here, dark wood and honey tones give a mellow, sophisticated feel.

ABOVE RIGHT This small bedroom has been well planned to keep furniture to a minimum, leaving space clear for a dramatic French bed.

OPPOSITE In this open-plan bedroom and bathroom a low partition doubles as a headboard, zones the space and creates some privacy.

Begin by thinking about all the ways you will want to use the space and incorporate these activities into your plan. Increasingly, we use bedrooms not just for sleeping and clothes storage, but for reading, watching TV, maybe even working. Sketch out some plans for the room, thinking carefully about use of space and the best position for furniture. Would fitted storage make better use of the room's dimensions than freestanding? Could you position the bed in the centre of the room and build hanging space behind it? Do you need to store clothes in here, or is there space in another room? Do your homework at

this point and you are less likely to make costly mistakes.

Think about what style you are drawn to. Sometimes, the room itself will point you in the right direction. A low-ceilinged bedroom in a country cottage demands a warm, relaxed look, whereas an anonymous, square room in a new-build home can take a more modern, chic style. Consider your budget, too. You may need funds for major work like joinery, electrics, flooring and plumbing. You will need to allow money for paint, wallpaper, fabrics and carpet, for fixtures and fittings like lighting, and for finishing touches like rugs, bedding, mirrors and artwork.

ABOVE All the colours in this bedroom are muted and subtle – mossy green, dusky pink and beige. This could look flat, but the satin bedspread brings subtle brightness to the scheme and creates a glamorous focus.

RIGHT Natural and neutral shades – brown, oatmeal and off-whites – combine here, creating a relaxed but grown-up scheme.

FAR RIGHT A powdery blue paint gives a vintage, cottagey feel to this room, but its colour is nicely broken up by pictures and warmed by the wooden bedside table, preventing it from feeling cool or sterile.

bedroom palettes

It's traditional to opt for calming colours when you're decorating a bedroom, but that doesn't mean the room must be awash with neutrals, or that you should rule out using splashes of bright colour.

Colour is very subjective. A shade that is refreshing to one person is garish to another; one person's warm is another's gloomy. There are no rules, therefore, about how to paint a bedroom, but it makes sense to steer clear of stimulating shades, or you may struggle to switch off.

Remember, too, that whatever colour you choose will be seen mostly in strong morning light and by artificial light at night, so find a shade that can cope with both extremes. If you stick to neutrals, work in lots of texture – rugs, throws, quilts or textured wallpaper – to add visual interest. Dark colours can be warming and sensuous and will help a large or high-ceilinged room feel cosier; olive green, teal and chocolate work well. Bright colours can be stimulating, and they also 'advance', which can make a room feel small, so if your heart is set on a loud shade, try using it as an accent on bedlinen or curtains, or paint it behind the bedhead. This will create focus and give the room personality, but won't distract you at bedtime.

BELOW LEFT **Black walls and black and white bedding – this bedroom works because it has been done simply and with conviction, with no fussy details to water down the monochrome scheme.**

BELOW RIGHT **If you like the idea of black and white in a bedroom, but don't want as strong a look as the picture shown left, opt for black and white stripes and plenty of light-reflecting materials, like this capiz shell lampshade, to lighten the effect.**

BOTTOM LEFT **An all-white scheme can work brilliantly in a bedroom, creating a calm, clean and serene atmospere with very little effort.**

BOTTOM RIGHT **A fabric-covered headboard brings colour and pattern to a bedroom and is comfortable to lean against, too. Here, the plum toile de Jouy print that has been used looks striking against the soft pink walls.**

ABOVE LEFT **This beautiful sleigh bed and matching bedside cabinet in rich, dark wood look stylish and timeless. A tall cabinet like this can make it hard to access the things on its top from a lying position – worth considering when choosing bedside pieces.**

ABOVE RIGHT **A good-sized chest of drawers provides useful storage and its top is also large enough to support a mirror and lamp. The armchair, positioned by the window, gives this room day-round appeal.**

RIGHT **A blanket box or wooden chest is a useful addition to a bedroom, providing storage and, when fitted with a cushion pad, a place to sit.**

furniture

From a simple bed to a room kitted out with wardrobes, cupboards, bedside tables and more, the bedroom can be as cramped or as clutter-free as you choose.

One thing is certain: you will need a bed. A good mattress is a must and the choice of what to put it on is huge. Divans often offer storage underneath and look elegant topped with floor-skimming sheets or finished with a dramatic headboard. For some vintage character, scour antique shops and markets for old iron bedsteads or French carved wooden frames, or try the high street for a modern take on the elegant sleigh bed or four-poster.

The bed need not be the focal point of the room. You may wish to incorporate a big antique wardrobe or tall chest of drawers. For further storage, consider blanket boxes, wooden chests and baskets. A whole range of pieces can operate as a bedside table: a desk, stool,

hatbox or chair. Floating shelves are a cool alternative. The foot of the bed is a good place for a more unusual piece, but think beyond the blanket box that traditionally stood here. A bench, an ottoman, even a desk, can all tuck against the end and function as a footboard.

If your room is large enough, consider incorporating some seating. An armchair or chaise longue will tempt you in during the day to read, relax or just daydream.

THIS PICTURE **To get** maximum use out of your room, think about where you can fit in hard-working, multi-tasking pieces. In this bedroom, a bedside table is actually a desk for catching up on paperwork or correspondence, while also being home to the book and drink that everyone needs to hand come bedtime. This choice of furniture only works if you can keep the desk clutter-free, to avoid paperwork encroaching on the calmness of the space.

■ When you're buying a mattress, don't be influenced by the term orthopaedic. It just means that the bed is a firmer specification from that manufacturer, not that it is designed for those with back pain.

■ 100% down duvets are super-soft as, unlike feathers, down is pliable and does not contain a 'spine'. Geese that live in cold climes produce the fluffiest down, so expect to pay more for a Siberian goose-down quilt.

■ Airing is essential for a natural down duvet and pillows. Give them a regular shake, to circulate air and stop the filling compacting.

■ When buying cotton sheets, look out for the thread count – the number of threads per square inch of fabric. Basic cottons will be around 150, good-quality sheets start at around 180, and anything above 200 is a luxury cotton.

■ Synthetic duvets are ideal for allergy sufferers, as they can be machine washed at 60 degrees, which wipes out dust mites.

■ If you use a blanket with your duvet, spread it underneath, but over a sheet, to prevent the air that traps the warmth inside the duvet being squashed out.

ABOVE The linear pattern of stripes on this blanket echoes the bars on the iron bedstead. It's a fresh look, made comfy with scatter cushions, which soften the bedhead and add warm colour.

RIGHT A thick feather duvet dressed in a crisp white cover and teamed with masses of soft white pillows is a classic look that works in almost any bedroom.

BELOW RIGHT An old-fashioned patchwork quilt teamed with white sheets looks elegant and provides ample warmth and comfort in summer.

In a room designated for sleep, the bed needs both to look great and feel wonderful, so that means mixing beautiful bedding with a quality mattress.

bedding & mattresses

If you have a comfortable bed you are, on average, likely to sleep for 42 minutes more each night than if your bed is not comfortable. So it's a good idea to invest in the most expensive mattress you can afford. Before buying, spend plenty of time lying on a new mattress in a variety of positions and, if you buy your base separately, remember to make sure the dimensions are exactly compatible.

Duvets come in a wide range, so fix a budget first. Choose between natural feather fillings and synthetic fibres. Natural materials feel luxurious, are breathable and draw moisture away from the body. They generally last longer than synthetics, too. The most basic natural filling is duck feather and down, which gives a cocooned feel, while pure down is lighter. A synthetic duvet is practical, because you can throw it in your washing machine, but feels less cosy than a feather filling. Duvets are very popular, but traditional blankets and quilts are a great way to add colour and texture. Try a mixture; blankets make a low-tog duvet warm enough for winter and give that tucked-in feeling.

THIS PICTURE A striped woollen blanket looks smart and graphic. Quality thick cotton sheets that can be folded deeply over the blanket increase its comfort – no risk of it tickling your chin – and keep the look crisp.

The bedroom is the place for romantic, indulgent window treatments. Just remember practicality – they must block out morning light and offer privacy, too.

window treatments

When choosing material for blinds/shades or curtains, soft, light-absorbing fabrics give a warm feel, while shiny, reflective surfaces create a cooler, more glamorous atmosphere. If you want an opulent look, allow extra fabric for curtains so that it pools on the floor. Remember that strong sunlight will bleach coloured material, so if your bedroom is sunny, go for a pale or neutral option.

Roman or roller blinds/shades work well on smaller windows, but can be cumbersome on wide windows, and if more than one is fitted across a single pane light will inevitably seep in. Layering works well at a bedroom window. Fit a practical roller blind/shade close to the glass, to block out morning light and provide privacy, then hang floaty curtains, lace panels or lush drapes from a rail fitted in front.

If your bedroom faces east, you will need window treatments that block out the early morning sun in summer. Have existing curtains lined with blackout fabric, or hang a blackout liner that fits behind your curtains, either on the same rail or clipped onto the curtain.

ABOVE RIGHT **When pulled up, Roman blinds/shades make a neat stack at the top of the window frame that is visible, so they remain a feature in any decorative scheme. Here, the linear pattern of this version grounds the scheme and is a good balance to the floor-to-ceiling floral wallpaper.**

BELOW RIGHT **In a plain white bedroom, pretty curtains hung on a simple rail add a welcome shot of pattern and colour. This floral yellow and orange pair are made from vintage fabric from a market.**

BELOW **Roman blinds/shades typically fold up neatly, but you can also have them made so that the material scrunches up into a pleasingly ruffled stack at the top, creating a casual, textural effect.**

OPPOSITE **Neat white roller blinds/shades fitted close to the windows block out light, while floaty curtains fitted in front offer privacy, filter bright light by day and soften the lines of this big window, too.**

■ As well as blocking out unwanted light, quality blackout fabric is often thermal-lined, so it reflects heat and can help regulate the bedroom temperature during the summer.

■ Shutters are a stylish alternative to fabric window treatments. Typically made of wood, their slats can be moved up and down to let light in or provide complete privacy.

■ Vertical blinds/shades are versatile and inexpensive, but can recall the office. Opt for Venetians in coloured metal or warm wood instead. They can filter light, cut it out totally, or pull up to let maximum light in.

■ If your bedroom is overlooked, consider fitting frosted film to some or all of the windowpanes. Available in a range of perforated designs, it allows light in, but provides complete privacy.

■ Modern, top-of-the-range blinds/shades offer solar protection, to prevent flooring or furniture becoming faded in the sun, and also block out heat.

■ Bottom-up roller blinds/shades are now available, which are great for providing privacy for dressing while still letting light in through the top half of the window.

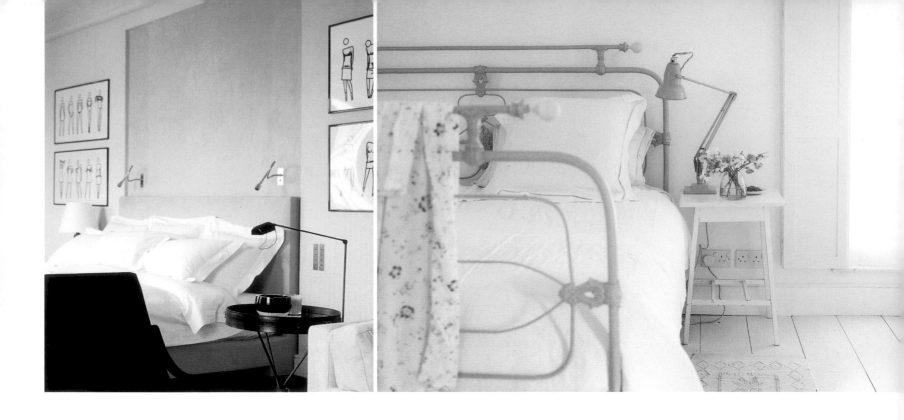

■ Consider fitting a light inside your wardrobe or cupboard space so that you can find clothes easily.

■ Wall lights fitted either side of the bed are a stylish way to provide reading light, but be sure that you will always want your bed in the same position before you install them.

■ Matching bedside lamps either side of a double bed give a stylish, symmetrical look to a bedroom, especially when sited on co-ordinating units.

■ The central pendant light often gets little use in a bedroom, but dress it in a twinkling chandelier or oversized shade and it will look good even if it's rarely used.

■ Rope lights, made of hundreds of LED lights inside a see-through cable, produce a warm glow – perfect in a bedroom. Try trailing them over a headboard or across a mantelpiece or shelf.

■ Candlelight is seductive and relaxing, ideal at bedtime. Light scented candles for subtle perfume as well as ambient light, but remember to blow them out before you drift off to sleep.

ABOVE LEFT Tiny directable wall lights are complemented by a floor light and traditional table lamp either side of this bed, creating a versatile mix of lighting.

ABOVE RIGHT Old Anglepoise lights frequently crop up at second-hand fairs and markets and can be spray-painted to refresh them. They are highly versatile, too. Point the head upwards for bright light, down for minimal light or simply direct it at your book while you read before sleep.

OPPOSITE, ABOVE Matching lamps and shades give a pleasing symmetry to this bedroom, which is continued with identical bedside units and neatly arranged pillows.

OPPOSITE, BELOW LEFT Wall-mounted lights that can be pulled out from the wall help direct the light and make it possible to forgo a bedside table, ideal in a small room.

OPPOSITE, BELOW RIGHT This is quite a spare, modern room, but it gets an instant touch of glamour and playfulness thanks to the sparkling chandelier. The dark glass drops give it a contemporary feel and match the rich purples and reds of this scheme.

Lighting can dictate the atmosphere of a room. Take time getting it right in your bedroom to suit morning dressing, late-night reading and everything in between.

lighting

A bedroom is used mostly at each end of the day. While it is a room to relax and prepare for sleep in – demanding soft light – it's also where we dress and put on make-up, which needs strong light. A mix of general, task and mood lighting is therefore essential. Flexibility is key, so ensure lights work independently of each other. Fit dimmer switches for fixed lighting and add freestanding lamps.

Most bedrooms are fitted with a single central pendant, but this provides a flat light that deadens texture, so supplement it with uplighters to create a soothing glow without glare. Downlighters provide an even background light, but are not good fitted above the bed, where the light will shine directly into your eyes. For bedtime reading, a table lamp works well, or go for task lighting in the form of a directable Anglepoise light. Wall-mounted reading lights are a great idea, and free up space on your bedside table.

OPPOSITE Painted white floorboards give this bedroom a cool, clean feel. They also reflect light into the room and are therefore particularly suited to small or dark spaces. White floorboards do show up dirt, crumbs and dark hair, so need regular sweeping or vacuuming, but are an easy way to create a fresh, uncluttered atmosphere.

ABOVE LEFT The rich, dark tones of the floorboards in this attic room help to anchor the scheme. Although a deep conker brown, their lightly varnished finish helps increase the feeling of light. They are softened by a simple rug in a neutral colour.

ABOVE RIGHT A neutral woollen carpet in a fairly dense weave teams good looks with practicality. It is soft underfoot, provides excellent soundproofing and is easy to clean, but also creates a calm neutral backdrop that suits the classic simplicity of this bedroom.

In many rooms of the house, flooring is all about practicality, but in the bedroom you can afford to be more indulgent and choose something that feels as good as it looks.

flooring

Bedroom floors experience little traffic and are seldom walked on by outdoor shoes, so a pale or deep-pile carpet can be enjoyed here. Beware of deep pile, however, if you suffer allergies, as they can harbour mites. Similarly, if you love breakfast in bed, bear in mind that vacuuming toast crumbs from a shag-pile carpet is hard work.

Natural fibres like coir, seagrass and sisal are hardwearing and look great, but can feel rather hard and prickly underfoot. A good alternative is coir-effect carpet, which has the look and texture of natural fibres, but is made from wool, so it's softer. Wooden boards are a great bedroom option. Wood is warm, stylish and practical. Go for either newly laid boards that are sleek, knot-free and seamless, or just strip and treat the original floorboards for a more relaxed look.

Rugs are a versatile asset to a bedroom, adding softness, colour, warmth and pattern. Choose a sensual sheepskin – next to the bed so it's the first thing your toes sink into in the morning – fluffy flokati or woven mats that add a shot of colour and can be machine-washed.

■ Carpets come in a range of constructions: loop, velvet, twist, pile or pattern. Those made with densely packed pile are the most hardwearing, while plush, velvet-pile and shag-pile carpets are super-soft and luxurious options.

■ The colour of your flooring can play visual tricks in your bedroom. Light colours recede walls and suit a small space, while dark tones make walls seem nearer, creating a cosy feel in a big room.

■ Good underlay will prolong a carpet's life, so don't cut corners on quality here, and make sure your new carpet is laid by a professional carpet-fitter.

■ Painting floorboards is a cheap and easy way to hide discoloured wood and ugly knots. Floor paints are available in a huge range of colours, too.

■ If you have a big budget and want a really individual look, bespoke rugs can be commissioned at many major rug specialists.

■ Take along colour swatches of the fabrics in your bedroom or a paint chart showing the wall colour when choosing rugs, carpet or floor paint, as it is very hard to remember colours accurately.

■ Invest in good-quality wooden or padded hangers/clothesrods for your clothes. Wire versions can stretch and misshape garments.

■ If you are having wardrobes built in, consider having them fitted with small spotlights, which can be fixed to the tops of shelves and over the rails to help you find clothes easily.

■ Pine furniture has fallen out of fashion lately, but the wood responds well to a coat of paint. Sand it down first, then prime it, before applying eggshell in the colour of your choice.

■ Free up storage space in your wardrobe by keeping rarely used or out-of-season garments in zip-up or vacuum-closure plastic clothes bags on a high shelf, in a spare room or in the loft.

■ Clear out your bedroom storage every so often and edit your clothes collection. If you haven't worn the item in the last year, give it to charity.

LEFT Mirrors are a key component of any bedroom, essential for checking your appearance when dressing. Here, mirror panels are used to front the doors of these built-in cupboards, giving them a glamorous feel. They also help to increase the sense of space and light, too – a bonus in a small bedroom.

FAR LEFT An exquisite wallpaper hand-painted with a design of birds and flowers is used to cover the doors along a wall of storage between a bedroom and bathroom, transforming it into a work of art. It's a clever and original way of introducing pattern and colour to a bedroom while also disguising a vast amount of wardrobe space that might otherwise look rather functional.

BELOW LEFT A mixture of open shelves and simple, plain cupboard doors gives this wall of storage visual interest. Keeping shoes, handbags or colourful clothes on open shelves allows you to enjoy their shape and pattern even when you're not wearing them, and makes finding what you want to put on easy.

Bedrooms should be relaxing sanctuaries, places to potter, dress, read and, of course, sleep. So it's vital to work in plenty of storage, because nothing spoils the atmosphere of what should be a peaceful haven faster than clothes strewn everywhere and a floor scattered with shoes.

clothes storage

The principal piece of storage in any bedroom will be the wardrobe, but do you go for built-in or freestanding? Custom-made wardrobes are not necessarily much more expensive than freestanding or flat-pack, and they make the most efficient use of space – vital in a small or oddly shaped bedroom. You can also tailor the storage to your own requirements: extra-high hanging rails if you have a lot of dresses, for example, or plenty of shelves if you have clothes that need to be stored folded. Freestanding wardrobes, on the other hand, are versatile – you can

change their position in the room – and you can take them with you if you move. If you like retro or vintage style, you can pick up old wardrobes on eBay or in second-hand markets for very little money. Whichever you choose, remember to allow for more rail space than you currently have. You are bound to need more in the future, so factor in an extra 20%. A generous rail will also allow your clothes to hang properly, without getting hitched up on their neighbours, and makes it easier to find each item when you're dressing.

THIS PAGE In this bedroom, an antique armoire provides a large amount of storage and looks wonderfully grand. The walls, decorated with a bold pattern painted directly onto the plaster, add further elegance, but plain walls would do just as well. White bedlinen and a simple bed are the perfect complement to this decorative piece.

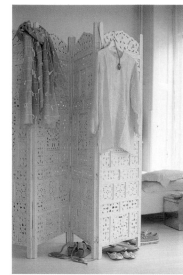

Whether you love the boutique hotel look or want the cluttered country vibe, finishing touches bring a bedroom to life.

finishing touches

Mirrors are an essential ingredient in all but the most spartan bedrooms and a floor-length design is vital for checking your appearance. Fit one inside a wardrobe door if you want to keep the space clean, or simply prop one against a wall. Take care to check what the mirror is reflecting, though. It won't look as dramatic if it's showing everyone all the boxes and bric-a-brac you store under your bed. Mirrors are easy to pick up second-hand, cropping up in antique shops and flea markets regularly, so keep your eye out for something with a fabulous frame or pretty mottled glass, a handsome sign of its age.

Pictures add personality to your room, but as less is often more in the bedroom, stick to simple images or small-scale prints, to add interest without dominating. Remember, too, that the eye feels most comfortable viewing rows of odd numbers, so it has a central image to alight on. A row of three pictures above a bed works very nicely.

As the bedroom is a personal space, it's a good place to display treasured photos or precious ornaments. As few people enter this room, delicate or special pieces are less likely to be damaged, too.

■ We so often keep them for the living room, but fresh flowers are an easy and inexpensive way to add colour and beauty to a bedroom. Stick to simple bunches of the same bloom, rather than fussy mixed bouquets, for a pretty but tranquil feel.

■ A screen makes an elegant addition to a bedroom and can be used to partially obscure the window for privacy.

■ Instead of hiding jewellery away in boxes, display it. Decorative hooks can hold necklaces, or you could drape them from the frame of a picture or mirror.

■ Hang favourite dresses or shirts from your wardrobe door, so you can enjoy their patterns and colours every day.

■ Seek out attractive old pieces that may not have been intended for life in a bedroom. Crystal cake stands, pretty teacups and vases can be used to hold jewellery. Old wooden boxes, tins and suitcases can double as storage and bring character to a simply styled room.

■ A welcoming scent is a key finishing touch for any bedroom. Burn scented candles or sprinkle eau de cologne over freshly laundered bedding for subtle perfume.

OPPOSITE, TOP ROW, LEFT TO RIGHT A single bloom is the only decorative element in this strictly all-white room, but helps prevent it from feeling sterile. The lone flower can be appreciated more because it stands out so clearly; this decorative Indian screen doubles as a place to display favourite clothes. Its perforated wooden design and pale colour prevent it from dominating the room, despite its size; a huge French mirror, resting against a wall, is both practical and beautiful. Scour antique shops and markets for large carved pieces like this one; three small prints create interest on the wall above the bed, while the cushions below, arranged more casually, are a nice foil to the symmetrical arrangement above.

OPPOSITE, CENTRAL ROW, TOP TO BOTTOM A bedside table is a great place to display a few favourite pieces. Here, a framed painting, some antique silverware and a shapely glass vase create an attractive and personal display; this old bust, now draped with jewellery, looks great amid a cluttered display of necklaces and knick-knacks on a chest of drawers; a full-size tailor's dummy gets to wear beautiful clothes in this bedroom and strikes a theatrical note, standing next to a brilliant red armchair.

THIS PICTURE Five pretty stems add a lovely finishing touch to this simple scheme, injecting a welcome natural note to the pared-down look.

Modern country style takes the best ingredients from the classic country look and blends them with contemporary touches. Natural materials are vital to anchor the look, so think cotton sheets, woollen blankets, flatwoven rugs and lots of wood. A classic country-style bedroom feels that it has evolved over time, with furniture casually positioned and displays added to and moved around. This relaxed, organic feel is at the heart of modern country style, too, which never looks overstyled or self-conscious and is flexible and welcoming. Colours are predominantly neutral or muted, with plainly painted walls, but fresh modern colours are used as accents – a bright cushion, a patterned rug, floral wallpaper on one wall.

Fabrics and textures that would not belong in a traditional country bedroom can look great in this modern version, so consider mixing in some light-reflecting silk, lush velvet or ethnic weaves. On cushions and throws, sequins or glass beads add sparkle, useful in a dark room, while decadently fluffy sheepskin rugs dyed a strong shade soften wooden floorboards and inject some colour.

Traditional country bedrooms would have a striking bedstead, often in iron or perhaps carved wood, but modern country opts for less obtrusive styles. A plain divan or slim four-poster will keep the look light and uncomplicated. Forget piling on blankets, eiderdowns and quilts and instead choose classically simple bedlinen in white or cream that can be draped with a blanket or throw in a warm shade. It's just one of the ways that the look feels cleaner and less cluttered than the original.

Hunt around in second-hand shops or markets for pieces that have seen a bit of life, for that casual, warm country feel. In addition to units, chests of drawers, old pictures and mirrors are easy to find and will inject personality into your space. Then throw in the odd piece of modern design – a dramatic floor lamp, designer chair or contemporary rug that will strike a modern contrast with any old pieces and original timbers or boards in the room, to bring the space stylishly up to date.

When well done, a modern makeover of the comfortable cottagey look combines its easy-going rusticity with a contemporary freshness.

modern country

■ Ditch the symmetrical look found in so many bedrooms for a more informal, unbalanced arrangement. Use bedside units of different sizes and styles, work in lamps with different shades and bases, or position a bed in a corner.

■ Keep walls simply painted to fit the modern aesthetic.

■ Floral fabrics are a stalwart of any country scheme, but a modern take also uses contemporary patterns, toile de Jouy, embroidery or ticking stripes.

■ Stick to unfussy window treatments like roller or Roman blinds/shades in a fabric that tones with the wall colour.

■ A woollen blanket or throw draped over a bed adds extra warmth and a subtle note of country style. Choose a plaid or stripe in a soft shade.

■ Keep the room uncluttered and let a few pieces of much-loved furniture take centre stage. Texture, warm wood and a little pattern or colour will prevent the room feeling sterile.

There are lots of myths about all-white schemes. They feel cold or sterile, they are not practical, they don't suit some rooms. None is true. In fact, with the right mix of ingredients, using white throughout a space is incredibly easy, stylish and versatile. Just follow a few simple tips.

Avoid using pure brilliant white paint, which has optical brighteners in it to give it a really sharp, stark effect. This can look too bright and clinical, especially in a bedroom. Instead, choose a basic white emulsion with a more chalky finish, or pick one of the hundreds of off-whites available on the market. Test them as you would a coloured paint, as you may be surprised how 'coloured' they can appear. What looks white in the can may seem purplish, peachy or grey once up.

For a totally white room, paint floorboards white or lay pale carpet, but remember that they take more looking after as both show up dirt and hair. If you want a little softness and warmth without spoiling the aesthetic, keep floorboards in their natural state – the glow of wood fits in well with an all-white room and adds a touch of warmth. Or consider using Danish lye, a traditional treatment that bleaches boards and stops them yellowing.

When it comes to furniture, an easy and inexpensive way to kit out a white bedroom is by picking up old pieces – chests of drawers, tables, chairs, cabinets – at second-hand markets. If need be, paint them with some white eggshell. It will hide old marks and ugly knots in the wood and transform even the most battered piece.

To prevent an all-white bedroom looking sterile or boring, mix in plenty of texture. On the bed, layer on blankets, embroidered bedspreads or traditional quilts. Scatter tactile cushions over or dot the floor with toe-tickling rugs in sheepskin or fluffy flokati. Work in some light-reflecting surfaces, too, for subtle sparkle and shine. Prop old mirrors against the wall or on a tabletop, choose photo frames made from glass, shell or glossy painted wood and hang a twinkling chandelier. This will all add personality and richness to a one-shade scheme.

Calming and uncomplicated, white is a great colour for a bedroom. Far from being cold, it can hit just the right note of serenity, perfect where relaxation is key.

white nights

■ Every paint manufacturer makes inexpensive standard white. Keep a pot to hand to paint over marks easily.

■ Shop around for old white furniture with a few knocks. It will fit in with the all-white look, but without looking too pristine and edgy.

■ Don't be too 'strict' about your white bedroom scheme. You might include grey or palest cream – use them on floors or old furniture – to introduce variety and interest.

■ Use baby wipes to clean marks and smudges off white paintwork.

■ Keep pattern subtle and restricted. A single wall of wallpaper, for example, or a delicately embroidered bedspread will add interest without spoiling the calm, balanced feel.

■ Bring in natural colour with plants and flowers. Put a few sprigs in a selection of old jars or glasses, or include the odd pot of an easy-to-grow plant like ivy or mind your own business.

When we think of florals we often picture a cottage pattern with big blossomy roses in pinks and reds, but there are numerous variations on this flowery theme.

romantic florals

From the Fifties-style florals revived by Cath Kidston to modern, abstract versions, from tiny sprigs dotted across an all-white background to oversized blooms amid a sea of colour, there is a floral to suit most tastes.

While florals add a touch of romance to any bedroom, they need not look ultra-feminine. Choose muted or earthy shades rather than pink tones, or pick a pattern of trailing stems with only the occasional flower, to suggest a floral style without splashing blooms all over.

The walls are the biggest surface area in any room, and a floral bedroom often incorporates wallpaper, which transforms a plain room to a flowery oasis in a few rolls. Use it on just one wall as an accent or take your bedroom to floral heaven by papering it on walls and ceiling for a cosy, but tongue-in-cheek look. Modern wallpaper designers usually have their own take on the classic floral, so check them out, or plunder the archives for old prints that still look fresh today.

Textiles with floral patterns are widely available. For the bed, pick a pretty duvet cover or have fun layering quilts, sheets and bedspreads for a more ad hoc look. Shop on the high street, or track down antique florals in specialist shops or on the internet. The window is another part of the room that can benefit from the romantic floral look. Pretty curtains peppered with sprigs or a Roman blind/shade in a bold floral pattern that can still be glimpsed when rolled up suit this scheme. You might even have a plain headboard upholstered in a floral fabric. Remember to keep an eye on the balance. Too many florals, in too many different designs, will look busy and chaotic, so stick to florals that tone in together and use them in just one or two places in the room.

For small hits of floral prettiness, look out for lampshades or cushions, wall hangings or beautifully painted screens that will contribute to the look without making it claustrophobic. And don't forget fresh flowers, too – the original and still the best romantic floral.

■ Mix feminine, curvy furniture, such as a French carved bed, with pieces that have a more masculine feel; a battered leather armchair or dark wooden chest of drawers.

■ Play with scale. Curtains adorned with oversized blooms will look great next to wallpaper with a small-scale pattern of tiny sprigs on a pale background.

■ Beware of the bedroom becoming too pink. Soft plums, mauves, sage green and watery blue are good colours to incorporate, and should be balanced by creams and antique white.

■ Old china can be bought cheaply at markets or junk shops and adds a shot of floral romance, on a small scale.

■ An old iron bedstead is the perfect partner for traditonal floral bedding. Many new versions of classic bedstead designs are available, or scour antique fairs and markets for an original.

Think about colours first. Grown-up glamour rejects whites and neutrals in favour of colours that are muted, but not sludgy. Watery blues, dusky pinks, greys, purples and mossy greens all suit a glamorous scene – nothing too bright, nothing too earthy. Deft touches of silver and gold can work, too, but keep them to a minimum to prevent the look becoming Versace-fied. Use colour on walls, bedding and accessories, but keep your flooring simple to help balance the look.

Furniture should blend beauty with practicality. A dressing table is a key piece. The perfect place to preen, it also looks pretty and elegant when not in use. Triple mirrors were typically fitted to dressing tables, so you can see your face from any angle, but they also help bounce light around the room and catch interesting reflections. A beautiful bed with a striking or unusual headboard is another essential ingredient. Team a tall, padded headboard with a plain divan for that boutique hotel feel, or hunt for an old French carved wooden bed, complete with part-padded head- and footboards, or an unusual metal frame. The bed must make a glamorous statement, even when dressed in plain linen.

Glossy and reflective surfaces are central to the grown-up glamour look. Freestanding mirrors propped against a wall and draped with sparkling jewellery look stunning, or look out for a mirrored console table, bedside table or dressing table. Choose wallpapers with a slight sheen and perhaps throw in a satin bedspread, to add a subtle glimmer to the bed.

An armchair is a great addition if you have space. Choose something elegant, like an ornate French piece, or tactile, like a thick-armed, low chair in velvet. It all adds to the impression that in this bedroom one can linger, relax and daydream.

Mix in a few splashes of luxury, too, that are wonderful to gaze at or touch: lush fabrics like velvet and silk; thick pillows and soft cushions, heaped on the bed; a chandelier or ornate lamp; silk curtains, pooling on the floor or tied back into deep sweeps. Anything pleasing to the eye and the skin is vital for a glamorous feel.

Any bedroom can be transformed from basic to glamorous. For pure grown-up glamour, just add luxurious touches, tactile fabrics and subtle colours.

grown-up glamour

■ Panels of vintage lace hung at a window look glamorous and help filter light and provide privacy.

■ A large, statement piece of furniture suits this kind of bedroom. If it isn't the bed, make it an oversized chest of drawers, elegant side table on which you can arrange favourite accessories, or an ornate French armoire that will hold all your clothes.

■ Curtains look more glamorous than blinds/shades, which are too neat and minimal for this style. Fit curtains to the floor for a luxurious feel.

■ Pay attention to details. Install pretty light switches, door handles, drawer knobs and sockets – you touch and use them every day and they can really lift the appearance of a room.

■ Grown-up glamour is all about quality, but not necessarily brand-new materials, so shop in both antique stores and on the high street when putting together this look.

- Neat, functional window treatments are key. Discreet, super-simple curtains work; Venetian or roller blinds/shades are perfect. Try vertical Venetians for an extra-masculine, 'officey' feel.

- The modern retro look is all about big, strong statements, so on walls a single, large painting will look better than several small ones.

- Shop second-hand for swatches of Sixties and Seventies fabric to make into cushion covers. Look for curtains, dresses and tablecloths to convert, too.

- Try hanging graphic wallpaper behind the bedhead. It will add personality to the room without distracting you when you are in bed.

- Keep surfaces clutter-free, so you can display one or two favourite objects – a coloured glass vase, original ceramics or a sculptural plant.

- Find original Sixties and Seventies wallpapers on eBay, or pick up a reproduction roll. Some manufacturers stock reissues of original designs, for a really authentic feel.

Take your bedroom back in time and plunder the best of Sixties and Seventies style, then update it with a few fresh additions for a super-cool, modern retro look.

modern retro

Sixties and Seventies style was a bold rejection of post-war austerity in favour of an optimistic and original look: graphic shapes, designer furniture, strong and earthy colours. It booted the stuffy, cluttered bedrooms of the Fifties out and brought in a bold new style.

Modern retro takes the best elements of that style. It incorporates those signature colours – brown, orange, mustard and green – and aspires to be symmetrical, masculine, ordered and uncluttered. It could feel austere were it not for soft flooring, bedlinen and upholstery.

Designer furniture suits this look, and there's usually room in a bedroom for a lightweight, classic chair. Think Eames' fibreglass armchair, Harry Bertoia's Diamond chair or Norman Cherner's iconic bentwood design. Fitted wardrobes with sliding doors are ideal, leaving space for stylish extras like a sideboard or console table. Choose pieces that are slim, unfussy and well designed.

Large bedside lamps are a feature of the modern retro look. A metal or wooden base with a big shade will do well, and keep the look symmetrical with matching lamps either side of the bed. A floor lamp is another stylish addition. If your budget allows, pick something dramatic like Castiglioni's iconic Arco light, designed in the Sixties.

Colour is key to capturing this look. Choose a neutral background palette of oatmeal or soft brown, then add accents of orange, lime, mustard, even gold. Don't be afraid to use black, either. Try it on lampshades, picture frames or cushions. Wallpaper was big news in the Sixties and Seventies, and most homes had papered rooms; designs were usually graphic or abstract, not floral.

Soften your scheme with stylish bedding. Sheets and blankets look more modern retro than a duvet. Blankets in muted browns or beiges over white sheets, perhaps a throw in a similar shade, a pair of cushions are enough: keep it understated and unfussy. Carpet suits this look, but where shagpile was first choice, a modern retro room looks better fitted with a plain, short-weave design. Pick a contrasting shade, or go for easy-on-the-eye neutrals.

bathrooms

design & decoration

Creating a new bathroom or updating an existing one is something you can't afford to do too often, but get it right and it will add value to your home in more ways than one. It is all about practicality plus wellbeing.

Today's bathroom must be functional, of course, but it should also be a sensual and sybaritic space, a private oasis where you can unwind. Getting this twofold formula right takes thought and careful planning, so before you start choosing hardware, consider exactly what you want.

Browse through magazines and websites for inspiration. Many bathroom manufacturers now provide room sets (both in-store and online) to show you how a finished design will look. Consider the shape and size of your bathroom and think what arrangement would work best in the space. If you have a tiny cubicle, perhaps a

wet room is the answer? Can you squeeze in a big, sculptural bath? Would a separate toilet be the solution to early-morning congestion? By analysing your needs at the outset, you'll save yourself time and money later on.

Once you have a favoured layout, think about what look you would like to achieve. Do you want a traditional bathroom or something streamlined and modern? A simple white scheme or strong colour or dynamic pattern? Today, there are so many different options for sanitary ware and surfaces; you may find a particular design or material will set the tone for the whole room.

ABOVE LEFT This streamlined modern bathroom is practical with its tiled surfaces, simple shower screen and stack of shelves. Though neutral, the room isn't dull; a chocolate-coloured mosaic floor adds visual texture.

ABOVE RIGHT Freestanding stone baths, placed in the centre of a room, make for luxurious bathing. Make sure the floor can bear the weight.

OPPOSITE The modern bathroom is no longer purely a utility space; it can be as individual and expressive as any other room in the house. Here, traditional fixtures and fittings have been mixed with more homely elements to create a very personal and comfortable bathing space.

ABOVE LEFT When planning the layout of your bathroom, make the most of the space. Position the biggest element – the bath – first because it will determine the design of the rest of the room. Here it is tucked along a wall, leaving a clear pathway to the door.

ABOVE RIGHT Here, a walk-in shower has been neatly fitted at the back of the bathroom. By installing clear glass doors and by keeping the flooring the same as the rest of the room, the owners have retained a sense of space.

RIGHT If you have a small bathroom, consider knocking it through into an adjacent bedroom to create a handy en-suite. This will also make both rooms feel larger.

OPPOSITE Built-in features, whether shower rooms or basin units, make the best use of space. Here an integral washing area fits neatly against the wall and also provides plenty of storage.

planning

Designing a new bathroom can be a fantastically creative experience, but don't forget that – above all – the space has to be functional and safe. It is essential to plan the project very carefully and to get advice about structural, plumbing and electrical issues before you start.

Just how much professional guidance you need depends on the size of the job, but if you are planning any major changes, it is worth calling in the experts. Architects, designers and even many bathroom suppliers can help you decide exactly which fixtures and fittings are right for the space and answer tricky technical questions. Is the water pressure sufficient for that power shower? Can the floor be raised to accommodate a sunken bath? Can the position of the toilet be changed?

You might be eager to start picking tiles and choosing colours, but it is vital to sort out the nitty gritty of the

room right at the start. Think about heating. Is there space for an underfloor solution, and could you afford it? Take into account the position of drainage pipes and consider how to conceal them (the professionals will help here). And don't forget about including built-in storage; the more you have, the easier it will be to keep the bathroom free of clutter.

One last, crucial, task is to consider the cost of a new bathroom. Shop around for good deals and be prepared to spend as much on advice and installation as you do on fixtures and fittings. Set yourself a budget and stick to it.

THIS PICTURE A child-friendly bathroom doesn't have to be garish or full of plastic toys. This elegant, monochrome space works well for adults and children alike with its practical wipe-down panelled walls, painted floor and hidden storage. Even the armchair has a washable loose cover/slipcover.

OPPOSITE With its bright colours and series of storage shelves, this simple bathroom is functional and fun. Products and towels can easily be put away (or out of reach, if necessary), keeping the bath surround clutter-free.

fitting in the family

If you don't have the luxury of multiple bathrooms, it is important to make sure the one you have caters to the needs of the whole family. Think about how and when the space is used and try to include family-friendly elements in its design so that it functions effectively at all times.

If you and your partner are always jostling for space in the morning, consider installing two washbasins instead of one, or even side-by-side baths if you have the space, the money and the inclination. The bathroom can be a sociable as well as a functional room, so take this into account when you are planning the layout and leave room – if you can – for a comfortable chair or cushioned bench.

If you have small children, try to make the design work as well for them as it does for you. Opt for baths and basins with rounded edges rather than sharp corners and make sure that the floor is nonslip, even when wet. Safety is a key issue in the bathroom, and with a little careful planning you can take practical steps to reduce unnecessary accidents. Underfloor heating gets rid of the need for radiators or heated towel rails with their exposed hot pipes, for example; a twin-ended tub (one with the taps in the middle rather than at the end) creates safe and comfortable space for a child at each end.

To reduce the risk of scalding, go for a mixer tap/faucet rather than individual hot and cold spouts or, to eliminate the problem altogether, opt for a thermostatic version with built-in temperature control. It is also sensible to include a pull-out shower handset in the bath surround, even if you have a separate shower, for easy hair-washing.

You want your bathroom to be clean and clutter-free, so do all you can to encourage your children to keep it tidy. Erect hooks at child height so they can hang up towels and flannels easily (plastic suction hooks work well on the side of the bath) and include plenty of easy-access storage space for bath toys, soaps and toothbrushes.

ABOVE LEFT **Letting the light through, a glass washbasin works well in a small or dingy bathroom and is also easy to clean. This wall-hung version suits its surroundings and takes up little space.**

ABOVE RIGHT **A traditional roll-top bath looks good in any bathroom and can be painted to co-ordinate with the colour scheme. Because the tub has no integral surround, however, you need to make sure you have somewhere to stash the soap. Here the adjacent cistern makes an effective storage space.**

OPPOSITE **Ingeniously designed, this small linear bathroom seems far more spacious than it really is. Partitioned with a glass screen, the shower area feels very much part of the room, while the streamlined, wall-hung basin unit leaves the floor clear and easy to clean.**

baths & basins

The layout of your bathroom may dictate the size of your sanitary ware, but what about the material and the design? Choosing from the array of styles can be a daunting task.

Selecting the bath should be first on the list because, as the biggest feature, it will dictate the look of the rest of the room. Consider which shape would suit the space best. A freestanding, central tub can look dynamic in a big room; a corner model could be the perfect solution in a smaller one. Don't be afraid to try before you buy. You are going to be lying in there, after all, so comfort is key.

Most baths these days are made of acrylic, which is warmer than steel and less likely to chip, but if your budget will stretch to it do consider the alternatives.

Natural materials, such as stone or wood, work brilliantly in the bathroom; or opt for a design in a cutting-edge material, such as lightweight resin or recycled plastic. These should offer you a wide choice of colour, too.

Choose a basin that complements the bath in shape and colour, even if it is not part of a ready-made 'suite', and consider carefully the design of the basin unit. Modern wall-hung versions look neat and streamlined, but make sure your walls are strong enough to bear the weight. Splashes are hard to avoid here, so ensure the basin and its surround can drain effectively, and invest in quality taps/faucets that work aesthetically with the room.

The neatest toilets sit flush to the wall so the plumbing is concealed, but make sure that you can still access the cistern and pipework. And do your bit for the planet by installing a dual flush system that will limit water wastage.

wet rooms

Showering in an open space, unhampered by steamy cubicle walls or damp shower curtains, is a luxurious and liberating experience. To make it work takes preparation.

Whether you want a self-contained wet room or an open shower within a bathroom, you need to make the room absolutely watertight before you start. The best approach is to get the area sealed by a professional, who will cover the floor and walls with an impermeable membrane. This can then be topped with your choice of covering; bear in mind that stone and tiles should also be sealed if porous.

The existing floor may need to be strengthened and should be sloped slightly so water can easily drain into the waste outlet. The outlet can be central or, better still, tucked neatly against the wall if you opt for a modern linear design. If there is space, consider underfloor heating.

Sealing a bathroom is an expensive business. To get the look for less, fit a shower tray so that it sits flush with the floor. Unless it is made bespoke, however, you will be restricted to standard sizes.

A wet room is just the place for a power shower, so hunt around for suitably extravagant water features. Think about installing a shower pump to guarantee a good jet. As for fixtures and fittings, wall-mounted models work best, allowing you to keep the floor clear. Include a small shelf or alcove for stashing shampoos and soaps.

THIS PAGE **In this light, Mediterranean-inspired bathroom the floor has been fitted with a concealed drainage tray, topped with a sealed wooden platform. This makes for a very neat and comfortable solution, with the waste pipes cleverly hidden from view.**

small bathrooms & shower rooms

With some careful planning and a few decorative tricks, even the smallest bathing area can be turned into a sybaritic sanctuary. Make sure the layout of the room is as efficient as possible, and use every available bit of space.

Think first about stealing space from elsewhere. If your shower room is cramped, can you raise the ceiling or drop the floor? Could you extend your mini bathroom into an adjacent bedroom, or create an en-suite with a screen or sliding door, which needs less room than a hinged one?

If this can't be done, build as much 'hidden' storage into a bathroom as you can, creating a cupboard in the area above the door, for example, or inside a panelled bath. Wall-mount fixtures and fittings and invest in space-saving kit – a corner bath or a fold-down towel rail/rod.

A shower room needs less space, particularly if you opt for a ready-made cubicle. Choose the biggest and most comfortable you can, with as many built-in features as possible. Some now come with integral seats, lighting and even steam or sauna options (though remember that these will demand good ventilation).

When it comes to decoration, choose surfaces that are light and reflective and use mirrors to expand the room visually. A giant one can effectively double the space; opt for acrylic over glass if the walls can't bear the weight.

ABOVE LEFT Storage is key in a small bathroom, so use wasted space for cupboards and shelves. In this tiny, high-ceilinged room, an ingenious high ledge provides double storage space, housing glassware on top and jewellery below.

ABOVE RIGHT A long thin space can make an effective wet room or shower. By wall-mounting fixtures so that all the pipes are concealed and by creating cut-out alcoves for storage, maximum space is left for showering.

OPPOSITE By carrying the white mosaic of the floor up onto the wall, the owner of this neat shower room makes the space seem larger. With its wall-hung basin and simple fixtures and fittings, it also feels clean and uncluttered.

FAR LEFT, ABOVE Colourful mosaic brings zest to the bathroom. Here a vivid yellow complements a deep blue bath surround to create a zingy modern look.

FAR LEFT, BELOW Deep red will add warmth to any room, and here sets off the patina of the marbled basin.

LEFT, ABOVE Bold colour can work brilliantly in a bathroom. Here, a vivid pink wall provides the perfect backdrop to a sculptural white tub.

LEFT, BELOW Wallpaper is an option in the bathroom, in a moisture-resistant version. Here, a pretty toile de Jouy creates a traditional feel.

RIGHT Unexpected colour makes any room interesting. Here, the soft lilac and curvy bath make a relaxing space.

bathroom palettes

White is often the first choice for the bathroom. Bright and pure, it can make the dingiest or tiniest space seem clean and airy. But strong colour and pattern can work, too, if you're brave enough to experiment.

Consider first what kind of look you are after: a bold modern statement or a pretty, subtle scheme? And flick through books and magazines to discover which colours and finishes inspire you. Buy tester pots of paint and get samples of materials you like – tiles, stone, wallpaper – so that you can see how they will work in your space.

A simple and effective option is to go for the monotone room, where one colour is used for walls, floors and surfaces. This wraparound effect creates a cohesive feel and works well when offset with white baths and basins. Or why not get your sanitary ware to co-ordinate?

Contemporary bathroom kit comes in all kind of colours, and an old bath can be repainted or repanelled to fit in.

A neutral scheme is also successful, particularly when teamed with natural materials. By keeping the backdrop subtle, the textures and patina of stone, slate or cork, for example, will shine through. Conversely, a bold, high-gloss look also works brilliantly, as well as being practical.

If you are after more dramatic decoration, consider creating a feature wall or floor. With countless options out there, from photo-wallpaper to intricately patterned mosaic panels, getting creative has never been so easy.

Today's bathroom is a sensual space. It needs good bright task lighting, of course, but also its antithesis – a soft glow to bathe by. The solution is in the mix.

lighting

OPPOSITE AND BELOW
OPPOSITE AND BELOW
A feature light can bring glamour to a simple scheme, but check that your fitting complies with safety regulations. To maximize the light in this tall, elegant room, the owner has installed mirrored cabinets (which also increase the sense of space) and used downlighters to highlight the washing area.

ABOVE RIGHT Bright lighting is not always what you want in a bathroom, so opt for a range of solutions to give you flexibility. Here, wall-mounted lights are supplemented by a giant decorative candle – perfect for a soft and subtle evening glow.

RIGHT An all-white scheme can do much to lighten a dingy or small bathroom, but add some curves to avoid it looking cold and clinical.

Safety has to be the first consideration when you are planning a lighting scheme for the bathroom. Water and electricity can be a dangerous combination and, thus, there are tight regulations governing what lights you can have in 'wet' areas and where you can put them. Before you commit to buying anything, check out the guidelines. However, the rules need not be restrictive. There is a wealth of interesting and innovative fixtures and fittings out there and, if you look beyond the standard bathroom kit, it is still possible to create an individual scheme that is right for you.

Whether you are revamping an existing bathroom or creating one from scratch, it's worth identifying first exactly how much light you need and where you need it. Rather than opting for the classic overhead solution, it is better to think in terms of layers of light or a scheme that mixes a variety of different options. You may want strong task lighting when you are shaving or putting on make-up, for example, but a much softer wash of light for an evening bath.

■ Safety is a key issue when it comes to bathroom lighting, so make sure to consult a qualified electrician before you start planning your scheme.

■ There are strict regulations about what lights can be used in a bathroom and where; for example, you may need to enclose bulbs. Gen up on the rules before you go shopping.

■ Don't limit yourself to one light source; your lighting needs will change at different times of the day. Combine bright task lighting with a more moody ambient option to give yourself flexibility.

■ To save on energy, maximize daylight wherever you can. Light colours, glossy surfaces and mirrors will all make the most of the available natural light.

■ Think carefully about the position of your lights. While you might want a brightly lit mirror, remember that an overhead light can cause unflattering shadows.

■ You don't have to stick to standard fixtures and fittings; consider the alternatives. There are so many innovative solutions available, from submersible bath lights to colourful fibre optics.

■ New flooring can sometimes be laid on top of old if the existing surface is dry, flat and stable. Get advice from the experts before you rip out what is already there.

■ In a shower area or wet room, it's crucial that the floor is not slippery when wet. Choose rougher, textured materials here to give good grip.

■ If you opt for coloured mosaic or ceramic tiles, use a grout to match, giving a seamless modern finish. And make sure the grout is mould-resistant and waterproof in a wet room or beneath a shower.

■ Intricately patterned mosaic will make an impact on the floor, but it is expensive. To lower the cost, opt for a few 'feature' panels in an otherwise plain floor.

■ The bathroom floor is often the smallest in the house, so it's just the place to splash out on a luxury material without breaking the budget.

■ Wood looks good on a bathroom floor, but use engineered boards to avoid warping.

LEFT Stripped wooden floorboards are comfortable underfoot and look good in a simple, homely bathroom, but remember that they are liable to warp if they get wet. To make them more durable, top with a waterproofing sealant but make sure that the resulting surface is nonslip. To discourage dust and make cleaning easier, it is also a good idea to fill any gaps between old floorboards with strips of wood or cork.

OPPOSITE A textured terrazzo floor can add visual interest in a sleek modern bathroom like this, and it is an extremely hardwearing option. Made from a combination of marble or granite chippings and concrete or cement, terrazzo comes in a wide variety of colours and can be laid in situ or bought as tiles. Topped with a sealant, a terrazzo surface is low-maintenance and usually nonslip.

Bamboo, concrete, vinyl, mosaic – options for the bathroom floor have never been greater. Make sure whichever material you choose will give you a floor that's comfortable underfoot and easy to clean, durable, functional and good-looking.

flooring

A new floor needs an under-surface that is solid and even – whether it's a concrete foundation or existing floorboards. And, if you are planning to top it with a heavy material like stone, it should be strong enough to support its weight. Get advice from a professional before you begin.

At this point, too, think about underfloor heating. It can work brilliantly in the bathroom, where it can warm up cold materials like marble or ceramic tiles and get rid of the need for radiators in what is often a small room. However, it is a luxury option and should be fitted by an expert.

Safety underfoot is paramount in the bathroom, so choose a material that won't be slippery when wet – natural slate, perhaps, or textured mosaic. If you must have a smooth stone surface, keep it away from the shower area and add a stable mat to prevent accidents. Don't forget, too, that stone is porous and needs to be properly sealed to prevent staining.

Alternatively, opt for eco-friendly cork or bamboo – both perfect for damp areas and sustainable. Lino and vinyl are ideal, too; easy to lay, they can also camouflage uneven floors and come in countless colours.

■ Opt for wall-hung storage where possible. Anything that keeps the floor clear will help you achieve an uncluttered look.

■ Before you assess how much storage you need, have a clear-out. You might find that you can reduce your bathroom bits and pieces dramatically.

■ Use the back of the door for storage. A piece of wooden peg rail, for example, can be just the thing for hanging damp towels and can be painted to match your colour scheme.

■ If you have bath products on show, make a feature of them: decant lotions and potions into attractive glass bottles, for example, and line them up on a shelf.

■ If your bath has no integral surround, make sure you have somewhere to stash the soap. A built-in mini niche can work well, or a suction-style soap dish.

OPPOSITE Painted white, the storage wall in this fresh and airy bathroom is very unobtrusive. With its series of cupboards, it can accommodate all the bathroom essentials – towels, toilet paper, soaps et al – allowing the owners to display only what they want to. An old glass jar makes a very attractive container for a collection of shells.

RIGHT The block-like built-in shelves in this minimal modern bathroom make it easy to keep the space ordered and tidy. Because they form part of the basin surround, they don't intrude visually into the space. A mini shelf-cum-mirror stand provides a home for smaller items and a useful bit of display space.

Damp towels; wet soap; half-empty shampoo bottles – the bathroom is a prime spot for mess. But with plenty of well-planned storage solutions, you can conquer the clutter and keep your bathing space calm, clean and tidy.

storage

If you are creating a new bathroom from scratch, build as much storage as possible into the fabric of the room itself. Carve alcoves into a shower wall for stashing cleaning products (if the wall is thick enough) or squeeze a cupboard into an awkward space at the end of the bath. In a large bathroom you could create a run of cupboards along one wall. Decorated to match the room, these will 'disappear' when the doors are closed.

Alternatively, build around your sanitary ware. A cupboard beneath the basin can house boxes and bottles without taking up too much space.

Or why not raise the bath slightly so that you can fit a couple of drawers for towels underneath? And invest in some ready-made 'secret' storage solutions: a mirrored cabinet, for example, or a hollow seat-cum-chest.

If your bathroom is tiny, maximize the potential of whatever you have. Hang hooks underneath a shelf so you can make use of the top and the bottom, for example, or buy a shower curtain with useful pockets.

You don't have to hide everything away, but keep what is on show neat and tidy, and choose containers that can cope with a moist environment.

ABOVE **Don't forget that the bathroom can be used as a display space. Instead of making do with a medley of pots and bottles, arrange your bits and pieces with a stylist's eye. Here, a collection of curvy glass bottles and textural shells makes a striking arrangement.**

ABOVE RIGHT **Candles make a perfect finishing touch in the bathroom, but make sure to keep them away from anything flammable.**

BELOW RIGHT **Don't be afraid to mix old and new. In this Thirties bathroom, a cutting-edge cabinet and some graphic Perspex art make a bold statement against the original panelled walls and leaded window.**

OPPOSITE **This light and airy bathroom might be functional, but it also has a very homely feel with its collection of personal bits and pieces. By bringing in a spindly French café table, a jug of flowers and a collection of pretty antique mirrors, the owners have turned it into much more than a utility space.**

Given a personal touch and some special details, the bathroom should become a space you can't wait to spend time in.

finishing touches

In a large bathroom, consider adding elements that aren't usually associated with utility spaces – an armchair, perhaps, or a shaggy sheepskin rug. Pieces like this will give the most functional bathroom a comfortable touch (soft furnishings used in a damp or humid environment need to be aired regularly to prevent mould).

If you don't have underfloor heating, consider installing a feature towel rail. Bathroom radiators now come in all kinds of innovative designs and colours. Alternatively, hunt down unusual storage items – an old-fashioned wall-mounted soap dispenser, for example, or a cutting-edge toothbrush rack.

The window is another great spot for self-expression. If you want a cottagey look, opt for old-style curtains (these will need regular washing); or invest in a statement blind, printed with a graphic image or even a photograph. For the ultimate sleek minimal look, do without a covering altogether in favour of frosted glass.

Finally, bring in decorative details. Whether it's a row of old glass bottles or a pile of pebbles, little extras can make all the difference.

■ If you don't want your windows to be permanently frosted, cover them with vinyl frosting instead. Window stickers now come in countless finishes and patterns, can be made to measure and peeled off when no longer required.

■ Get creative with the side of a bath. Cover plain wood panels with a giant laminated photograph, perhaps, or cut a piece of coloured Perspex to fit, and light it from within so that it glows in the dark. (Remember to get advice about the safety of any light fittings in the bathroom.)

■ Bring in fresh flowers. Though any arrangement has to be changed regularly, a floral display will transform the room – even if it is only a bunch of daffodils. Some houseplants are happy in bathrooms, too.

■ The bathroom is the most sensual space in the house, so make it smell nice. Avoid chemical air fresheners; opt instead for scented candles or natural perfumes. A few hyacinths or a bundle of dried lavender, for example, will do wonders.

There is something very homely about an old-style bathroom. Think curvy roll-top baths with twisty copper taps/faucets; wicker laundry baskets; simple scrubbed floors in stone or wood. It's an honest, unpretentious room, which can work well in a contemporary setting as well as being just the thing for a period town house or country cottage.

Traditional fixtures and fittings, from a old butler's sink to an Art Deco shower mixer, can be tracked down at salvage yards or on the internet. If it is in good condition, don't expect such bathroom kit to come cheap; if it isn't, take into account the cost of getting it reconditioned. Alternatively, opt for reproduction pieces, which combine classic looks with the advantages of modern technology.

A traditional bathroom should be familiar and comforting. Choose classic colours for walls and woodwork and avoid garish tones. Shock value is not what you are after. Use wallpaper, if you like, and add the odd soft furnishing – curtains, perhaps, or a pile of cushions on an armchair (these will need regular airing).

Accessorize with old-fashioned pieces – a vintage bath rack; a block of traditional soap; pretty glass storage bottles. Just don't be tempted to bring out the tin bath.

An old-fashioned bathroom has to function like a new one: recondition antique fixtures or buy reproductions to give you a classic look with all the mod cons.

traditional style

■ Stick to natural materials for floors and surfaces – stripped wood, stone or ceramic tiles. Stainless steel and vinyl are not what you want here.

■ Add a homely touch with floral fabrics or wallpaper, but make sure you buy a wipe-down version, specifically made for humid environments.

■ If your old bath is chipped, get it re-enamelled. You can buy DIY kits, but to get a really good result it is best to employ an expert.

■ A copper bath will give you old-style looks in an instant and will naturally retain the heat. Hunt down an antique or buy a reproduction or new design.

■ The traditional bathroom should not be a minimal space. To make it feel lived in, bring in collections of old glassware, mirrors or pictures (but make sure the latter are well sealed, to protect them from damp).

■ Include fabric washbasin 'skirts' and shower curtains (with a plastic liner).

White brings with it associations of purity and cleanliness, and thus is often an automatic choice for the bathroom. Bright and light-enhancing, it can freshen up dark or dingy spaces and blur the boundaries of a tiny room to make it seem larger. What's more, a white scheme is supremely versatile, catering to all tastes from minimal to smart Scandinavian to vintage washroom style.

For a wraparound white look, choose a tone that has an element of warmth in it to prevent the room looking too cold or clinical. And – for the same reason – opt for baths and basins with a bit of a curve to soften the effect. Wooden floors can be whitewashed or limed for a subtler finish; walls could be painted in chalky distempers or shiny gloss – whatever your preference.

To add visual interest in an all-white room, turn up the emphasis on texture. Invest in some curly candlesticks; hang a diaphanous shower curtain; or add waffle towels. A white bathroom can be high-maintenance, so opt for practical hardware and surfaces to make cleaning easy.

Bright, fresh and light-enhancing, an all-white scheme is perfect for the bathroom, but remember to add some curve and texture to soften the look.

classic white

■ If you opt for an all-white bathroom, think about adding pattern in unexpected ways. Slatted shutters at the window will cast fantastic linear shadows on the floor, for example; set against a plain background, a curvy basin will become a sculptural focus.

■ Don't opt for cold, blue-whites; instead choose warmer tones or creamy whites, which will glow in the sunlight. Think laundry rather than clinic.

■ The all-white bathroom demands a bit of maintenance. Wash surfaces and furnishings regularly to keep it looking fresh and clean.

■ Don't be afraid to add an accent of bold colour. A brilliant cushion, vivid towels or even some coloured lights will lift the decorative scheme and add visual interest.

■ Texture is key in an all-white space, so bring in the contrasts, whether rough and smooth or glossy and matt.

With its fresh, calming colours and natural textures, a seaside theme will give any bathroom an honest, outdoorsy feel, and it will cost you little to achieve.

coastal style

A dip in the sea is nature's most elemental bathing experience, and by decorating your bathroom coastal-style you can bring a bit of that outdoor energy to the most urban space.

Keep the look simple and put the emphasis on natural tones and textures. The seaside offers a host of tried-and-tested colour combinations – aqua and sand; turquoise and stone; seaweed-green and sky-blue – ready to be exploited. Stick to natural, organic paints if you can, rather than sophisticated glossies: the look you are after is more distressed beach hut than smart seaside chalet.

Opt for natural materials, too, for floors and surfaces: stripped wooden boards, perhaps, or cork or rough stone tiles. For more texture underfoot, you can even sink pebbles into concrete or resin (search on the internet for suppliers) or buy some ready-made pebble mosaic tiles. These will give you that beachy look in an instant.

Tongue and groove panelling – reminiscent of old ships' cabins – will enhance any maritime theme and is perfect for covering up uneven or pitted surfaces. Use it for the walls, the side of the bath or even the ceiling. The authentic stuff is made of individual planks of softwood, but today you can also buy ready-grooved MDF panels, which are easier to fit and inexpensive. Both will need to be properly sealed to make them moisture-resistant, so get some expert advice before buying.

Choose seaside materials for rugs and furnishings, too – a coarse coir or seagrass bathmat, perhaps, or a rattan armchair – and opt for simple, rustic sanitary ware. Finally, bring in a few desert-island accessories – a driftwood stool, a basket of shells, a natural sponge – or go for a nautical theme with toy boats, anchors or coils of rope.

■ Keep your colour scheme to seaside shades: sandy ochres and yellows; sea-greens; aqua blues. These naturally harmonious colours will always look good together.

■ Natural materials like cork and wood are perfect for a coastal theme. They will also allow your bathroom to breathe, helping to prevent mould.

■ For this style, peeling paint and distressed furniture are just what you want. Hunt down second-hand bits and pieces or buy new 'vintage' items – but make sure they look authentic.

■ For a light-hearted coastal feel, add fun seaside elements. A length of stripy deckchair fabric, for example, can make a brilliant blind/shade.

■ As well as photos and pictures, display found objects on the wall. Even a gnarled piece of driftwood can become a sculptural focus.

Contemporary hotel bathrooms are luxurious and indulgent. Beautifully designed and free of domestic clutter, they offer a vision of the ultimate bathing experience. Recreating such an extravagant space at home is beyond most budgets, of course, but you can steal inspiring designer elements or ideas.

A statement bathtub will instantly give five-star glamour, whether it is in hand-carved stone or sparkling mosaic. Set it in the middle of the room for maximum impact, but make sure first that your plumbing can cope with central drainage. Alternatively, splash out on a sunken bath. This can't be undertaken lightly – you will need to raise the floor and create steps up to the bathroom – but can be very effective. The infinity bath, created as a tub within a tub so that water can brim to the top of the inner shell and pour over the sides, is also a luxurious option, particularly when filled from the ceiling with a waterfall-like jet.

In a bathroom like this, you want a shower that cascades, so hunt around for extravagant water features; giant showerheads or rain panels that drench rather than dribble. Prices aren't necessarily prohibitive, but check that your water pressure can cope or fit a new pump.

Glamour can come as much from your bathroom surfaces as the fixtures and fittings, so flick through magazines to see what appeals. Quality counts, so buy the best material you can afford – whether it's smooth natural stone, patterned mosaic panels or rich dark wood – and use it wherever your budget will allow. Just a strip of golden tiles, for example, will lift an otherwise plain bathroom to a new level.

And don't forget to tap into modern technology. It is constantly evolving, so keep up to date and consider what could transform your space. A shower with MP3 connection, perhaps; a bath you can fill remotely at the touch of a button; a chromatherapy feature to flood the water with coloured light? Finally, add a little luxury in the details with top-quality towels and cleansing products.

A designer bathroom may be beyond your budget, but by stealing ideas from hotel suites you can bring a bit of five-star luxury to your own bathing space.

hotel glamour

■ Before you splash out on designer fixtures and fittings, make sure that they will function effectively in your bathroom. You may need to get your water pressure checked, for example, or install a new pump for a power shower. Get advice from the experts before you begin.

■ Choose fashionable toning shades for the walls, floors and surfaces. A one-colour room will always look chic.

■ Half the appeal of a sleek hotel bathroom is that it is calm and uncluttered. Achieve the same effect by building clever storage into your space (see page 143) and keeping mess to an absolute minimum.

■ In a plain bathroom, make light a decorative element. Invest in a chromatherapy shower, create your own illuminated bath panel or simply install some recessed floor spots.

children's rooms

THIS PAGE A young person's room works as a place to study, entertain friends, read and relax in, as well as to sleep and dress in. So in addition to a bed and storage, it must house a desk, computer, kit and books, too.

RIGHT Colourful painted furniture and a pretty bed give this little girl's room a bright, cheerful feel. Positioning a bed next to a window is not safe, as the child could jump or fall out, so here it's been placed at an angle with the window a safe distance behind.

design & decoration

When designing and decorating a child's room, flexibility is key. Children's rooms need to change and evolve as fast as the child does. From a calming nursery to a high-tech teenage hangout, the room must be adaptable, well-planned and creative.

A child's room should reflect his or her personality and preferences, while also remaining similar in style to the rest of your home, so it fits in. Involve your child in decision-making; young children can feel very upset when their room is transformed and familiar pieces in it changed, so let them make some choices to reduce the risk of their feeling unsettled.

That said, your input is essential. Do not trust a four-year-old to pick a scheme that he or she will still love in six months' time, so avoid Spiderman wallpaper on every wall, as your son may prefer Batman in a few weeks, but do leave a wall free where he can hang posters or pictures, which can be swapped easily.

Pick furniture that can be adapted, to accommodate a child's ever-changing interests without compromising your own sense of style too greatly; wooden furniture that can be painted, a dressing-up box that can double as seating, a shelving unit that can be wall-mounted once the child is taller. Then have fun with inexpensive accessories like lights, wall stickers, rugs and bedding, to create a space that is both stylish and child-friendly.

planning

Children's rooms demand as much planning as the more public rooms in your home. Your child's tastes and interests should be reflected, there should be easy-to-access storage and it must be able to switch from play area to sleep space in moments.

If you are starting from scratch, choose flooring that marries practicality with comfort. Children spend a lot of time on the floor and need a comfortable surface. On walls, go for neutral tones and liven them up with textiles and accessories. Funky bedlinen and rugs add colour cheaply, so you may be happy to let your child choose.

If you want to use bright paint or wallpaper, try limiting it to one feature wall, so it's less time-consuming and expensive to change. Children love bright colours, but they can make a room feel small and have a stimulating effect, which might prevent a child sleeping well.

Although adults often love clutter-free living, children like having their things around them and should be able

ABOVE This baby's room has a chic, grown-up style, but still includes all the essentials for the first year of life – clothes storage, a cot and a comfy chair for feeds and bedtime stories.

ABOVE RIGHT If your children are to share a bedroom, a bunk bed is the ultimate space-saving sleeping arrangement – and always popular with kids.

RIGHT Classic furniture like this wrought-iron bed and tall chest of drawers are given a childish edge with colourful bedding, soft toys and a fluffy sheepskin on the floor.

to access them easily. So, rather than built-in drawers and cupboards, go for a mix of closed storage and open shelving, baskets and crates, so the room can be tidied quickly – by your child – but toys are still easy to get at.

Kids and teenagers like posters and their own artwork on their walls, but instead of using tape try pinning them to large corkboards or buy magnetic paint. Blackboard paint means children can chalk up their own designs.

OPPOSITE This room has been planned to allow plenty of desk space, a vital ingredient of a child's room, whatever their age. These wooden desks have a beaten-up look that is warm and appealing, and come with handy storage sections built in. A high shelf above provides space to display favourite pieces, while metal lockers create secure storage, ideal in a shared bedroom.

babies' rooms

A baby's room must tick certain boxes if it is to be a good environment for the first year of life. It needs to keep a constant temperature, fulfil specific lighting requirements and be comfortable and calming. Little furniture is needed, but the right atmosphere is key.

Research suggests that pastel shades comfort babies, so choose delicate, chalky colours and avoid anything too bright. Pay careful attention to lighting. Strong natural light is the enemy of good sleep, so make sure you have adequate window treatments fitted for daytime naps and to prevent early waking. A blackout roller blind/shade with curtains hung in front will block out most light, as will shutters. Dimmer switches mean you can keep light soft for bedtime and night feeds, brighter for dressing and play.

Choose a soft carpet or rug so baby can lie down and crawl. Fit a thermostat to the radiator so you can regulate the room's temperature – overheating has been linked to SIDS (Sudden Infant Death Syndrome). Make sure all sockets are covered and electrical leads hidden behind furniture or clipped to the wall. Avoid putting the cot near a radiator, as baby could burn his or her fingers or overheat, or near a window, which can be draughty.

ABOVE LEFT Baby clothes are so pretty, it's a shame to store them in drawers. Here, peg rails allow them to be displayed neatly. Choosing what to dress baby in is easier, too, when you can see her clothes at a glance.

ABOVE RIGHT A cleverly designed wall of built-in storage includes open shelves with baskets for nappies, cotton wool and creams, and a pull-out changing table.

RIGHT Simply furnished with neat, built-in cupboards, a comfy armchair and classic cot, this nursery looks fresh and timeless.

OPPOSITE Young babies respond to black and white images, so this graphic, coiled shelving would be a treat for them to gaze at. Positioning the cot in the middle of the room leaves the entire wall clear so the shelf can wind its way all over it.

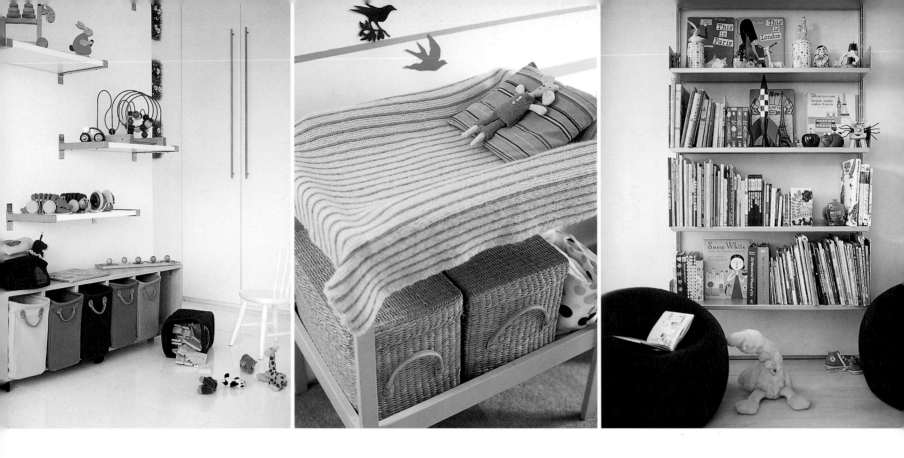

nursery furniture & storage

Comfortable, good-looking furniture and versatile storage are just as essential in the nursery as they are in the kitchen or living room. Look for furniture that will last, suiting your child from a few months old to several years.

You don't need a wardrobe at this stage in your child's life – tiny baby and toddler clothes can be stored flat – but a chest of drawers is essential. Try to include a bookcase, too, and easy-access storage for toys and teddies. Baskets, crates and buckets work well and allow a child to see what's inside. Store the baskets on high shelves to return the room to calmness at bedtime.

A standard cot will last a child around two and a half years, while a cot bed, which is slightly larger, lasts five years. If you buy a second-hand cot, always buy a new mattress, for health and hygiene reasons.

Include a chair in the room if you have space, so you can sit comfortably when feeding baby at night or bedtime. Chairs designed especially for breastfeeding in are available, but they are expensive, so simply choose a comfy armchair that you can both snuggle into for bedtime stories once your child reaches toddlerdom.

A changing table is a good investment, particularly if you suffer from back pain, as bending to change nappies on the floor creates strain. Otherwise, buy a changing board that fits over the cot – an inexpensive alternative.

ABOVE LEFT Colourful baskets hold everything from train track to teddies and live neatly in this wooden unit.

ABOVE CENTRE A changing table, which has storage space below for nappies and wipes, allows you to change baby without bending.

ABOVE RIGHT Arrange books on the lowest shelves so a child can reach them, using higher shelves for display.

RIGHT A chest of drawers is vital in a nursery for clothes storage, but don't feel you have to choose a piece purpose-made for that room. This elegant French-style chest looks beautiful in the nursery, but would look just as at home in an adult's bedroom.

OPPOSITE A clutter-free nursery feels relaxing and calm, important for both mother and baby. This cot bed will last until the child is around five, while the squashy armchair will be big enough to fit a parent and child at story time for many years.

girls' rooms

Girls often take a great interest in how their room is decorated, so have fun choosing pretty shades, stylish furniture and colourful accessories together.

It's a generalization, but girls tend to be more tidy and organized than boys and enjoy arranging their belongings attractively. Provide plenty of open shelves, box shelves or other surfaces for them to arrange favourite things on.

Girls also tend to favour pink, but beware – the love affair with this shade can dwindle and die by the time they are six or seven, so use it with restraint. Instead of Barbie pink, introduce your daughter to brighter shades of fuchsia, magenta or salmon. Use on one wall to make an impact without dominating, or keep the walls neutral and work in some colour on curtains, bedding and rugs.

Then have fun personalizing and prettying up the space. Bunting or fairy lights add colour, tacked to a wall

or hanging from shelves, while a simple canopy made from inexpensive coloured muslin, draped around the bed, will make her feel like a princess. Colourful cushions on the bed or used on the floor are welcome. Keep cuddly toys on the bed during the day, but at night limit your daughter to one or two and store the rest in a basket by the bed – teds can harbour dust and trigger allergies.

ABOVE **A canopy made from fine pink fabric, suspended from the ceiling, can be drawn completely round this bed or luxuriously draped over the headboard. Plain bedding and a neutral wooden floor stop the look from becoming oppressively girlie.**

LEFT **Lilac is a popular shade with girls and creates a calm atmosphere when painted on walls. Touches of hot pink and red liven it up.**

FAR LEFT **Lilac and strong pink shades make this play space for a family of girls really pop. The table can be moved to one side to clear the space for games.**

OPPOSITE **Wallpaper samples have been pasted to the wall behind this bed to create a pretty patchwork effect that's picked up in the mismatched cushions and bedding.**

boys' rooms

It's easy to assume that little boys are oblivious to their environment, but that's not true – they can take a great interest in how their space is organized, what colours are used and where pieces are positioned, so involve them at each stage.

Boys often love bright colours and might want them on their walls, but strong shades can make a space feel claustrophobic. Try using them just on furniture or woodwork, a chimneybreast or curtains, or let your son choose a zingy duvet cover or rug.

Interesting second-hand furniture often appeals to boys. Old lockers, metal trunks, school desks with the traditional hinged lid or beaten-up suitcases may intrigue them and will add tons of character to the room. Or buy sturdy wooden pieces from second-hand shops and refresh them with a colourful coat of paint and some fun handles or knobs.

A bookcase is important. Those that store books with covers facing out make it easy for a child to find the book he's after. Then make the most of fun, inexpensive decorative products. Wall stickers that can be repositioned again and again allow him to personalize his walls, or buy a stencil and paint footprints, grass or a train track onto floorboards.

ABOVE LEFT This funky, Sixties-inspired storage unit in a teenager's room has space to hide stuff away and open shelves to display trophies and favourite items. There is also room for a TV and amp, so that floor space remains uncluttered.

ABOVE RIGHT With a head- and footboard that look like fencing, this bed gives a quirky, individual vibe to the room. Simple bedding in navy blue matches a blue-dyed sheepskin, and walls are kept neutral to give the room a feeling of space.

RIGHT A bold combination of colourfully painted furniture and walls works well in this boy's room because the shades used are of equal strength and distracting clutter is kept to a minimum.

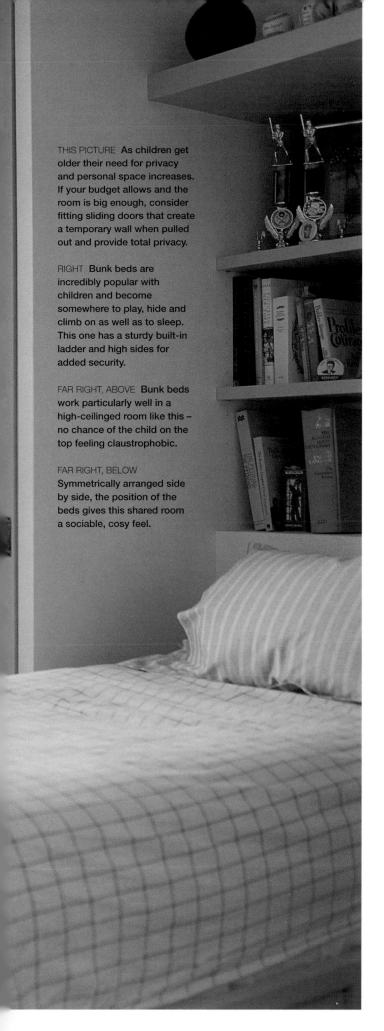

THIS PICTURE As children get older their need for privacy and personal space increases. If your budget allows and the room is big enough, consider fitting sliding doors that create a temporary wall when pulled out and provide total privacy.

RIGHT Bunk beds are incredibly popular with children and become somewhere to play, hide and climb on as well as to sleep. This one has a sturdy built-in ladder and high sides for added security.

FAR RIGHT, ABOVE Bunk beds work particularly well in a high-ceilinged room like this – no chance of the child on the top feeling claustrophobic.

FAR RIGHT, BELOW Symmetrically arranged side by side, the position of the beds gives this shared room a sociable, cosy feel.

shared bedrooms

Many children love the security and sociability of sharing a bedroom with a sibling. Organize the space well, so that each child has an area of his or her own.

Where you position the beds in a shared bedroom is crucial. Single beds side by side look cute and symmetrical, but it's sometimes better to put them at different angles, so the children can't easily see and distract each other. If the room is not a simple square or rectangle, exploit its odd angles by tucking beds into corners, creating a sense of privacy, important for older children.

Alternatively, opt for bunk beds. They are great space-savers and kids can use them to climb and play on, as well as for sleep. Make sure the ladder is sturdy and that the sides are sufficiently high to prevent the child on top falling out. Many bunk beds have the bonus of built-in storage underneath – another space-saver. Whether bunks or singles, fit a wall light or table lamp by each bed, so one child can read without disturbing the other.

Low-level, freestanding shelving units make great room dividers and provide lots of storage, too. Choose one that can be accessed from either side, or a unit on castors so it can be moved to open out the space or create personal zones.

teen bedrooms

Teenage bedrooms need to be more than just a place to sleep – they become a private place away from the family where the young person can relax, express their interests and entertain friends, too.

While children have a lot of toys, teenagers have a lot of equipment. Computers, video games, TVs, stereos, hairdryers, guitars, skateboards, amps…it will all need incorporating into their space, so work in as much storage as possible. As well as all this kit, the usual bed, wardrobe and chest of drawers must find a space, and make sure there is room for a desk for studying. It should be equipped with adequate task lighting for late-night revision sessions, too. If space is limited, a mezzanine-level bed with desk and storage beneath is a great choice, and cool, too. Find this type of bed in large furniture stores or have one built to your specifications.

Your teenager will also want to choose what goes in the room. If your budget doesn't stretch to the furniture of their choice, let them pick new bedding, rugs or window treatments, which can radically alter the look of a room without breaking the bank. Get them to paint the room, too. Finally, privacy is key for teenagers and should be respected. They may want a lock on the door!

ABOVE **Teenagers should be able to personalize their space so it reflects their diverse interests. Here, a collage of images tacked to a wall does just that and looks great, too.**

ABOVE RIGHT **A desk in the bedroom need not look ugly or out of place. Scour second-hand markets for a good-looking vintage piece that will bring real character to the room.**

OPPOSITE, ABOVE **Storing guitars and skateboards on the wall keeps them safe and prevents the floor from becoming cluttered.**

OPPOSITE, BELOW LEFT **Teenage bedrooms are a place to entertain as well as sleep, and the elegant sofa in this girl's room provides space for her to relax alone or socialize with friends.**

OPPOSITE, BELOW RIGHT **A long run of built-in work space suits a household with several teenage children and makes efficient use of space. Hammocks hung behind give them room to relax when study is over.**

■ Night lights and wall lights that look decorative whether on or off come in many designs – choose them in the shape of a flower, moon, star or football.

■ Illuminated globes create subtle light and make learning about the world appealing and accessible.

■ Once children can read, incorporate a reading light next to their bed, fitted with a low-wattage bulb.

■ A single central pendant light creates a very flat, unhelpful light, so always incorporate several light sources in your child's room to boost it. Some wall lights, task lights and soft, ambient light are necessary, and dimmer switches will give even greater control over brightness levels.

■ Make sure hot light bulbs are never within reach of curious fingers. Choose a lampshade that conceals the bulb, or fit lights high on walls, out of reach.

■ Coloured bulbs create atmospheric light that children often find appealing, but are not useful for reading, working or playing, so don't rely on them as the sole light source in the room.

THIS PICTURE A flexible light like this clip-on design can be pulled down to illuminate a book or turned up or towards the wall for more general light. It can also be unclipped easily and moved to another location, as required.

OPPOSITE This wall light produces a broad wash of light on the desk below, ideal for working by, and leaves more space on the worktop for books, stationery and a computer.

ABOVE RIGHT Task lighting like this hinged light is vital at a workstation, especially for evening study or close work like sewing or drawing.

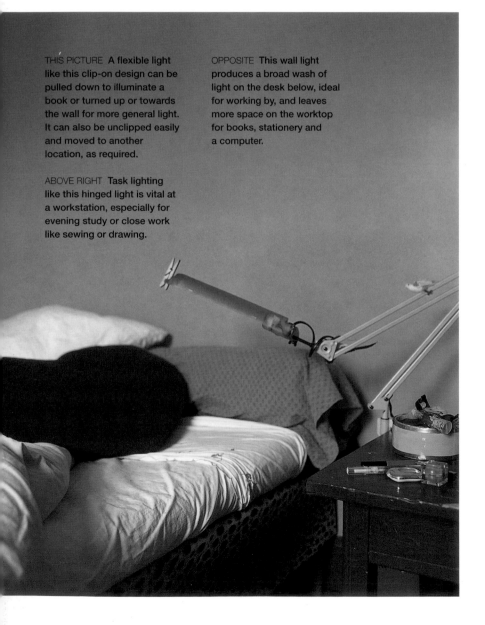

You will need different types of light for different ages, but a few basics will last from baby's first year into teenage times.

lighting

Toddlers often like a small amount of light in a room during the night. It helps them sleep better, as they feel more confident. Night lights that create a soft glow, either in table-lamp style or wall lights, are widely available.

Fairy lights or rope lights are great in kids' rooms. They can be strung across shelves, mantelpieces or curtain rails or just pinned on a wall to create an ambient glow that acts as a night light, too.

Dimmer switches are very practical, as they allow you to turn a wall or ceiling light down very low for night-time feeds, soothing bedtimes or checking a sleeping child. They can be left on low for a child who is afraid of the dark, then put on full when needed.

Directable spotlights are a good option, too, available as wall-mounted or clip-on spots, or in lamp form, like the classic Anglepoise. They can work as a reading lamp, be turned towards the ceiling or wall for a softer light and, when a child gets older, make good task lighting to do homework by.

Children spend a great deal of time on the floor. When you choose flooring for a child's room, comfort is a key consideration.

flooring

TOP A brightly striped rug picks up the colours on the walls of this nursery and pulls the scheme together.

ABOVE This giant foam jigsaw is big enough to cover much of the floor in a child's room, is comfy underfoot, fun to assemble and can be packed away easily.

RIGHT A Tintin rug softens the wooden floor and gives children a comfy place to sit and play in this themed room.

OPPOSITE Bright colours have been used in this bedroom, but with a degree of control. The orange on the wall continues on the patterned bedding and rug, while neutral wooden floorboards help anchor the look.

Let's start with what you don't want. Although hardwearing, natural fibres like sisal and seagrass are too rough for children's delicate skin. Deep-pile carpets, while beautifully soft, can trap dirt and crumbs, not practical for children, and also harbour the dust mites that can irritate children with allergies and eczema – conditions very common in childhood. So if you'd like a wall-to-wall floor covering, choose a short-weave carpet that has been treated with protective Scotchgard, so it's stain-resistant and easy to vacuum.

Wooden floorboards are also practical. Easy to clean and good-looking, they can be softened with rugs and mats, making them kind to floor-dwelling kids. In a dark room, go for painted floorboards in a pale shade that will make the room seem brighter and larger.

Vinyl and rubber flooring are other appealing choices, combining practicality with good looks. Rubber comes in a huge range of colours, is slip-resistant – ideal for kids who like to run around in their socks – and makes it easy to wipe up spills.

■ Make sure any gaps in old wooden floorboards are filled – small children love to 'post' things through them. Sand down any rough sections and check for protruding nails or splinters, too.

■ Use a mix of flooring to zone your child's space. Choose a cosy rug for by the bed, where he or she can sit quietly to read or draw, and a practical, wipe-clean surface in activity areas.

■ Soften and brighten wooden floorboards with cotton mats or rugs that can be machine-washed.

■ Shaggy rugs can hold mites and mess, and they do not provide the smooth surface kids need to put jigsaws together, stand play figures on or push toy cars over, so use them sparingly or not at all.

■ Rugs can be educational and fun. Many children's stores sell rugs with a world map or streetscape designs.

■ Choose a hardwearing fitted carpet in an oatmeal shade or with a flecked pattern – both are good at disguising marks and crumbs. Stripes will make any room seem longer or wider and also provide 'tracks' for children to drive toy cars along.

■ Children often have a great many toys but only become attached to a small selection at any time, so try rotating them, storing some on high shelves or in cupboards for a few months, then swapping them. It gives the child a sense of having 'new' things; they can focus on them clearly and enjoy them more.

■ Boxes on castors that can be stored under a bed help keep mess under control and floor space free for playing.

■ Hanging baskets and mesh cylinders that can be suspended from the ceiling or hung on the back of a door are great for storing and displaying soft toys.

■ If your child is at reading age, labels on drawers and boxes help with easy identification and organizing.

■ Choose units with solid bases, rather than legs, so that toys can't get lost underneath.

■ Avoid cupboards, trunks and chests with locks; a little one could get trapped inside.

■ Choose baskets and buckets with lids. Toys can be casually tossed into them at bedtime and, once the lid is on, the space looks tidy and uncluttered.

■ As well as closed storage, work in open shelving for displaying favourite things, artwork, certificates and family photos.

ABOVE **This multi-tasking tiered wooden unit provides lots of flexible storage in quite a small space and also acts as steps up to a mezzanine bed. The bright pink paintwork gives it extra personality.**

ABOVE RIGHT **A built-in wall of cupboards need not be the preserve of adult bedrooms, and is helpful in keeping a child's room tidy. Simply slide back the doors and all their toys are quickly accessible.**

BELOW RIGHT **A distressed wooden wardrobe looks perfect in this colourful, highly individual bedroom. Old wooden pieces like this can quickly be given a fresh new look with a coat of paint.**

OPPOSITE **This vintage locker unit looks incredibly stylish while also providing masses of storage, so it's perfect in this shared bedroom. The tough metal frame and doors make it hardwearing, too, and impervious to knocks or bangs. Trawl second-hand stores or flea markets for something similar.**

Sturdy furniture that can take a little rough handling and easy-to-access storage will cater for all your child's needs, from infancy to the teenage years.

storage

Choose a wardrobe with a height-adjustable rail so it can fit bigger clothes as your child grows. Adjustable shelves on bookcases are also useful as large picture books are exchanged for paperbacks.

Second-hand furniture that looks better with the odd bump and chip is a safe bet and economical, too. Old wardrobes, shelving units, chests of drawers and boxes crop up at markets and can be revived with a coat of paint and some decorative knobs or handles.

To encourage your children to clear up, provide adequate, easy-to-access storage. Rather than stackable storage, choose big toy chests, baskets and buckets that make tidying easy. Different-sized boxes and small drawer units keep small toys and stationery under control, too. Position some storage at child level and consider building in high shelves or cupboards for those pieces you don't need so often, like bedding, out-of-season clothes or excess toys.

Children respond positively to colour and aren't fearful of living with bright shades. Take advantage of their youthful enthusiasm and have fun with ultra-brights.

ultra-brights

■ Use some vibrant wallpaper as a feature on one wall. There are plenty of funky florals, lively patterns and cool abstracts around, and a single roll won't break the bank.

■ Choose colourful furniture that can stand against a colourful wall – painted wooden pieces or brightly upholstered chairs and beanbags look great.

■ Hang a bright roller blind/shade at the window. The strong tone will make an impact, but the unfussy roller

design will keep this injection of bright colour looking crisp and controlled.

■ Bring the brightness down to floor level – a surface that sees a lot of action in a child's room – and leave the walls white. The eye will be drawn downwards, which is also a useful effect in a high-ceilinged room.

■ Create a feature wall behind the bed or cot, so the child isn't directly facing it while lying down and will not be distracted by the bright shade.

Children instinctively prefer strong colour. They dress, draw and paint using bold primary shades and are less drawn to ambiguous neutrals or soft pastels than adults.

There is an argument that says bright colours are too stimulating in a bedroom, but children don't always find them so. Most children can easily switch off from their surroundings once it's time to sleep, so feel free to experiment with fresh, bright shades.

If you want to introduce some ultra-brights to your child's room, try painting a feature wall and keeping the others white. Or just accessorize with brights. From rugs to duvet covers, canopies to curtains, there are masses of ways to inject colour into a child's room without splashing it all over the walls. Children's furniture is often highly coloured – think plastic buckets, painted wooden units and even colourful bed frames and cots. Anchor any scheme with wooden floorboards or a neutral carpet to give it some balance and you can't go far wrong.

Have the courage of your convictions and be bold. Stick to the same intensity of bright throughout. A brilliant blue chest of drawers will look great alongside red plastic storage boxes and a strong, stripy duvet, but less impressive against a pastel wall or wishy-washy rug. Stick with the bright colours for a cohesive and confident look.

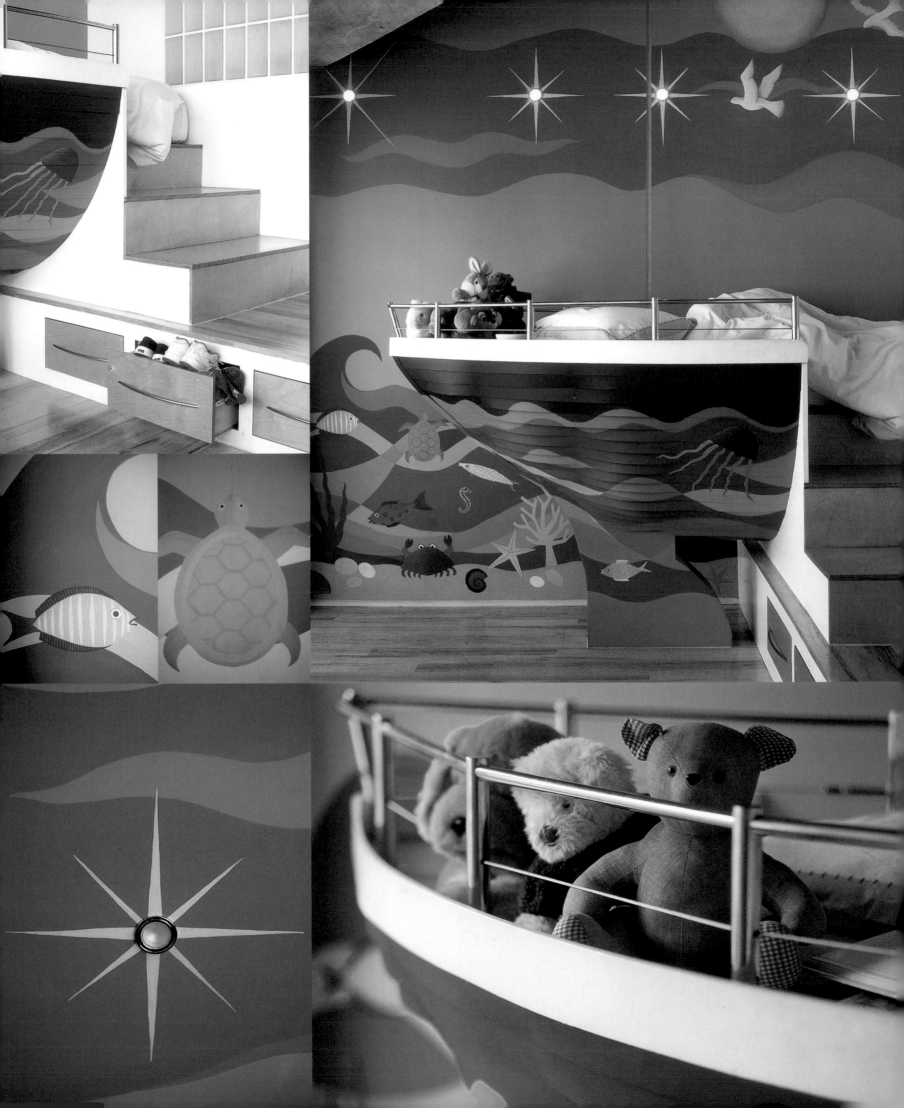

A child's room is one of the few in the house where your imagination can run wild. Creating a unique space can be exciting and, for your child, magical.

customized bedrooms

Theming your child's room is a useful first step towards creating a customized space. Does your child love pirates or princesses, the seaside or the jungle, dinosaurs or diggers? Begin by creating a mood board of images, cuttings, stickers and favourite characters that can help you and your child devise a workable theme for the room. Keep it fairly simple and clear – you may be overstretching yourself and your budget if you imagine you can have hand-

painted murals on every wall and a bespoke bed. One wall painted with a trompe l'oeil or one key piece of furniture that has been made to your design, with some less expensive accessories, is a good starting point.

The bed is often at the heart of a bespoke scheme. A carpenter will be able to incorporate a bed into a shaped exterior, so it can look like anything from a racing car to a boat to Cinderella's carriage. You could create a bed on a platform, or one enclosed by sliding doors or curtains, to give your child a hidey-hole.

Murals are another beautiful and imaginative addition to a child's customized room. Paint a seascape or landscape on a wall over which your little one's imagination can roam, or paint a starlit sky or cloudy sky on the ceiling. You could include favourite storybook or cartoon characters, but if in doubt, play safe and stick to an image that your child will not quickly outgrow. Unless you are a skilled artist, painting a mural is a job for a professional, but a good artist will be open to your ideas and willing to be directed by your suggestions.

■ A customized bed or hand-decorated wall is expensive and permanent, so be sure your child will enjoy it for a good number of years before you go ahead.

■ Rather than getting bespoke furniture made, commission a carpenter to modify an existing piece.

■ If your skills or budget do not stretch to a mural, customize walls with stick-on graphics. They are easy to put up and come in a range of patterns.

Pink can work well on walls, because it is both colourful and relaxing; just right in a room where you need to sleep. Stick to redder tones for a soothing vibe, and pale pink for a fresh feel. Take it across four walls for an uncompromisingly pink effect, or go for a super-bright shade on one wall, where it can create an impact without making the room feel claustrophobic.

For a really colourful effect, team pink with other shades from the same palette: warm reds, rich purples and lilac. Or mix it with other strong shades, but in moderation: fresh green, sky blue and sunny yellow can all work with a splash of cerise.

If your daughter demands pink furniture, shop around at specialist children's furniture retailers, or just paint wooden furniture in the right shade of eggshell. This is inexpensive and allows you to choose from a vast spectrum of pink-toned paints.

It's easy to accessorize with pink. From cushions to curtains, bedding to artwork, there is a host of pieces available. Restraint is key. Blend in enough cool white, neutral shades or very pale pink to balance the look and give it breathing space. A pink rug on white floorboards is far more eye-catching than a pink carpet. It's all about giving the eye little pools of pink to settle on. If you go for all-pink walls, team them with plain, pale bedding, a neutral carpet or white furniture to break up the effect.

Girls often love pink, but forget sugary shades and explore a world of sophisticated cerises, vibrant magentas and delicate pastels that will satisfy both your daughter's and your own sense of style.

thinking pink

■ Pink gingham or ticking stripes are a classic way to bring pink into a child's room, and will appeal to grown-ups, too. Use them on simple roller blinds/shades, bedding and cushion covers.

■ For a retro pink feel, find old curtains and fabric at markets and make them into cushion covers. Or get the vintage look by cutting up old damask, with its faded, tea-rose tones.

■ Create an understated pink look with rope lights or fairy lights fitted with pink bulbs. They produce a subtle glow, warming up white walls.

■ Remember your daughter may fall out of love with pink once she approaches her teenage years, so make sure that the majority of pink ingredients in the room can be easily and inexpensively changed.

Teenage boys rarely go for the minimalist approach to decoration – more is definitely more. Their 'toys' need to be out, but ordered – and that takes planning.

boy zone

■ Floors can easily become dumping grounds. Incorporate plenty of open shelving so it's easy and quick to store away books, shoes, CDs and other kit.

■ Make sure there is plenty of flexible lighting, to cope with different hobbies and activities. Clip-on spotlights are incredibly versatile and provide strong, directable light.

■ Framing favourite posters will protect them and instantly make them look smarter, while also avoiding the need to use sticky tape or Blu-Tack to hang them, which can damage paintwork.

■ Encourage your son to switch off all his electrical gear at the socket when not in use, to save power wasted on standby lights and sleeping computers.

■ Lots of electrical equipment means lots of electrical wires and flex. Make sure they are trained neatly away from the open floor, to prevent accidents.

Most boys, given half a chance, will happily live in an untidy space. Of course that's a generalization, but boys are often less bothered by mess than girls and would always rather spend time on their interests than on tidying. To help impose a little order into their space, work in practical storage that requires minimum effort to use. Sometimes, even hanging clothes on a hanger seems too wearisome, so put up pegs and hooks so shirts and jackets can be casually thrown onto them. Lidded baskets that can hold shoes are also useful and, if strong enough, can also double as seating.

If your son is into sport, his room may be home to anything from skateboards to wetsuits to football kit. Floors can quickly become cluttered with kit, so find ways to store stuff up and out of the way. A rack that skateboards or tennis rackets can slot into will keep them safely off the floor, and a net suspended from a hook can hold footballs, helmets or shin pads.

A desk is essential; deep enough to house a computer and printer. You can pick up huge old desks at second-hand shops or look around for an adaptable modern version, with a pull-out shelf for a keypad or integrated shelving above. No matter how small your son's room, you should be able to find something to fit. If awkward dimensions are proving challenging, ask a carpenter to build a desk and shelves in an alcove or across a corner.

If music is your son's passion and he needs room for a keyboard, guitars or mixing desks, it might be worth moving the traditional wardrobe and chest of drawers out to a spare room or the landing so that he can keep his kit close to hand and out of reach of family life. CD racks are available in dozens of designs and will encourage him to order his collection, while small drawer units or under-bed boxes are also great space-saving storage options.

Young children need a table or desk for all kinds of activities. Practising their writing, drawing and painting, sticking and making, jigsaw puzzles – they all demand a wide, wipe-clean surface that is the right height for a child to sit up at. Children's tables can be rather small, so position two together to make a longer run, or buy a second-hand kitchen table and cut the legs down to make it lower.

Storage for pens, glue, art materials and paper needs to be positioned close to hand. A simple row of shelves alongside the table or just above (but not out of reach), topped with boxes and trays that can neatly hold paper and colouring books is a good idea, while old glass jars, jugs or mugs can keep pens and pencils tidily on the desktop.

A desk remains key for older children and teenagers, too. It is somewhere to study, draw, paint, sew or arrange favourite objects. In later years, it will become home to a computer or, when topped with a mirror, can double as a dressing table. As the child grows taller, so too can the height of shelves arranged above, there to hold not just books, but CDs, study materials, holiday souvenirs and pictures.

The need to personalize one's space becomes greater the older one gets, so as your child becomes a teenager, work in flexible pieces that they can leave their mark on – furniture that can be painted the colour they choose, an unusual chair, shelves that can become crammed with significant pieces.

Add corkboards or magnetic boards to an older child's room so they can pin up photos, postcards and certificates. Their bedroom is so much more than a place to sleep; it is the one space in the house that is uniquely theirs, a place to rest, but also entertain, study, listen to music, surf the internet, practise an instrument or just read. Flexible furniture, plenty of storage and space-saving ideas will help their room work hard and meet all their growing needs.

From preschool sticking and gluing to teenage study, from practising the flute to making a den, children's rooms are places of activity, as well as calm and sleep.

action stations

■ If your young child's bedroom is also his or her chief activity area, consider laying practical flooring such as rubber or vinyl over some of the floor, so it's easy to clean up spills and scuffs.

■ For an older child, try to find a desk large enough to fit the computer on one side, so there is still a decent-sized work surface for writing, painting or sketching, to encourage all facets of your child's creativity.

■ Good lighting is essential in a room that multi-tasks. Work in general light with ceiling and wall lights, then add directable task lighting for close work and soft, ambient lighting for relaxing.

■ Try to zone the space so there is a calm area, too. Position the bed facing away from the main activity area, so the child isn't distracted when trying to sleep.

■ A chair on castors allows an older child to move quickly between desk, drawers and shelving without getting up.

home offices

design & decoration

Whether you work from home full-time or just need somewhere quiet to tap away at the computer, creating a home office is a necessity these days. But if you haven't got a room to spare, where can you put it and how can you make it work with the rest of your living space?

ABOVE **Choose a calm, uncluttered space for working – whether it's an unused bedroom or the end of the kitchen table – and make sure you have lots of storage for all the office paraphernalia.**

ABOVE RIGHT **Foldaway features are extremely useful in a home office – particularly if the room is also used for another purpose. Here an ingenious fold-down desk and a giant cork noticeboard can be shut away behind a sliding panel when not in use.**

OPPOSITE **If you haven't a separate space in which to house your office, tuck it into the corner of another room, as here. A neat arrangement of sleek wooden filing cabinets, desktop and storage, this workstation is highly efficient but takes up little space.**

If you don't have a study, think where you could house an office. Could you convert a junk room, perhaps, or put a workstation in the loft or on the landing? If you are short of space, could you section off part of a large living room or create a mezzanine level in a high-ceilinged bedroom? Consider what you can afford and get advice from an architect if you want to make structural changes.

A cheaper solution is to double the function of a room so that it can play the office role part-time. A spare room could be work space by day and guest bedroom by night, for example. The key is to keep the décor neutral and to be organized, so one function doesn't intrude on the other.

The bonus of creating an office in your own home is that it needn't look corporate or dull. You will have to accommodate all the technology, but you can make the room as comfortable and colourful as you wish. Keep in mind that certain colours can affect your mood and try to keep clutter to a minimum to help concentration.

RIGHT Don't buy new office furniture for your home work space; make use of what you already have. Any table can function as a desk if it is big enough to work at and the right height for you, while storage comes in many shapes and sizes. Here, a tall open shelving unit houses cane baskets. Good for categorizing clutter, they can also be moved around easily.

OPPOSITE When you are planning the layout of your office, take into account exactly what you need to accommodate: a series of box files, perhaps; a stationery cupboard; room for two people to work at once – as here. Addressing your needs at the outset will help you achieve a result that is just right for you.

planning

Today's home office can be a fixed, functional space or something altogether more fluid – a computer at the kitchen table, for example, or just a laptop and a mobile phone. Decide what is right for you and then plan the space down to the last detail to make sure it delivers what you need.

In any office, technology is a top priority. Consider just how much equipment your work space will need to accommodate and devise a layout to suit. The last thing you want is for your office to become a hotch-potch of ugly grey machines, so think how to arrange them neatly and discreetly so they won't dominate. Could you house a printer or a photocopier in a shelving unit, for example? Could the modem be stashed beneath the desk?

Although wireless technology is developing rapidly, many machines still need plugging in. Avoid trailing cables by positioning related equipment together and install extra electrical sockets wherever needed. If you

have a fitted desktop, cut a hole at the back so that wires and cables can be channelled away from the working area, and use cable tidies to keep mess off the floor.

If your home office is located within another room, think of ways to separate it off. After all, you don't want to be thinking about work when you are relaxing in the living room, for example. If a permanent partition is not an option, consider positioning your office space behind a screen or a large piece of furniture. A tiny workstation can even be shut up inside a large cupboard when not in use.

Good and copious storage is a necessity, so make sure you have enough. If you are constructing an office from scratch, get as much built in as you can; if not, opt for freestanding solutions, making sure that whatever you choose can accommodate your equipment. An organized office not only looks better, it is far easier to work in, too.

Flat-pack and fold-away elements always work well in a home office – particularly if it is in a shared space. Consider putting a flap-down desk against a wall or within a cupboard. Flexible features like this can easily be tucked out of sight when not in use.

ABOVE Why not convert your garden shed or invest in a ready-made outdoor office? Equipped with the necessary technology, this will give you a well-defined work area and, by being away from the house, help you to maintain a healthy work–life balance. Working in the garden should prove quiet and calming, and will offer the shortest commute ever.

workstations

Today's home office needs to be ultra-efficient and equipped with the latest technology, but that doesn't mean it has to have its own dedicated room. A compact workstation can include all the elements of a larger office but can be slotted against a wall or tucked into the corner of another space.

So where should it go? Ideally, the location should be well-lit (natural light is best), quiet and set apart from the hurly-burly of daily life, so you won't be interrupted. A workstation won't take up too much room, so consider setting it in an in-between space, such as a half-landing or the end of a hallway, if it doesn't get too much traffic. Have a look at your home and work with what you have.

Apart from computer kit, a workstation requires three basic ingredients: a desk, a chair and storage. You can buy modular units ready-made, so investigate these first and consider if any combinations would be right for you. Alternatively, take the DIY route and design your own (an architect or designer can help here). It might cost more, but a custom-built workstation will fit its allotted space perfectly and give you exactly what you want.

Make sure your desktop is fitted at the right height and don't be tempted to skimp on your office chair. Choose an ergonomic model that is comfortable, supportive and adjustable to avoid bad posture and back pain.

corner offices

A computer on the kitchen worktop; a bureau in the bedroom; a desk in the living room – the home office is often squeezed into borrowed space, but that doesn't mean compromising on function or style.

In a dual-purpose room, the key to success is to create defined areas for each function, so that one doesn't intrude on the other. One way of doing this is to partition the space physically, perhaps with sliding doors, a fabric curtain or a simple screen to divide your work area from the rest of the room. This will give you the advantage of a distinct office space as and when you need it.

If you opt, instead, to keep things open, make the office element as unobtrusive as possible. Rather than buying in standard utilitarian furniture, choose pieces that will fit in with the look of the rest of the room. An old wooden desk, for example, could be just the thing for your computer as long as it is the right height and big enough to work at. If you don't have anything suitable at home, hunt around for old office fixtures and fittings that will slot neatly into your decorative scheme.

Ideally, choose pieces that come with integral storage space, so you can contain your office paraphernalia or shut it away when not in use. Planned carefully, a corner office shouldn't dominate the rest of the room.

ABOVE LEFT Old office or factory fittings can make a quirky workstation; just check they are comfortable to sit at. This unit, with connected stool and storage boxes, provides a neat solution.

ABOVE RIGHT An old bureau – the ultimate mini-workstation – can function effectively in a modern space. This mid-20th-century model fits neatly in a corner and provides a desk and storage space without taking up too much room.

OPPOSITE Office furniture doesn't have to be modular and modern; in a traditional setting, worktops and swivel chairs will look out of place. In this elegant, panelled room, a grand desk and Louis XV-style chair are unobtrusive and make an effective work area.

You can't have too much storage in your home office. Whether you opt for a built-in solution or freestanding furniture, include more than you think you need and make sure it is suitable for the task.

large storage

OPPOSITE A wall of storage can be the perfect solution in a small room, because it intrudes little into the central space. Whether you opt for open shelves, closed drawers or a combination of the two, make sure they are big enough to house your possessions, and keep things you use frequently in the most accessible spots.

BELOW LEFT A series of identical boxes can make a useful filing system. Not only are they capacious; they can easily be moved around to wherever needed. Stack them up neatly, as here, for a seamless look and stick a label on the end if you need to identify the contents.

BELOW RIGHT A flexible shelving system comes in handy in the office, allowing you to create storage spaces that are just the right size for your equipment.

RIGHT Make the most of any wasted space by using it for storage. Here, three large filing cabinets slot in neatly beneath the built-in worktop.

In a small office, integral storage works best. A wall-to-wall system of shelves and cupboards, for example, will give you copious places to put things but it won't intrude on the room. Similarly, if you fill an alcove or disused chimneybreast with shelves, you will create a practical storage solution without compromising the central space.

A mixture of open and closed storage works well because it allows you to display certain elements and hide others, but remember that an open storage box or shelf will attract dust. One solution is to shut up your storage with see-through doors (in glass or lighter Perspex, perhaps). Solid cupboards are the answer in a dual-purpose space, however, so that your office equipment can be invisible when not in use.

Build flexibility into your work space, too, so that you can easily accommodate new office kit (adjustable shelves are a good option) and put large freestanding storage on castors to make it mobile.

■ If your office is housed in a room that has another use, opt for enclosed storage so you can shut your work away when you have finished for the day.

■ For the ultimate now-you-see-it-now-you-don't office, create a mini-workstation inside a cupboard. Remember that you will need to fit internal plug sockets here for computer equipment and the phone.

■ Invest in a desk with integral storage. Multi-level models with overlapping tiers, for example, will allow you to stack monitor and keyboard on top of each other – a practical and space-saving option.

■ Freestanding storage solutions won't fit your space exactly but will give you more flexibility, allowing you to move things around if you need to. Put heavy items – such as filing cabinets – on castors, if possible, to make them mobile.

■ Clear out your office regularly: old files and paperwork can be stored in a loft or cellar, leaving you more space for your current bits and pieces.

- Reduce your paperwork by scanning important documents or articles and storing them digitally – but remember to back up your files regularly.

- In a small home office, make the most of every available bit of space. Suspend a fabric shoe tidy in an awkward corner and use it for storing folders and files, or invest in a hanging filing system which can be hooked onto the back of a door.

- Turn the wall above your desk into a giant noticeboard. Not only will it keep your worktop clutter-free; it is just the place to pin up inspirational bits and pieces.

- Bring in some unconventional containers to add a quirky and personal look to your work space: use an old cigar box as an in tray; recycled tin cans for pens and pencils; a toast rack for cards and invitations.

- To make your desktop neat and tidy, choose uniform storage containers. A row of stainless-steel pots, for example, or a series of wooden boxes will look smart and organized. If you do opt for a disparate collection of containers, stick to one colour to unify them.

ABOVE Desk tidies don't have to be dull. Anything can work for pens and pencils, so hunt around for something you like.

RIGHT If you have many odds and ends to organize, store like with like so you can easily find what you need. This collection of pencils and brushes may not look ordered but, stashed in separate tins, each is easy to identify.

BELOW RIGHT Any container can be used for storage, from wooden chests to old tin cans. Think lateral and make use of things you already have.

OPPOSITE Even old vegetable crates can make good storage containers. Practical, edgy and eco-friendly, they are the perfect finishing touch in this quirky, contemporary office.

It is easy for a home office to become overtaken with clutter. Keep your work paraphernalia under control by bringing in some useful storage containers.

small storage

There is a huge variety of office accessories on the market, from the classic tubular plastic desk tidy to smart letter trays in leather, wood or stainless steel. If you are buying new, choose a style you like and stick to it. A uniform set of storage containers will do much to make your worktop look organized. Similarly, opt for identikit magazine files in one or two colours, or buy plain ones and cover them to match your office. Lined up in a row, they will bring instant order to your bookshelves.

Don't feel you have to buy in a quota of standard office kit, however. You may have just what you need already to hand. A collection of vintage tins or some old wooden boxes, for example, can make great organizers, or you could even recycle tin cans or shoeboxes to make unconventional storage containers. Not only will these add a quirky edge to your home office, they are eco-friendly options to boot.

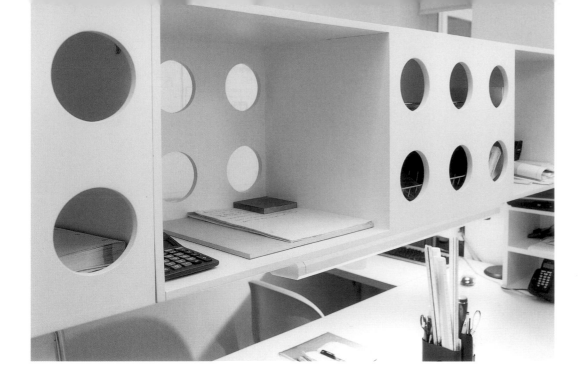

In a home office, more than anywhere in the house, it is crucial to get the lighting right. A badly lit work space can lead to headaches and eyestrain.

lighting

Daylight is the easiest to work by, so if you are creating an office from scratch try to site it in a naturally well-lit location. If you can't, consider other ways of bringing in the light: could you install a skylight or create an internal window, perhaps, to make the space brighter? Failing that, bring in bulbs that simulate daylight.

Supplement sunlight with a mix of ambient and task lighting so you can create the level of light you require. A central pendant or ceiling spots will give you good general cover, but you will also need targeted lights to illuminate your desktop effectively. In-built solutions can work well if they are strategically placed (under an eye-level unit, perhaps); freestanding lamps will give you greater flexibility. Opt for jointed models – such as the classic Anglepoise – so that you can easily change the direction of the light. If more than one person works in the office, make sure there's sufficient task lighting for everyone, and always turn off lights when not in use.

■ In summer you will need to screen out brilliant sunlight to prevent computer glare and excess heat, so make sure your windows can be covered without losing the light. Diaphanous curtains or vinyl frosting applied to the lower panes are good solutions.

■ Effective task lighting is particularly important if you will be using the office at night. Bright overhead illumination is not what you want here.

■ Build adaptability into your lighting scheme so that you can create just the amount of cover you need. Take advice from an electrician and install adjustable solutions, such as dimmer switches, to give you maximum flexibility.

■ If your office is stuck in a gloomy space, consider using full-spectrum bulbs, which simulate daylight more effectively than ordinary light bulbs. Some can also help alleviate symptoms of SAD.

■ Electric lighting consumes copious amounts of energy, so keep the environment in mind when you are kitting out your home office. Switch to low-energy light bulbs (daylight versions are available) and always turn off the lights at the end of the day.

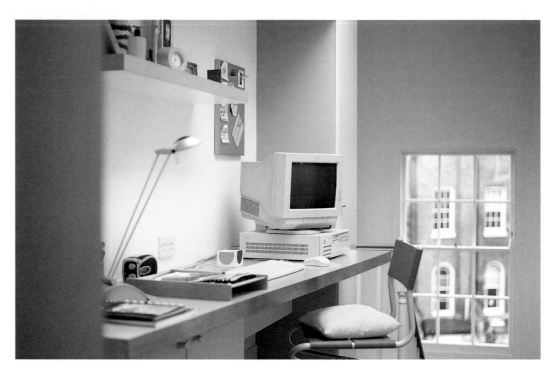

■ Your desktop needn't be dull. Give it a curvy edge or top it with an interesting material (vinyl or rubber tiles, perhaps) to achieve a distinctive look.

■ Create an eye-catching feature wall with something that inspires you, whether it's wallpaper, a blown-up map or a giant black and white photograph.

■ Display fresh flowers. Not only will they bring a bit of life to your work space; they should make it smell nice to boot. Just remember to replace them once they are past their best.

■ As well as books, files and folders, think of displaying more unusual things in your office space. Overscaled items can work well, such as giant wooden letters, a station clock or an outsized calendar.

■ Colour-code your folders and files to make an easy and good-looking filing system. Don't over-complicate it; just two or three tones should do the trick.

ABOVE LEFT Bring in accessories that suit the style of your home office, but don't go over the top. An uncluttered space is still the ideal. Here, a graphic lampshade and some colourful textiles liven up a traditional study area.

ABOVE RIGHT If your workstation is in an open space, like this office-on-the-landing solution, think carefully about its decoration. Here, a predominantly neutral scheme has been used so that the work area doesn't stand out too much, but the space has also been given a burst of energy with zingy accents of orange and lemon yellow.

OPPOSITE Your home office might be a functional space, but that doesn't mean it has to look dull or corporate. Apply the same decorative eye to your work area as you would to the rest of your home, and make it somewhere you want to spend time in. Here, a soft white scheme and a mix of individual furniture and pictures make for a pretty and personal work area.

Although functionality is the key ingredient in the home office, don't forget to decorate it. Adding colour, pictures and personal details will make it a far nicer place to be.

finishing touches

Just because this is a working space doesn't mean you need to temper your taste. What works for you in the rest of the house should work for you here, so put up floral wallpaper or photos if they inspire you. Think what colours would work best with the light; what flooring is appropriate; what window treatments you'd like.

A shared space, however, demands a different approach. Here, your workstation needs to slot into the general scheme, so consider the other role the room has to play and decorate accordingly. Though you might paint the walls all one colour, using different or raised flooring for the work space can be a subtle way of defining it without making it too obtrusive. A colourful rug would also be effective. Though you want your home office to be efficient and uncluttered, don't leave it bare. It is a *home* office, after all, and calls out for a bit of comfort and character.

There are countless ready-made office systems on the market, so if you want to buy off the peg, trawl the high street and internet to find out what is available. To save time and effort, have an idea of what you want before you start. What size workstation do you need? Which finish would suit your space? How much do you want to spend? Prices depend on material and quality, so set a budget (and remember you usually get what you pay for).

Any fitted system will offer office components in fixed sizes, whether shelves, desktops or drawers, and many suppliers will allow you to mix and match different elements to create something that will work in your space. Try to include as many adaptable features as you can to give yourself maximum flexibility. Opt for adjustable shelving, fold-down desks or light fixtures that can be moved to different positions, for example.

Always include more storage than you think you need (you will fill it). Closed cupboards give a neat, streamlined look; open storage boxes offer you easy access to your bits and pieces and also give you a useful display space. A combination of the two is often the best solution.

The one-wall home office makes the most economical use of space, particularly when a desktop is incorporated into the design. This linear system is streamlined and good-looking but it is not necessarily the most ergonomic solution. A corner office, by contrast, will create a self-contained 'work triangle', allowing you to move with ease between the prime working spots – the computer monitor, the desktop and the filing cabinet, for example – possibly without even leaving your chair.

If you can't find a suitable ready-made solution, consider a bespoke office. Get quotes from architects or designers and give a very detailed brief. Discuss what size the shelves should be to accommodate your box files; how many drawers you need; at what angle you would like the desktop. Getting something custom-made is the ultimate indulgence, but you will end up with a working space that is perfect for you.

Whether shop-bought or custom-made, a fitted office system makes good use of space. With adaptable elements, it can be both functional and flexible.

purpose-built offices

■ Ask suppliers if they offer a fitting service for their off-the-peg office systems. If not, measure up and make a floor plan yourself so you know exactly how much space you have to play with.

■ Note down the exact position of your electrical sockets and, if you need any extras, get them fitted before you start.

■ Don't forget that any open storage system will only be as tidy as you make it. If clutter is problem, closed cupboards may be a better bet for you.

■ If you haven't much space, choose smaller purpose-built pieces of furniture, such as the hard-working old bureau, which gives you a whole office in miniature.

■ Even an off-the-peg office system can include custom-made elements. Combine shop-bought pieces with bespoke to create just what you need.

■ Planning from scratch means you can create good task lighting and hide trailing wires and cables.

The best thing about creating a working space at home is that it need not look like a corporate office. You can do away with the formula of functional grey furniture, uniform filing units and flickering strip lighting and create an individual and expressive space that is just right for you.

You will still need the key office ingredients, of course – a desk, a chair and storage – but these don't need to be purpose-built. For a less structured effect, gather together an ad hoc collection of furniture, but make sure that whatever you choose is practical and comfortable. Think what you need in your office and look around the house to see if you can use something you already have, or hunt for interesting second-hand or vintage pieces.

A freeform office should be a fluid and adaptable place, so opt for freestanding furniture that you can move around at whim, and don't let your display space stagnate. Show off different bits and pieces week by week, or even day by day, to keep your work area alive. While a streamlined, ordered office is not what you are after here, do try to keep clutter at bay. Even in a freeform office, you need a bit of space to be creative.

Unstructured and adaptable, the freeform office should give you the space to be creative. Just remember not to let the clutter get out of control.

freeform offices

■ Make sure the essentials are in good working order – the phone, the electrics, the modem. Even a freeform office needs to be functional.

■ Mix and match different pieces of furniture for an idiosyncratic look. Make sure to find a comfortable chair and storage that is fit for purpose.

■ Turn your working area into a display space. You don't need collections of art or recherché artefacts to make it look good. Pinned with a collection of interesting bits and pieces, even a noticeboard can make a visual impact.

■ Rather than a dull filing cabinet, choose more unconventional storage options. Hang bags or baskets from hooks on the wall to accommodate your office kit, for example.

■ Surround yourself with things you love. Whether it's a family painting, an antique desk lamp or a knitted cushion, old favourites will inspire you and make you feel at home.

open-plan living

why open-plan?

Whether you want to knock two rooms into one or crave a giant do-it-all living area, an open-plan space has become the latest must-have. Free-flowing and flexible, it seems perfect for modern life, but why is it so popular?

The domestic interior used to be a very fixed and formal affair. There was the kitchen for cooking; the dining room for eating; the study for working. A hundred years ago this formula made sense, but today it seems outmoded and the separate rooms inappropriate for modern life. People like to chat with their friends as they cook; rustle up supper at the kitchen table; surf the net while the kettle boils. An open-plan layout offers just this flexibility.

It will also, of course, maximize the sense of space and light. Freed of dividing walls, even a small home can seem spacious. Think of combining a tiny bathroom and small bedroom to create one large sleeping and bathing space, or making the downstairs one multi-purpose area.

In new houses and loft-style apartments the open-plan layout has become standard, particularly downstairs, but in an older house some restructuring will be in order. Plan what you want to do, get advice from a structural engineer or an architect and cost the project carefully. Knocking down walls is a job for a professional, particularly if the walls are load-bearing.

OPPOSITE **By knocking out a dividing wall to connect the dining and sitting rooms, the owners of this elegant home have created a spacious and free-flowing space. Though each area retains its original function, the two are unified with a palette of muted neutral tones.**

ABOVE LEFT **The decorative scheme has to be carefully considered in any open-plan space. Here, the colours of the dining chairs are echoed in the sitting-'room' cushions to connect the two areas visually.**

ABOVE RIGHT **To maximize the feeling of space, this minimal living area is completely open, with the same white paintwork and sleek flooring throughout. Only the furniture defines the function of each area.**

pros & cons

An open-plan interior will give you space, light and freedom of movement, but before you start knocking down walls, think about the drawbacks, too.

One large, transformable space, rather than a series of rooms, allows you to organize the layout just as you like – and reconfigure it at whim. If you spend little time cooking, for example, minimize the kitchen area and leave more room for eating or lounging. If you sometimes work from home, create an ad hoc office wherever you like. And open-plan is perfect for entertaining – from six to sixty – as long as you have the right furniture to make it work.

LEFT To make an open-plan area hang together visually, use similar colours and materials right across the space. Here, warm wood and a neutral palette give a cohesive look to a contemporary living area.

BELOW Don't be afraid to use partitions if you need to. Here, a glass screen separates off the dining area without blocking out the light.

Without dividing walls, it can be tricky to know how to partition a space. In a do-it-all downstairs, for example, how can you separate each zone? How do you give a multi-purpose space a cohesive visual identity? Could you cope with a boundary-less area and keep it tidy?

Then there is the noise factor. Every sound, from the television to screaming children, will carry right through an open-plan interior. You won't have to worry about slamming doors, of course, but will you manage without a spot of quiet, private space? Cooking smells, too, may permeate and, while you may have acres of space, any open-plan area is harder to heat than an average room.

ABOVE **Without walls, you will need to find a different way to divide space. If you don't want to use screens or partitions, use the furniture itself to define the function of each different zone. Here a table and chairs create a 'dining room' at one end of an open-plan living area, while armchairs mark out the separate sitting space.**

RIGHT **Another way of demarcating individual zones within an open-plan room is to use flooring. Here, a spotty rug defines the sitting area, separating it visually from the rest of the space.**

OPPOSITE, ABOVE **It is a good idea** to divide an open-plan space into practical utility zones and relaxing comfort zones. In this contemporary apartment, the kitchen has been tucked to one side and is neatly separated from the main living area by an island unit.

OPPOSITE, BELOW LEFT If your kitchen is left completely open to the rest of the space, remember to keep things tidy. Shutting the door on dirty dishes is no longer an option.

OPPOSITE, BELOW RIGHT **A** curving vintage light creates intimacy in the dining space.

ABOVE RIGHT **An interesting** mix of old and new, this eclectic open-plan living area could look disjointed or messy. By keeping the palette neutral, however, and by using the same glossy painted floorboards throughout the space, the owners have brought the disparate elements together.

BELOW RIGHT **In any open-** plan or semi-open-plan space, you need to think carefully about the decoration to make sure different areas don't jar with each other. Here, white paintwork has been used throughout and the colour of the dining table is echoed in the adjacent wall hanging.

cooking, living & eating

Opening up the kitchen, dining room and living room to create one do-it-all downstairs space can prove very liberating, but how do you start?

First consider your needs and priorities. Are you a great cook who needs a big kitchen? Do you want a large dining table to accommodate friends? Would you rather give most of the space to a giant modular sofa? Think what would work for you and plan the layout on paper.

For practical reasons (extractor fans, water supply and so on), it is generally best to position the kitchen against a wall. This will allow you to incorporate lots of storage – a must in any open-plan space – but remember that it should also connect to the surrounding space. Installing an island unit with an integral hob is a good solution, as it allows you to face the living area as you cook and it will also partially screen the kitchen and any dirty dishes.

Remember that in an open-plan space furniture will be viewed from all sides, so choose pieces carefully, and opt for multi-purpose or adaptable models – an extendable dining table, perhaps, or a bookshelf-cum-screen.

sleeping, dressing & bathing

Your bedroom and bathroom should be peaceful, personal spaces, so how can you incorporate them into an open-plan scheme? The trick is to use ingenious partitions to give you privacy without doors.

If you are creating an open-plan apartment from scratch, position your bedroom at the margins of the space so you can transform it into a private cocoon. If you are working with an existing interior, incorporate flexible partitions into the architecture so that you can shut off your sleeping space when you need to. During the day you might be happy for your bedroom to be on show, but at night a secluded sanctuary is what you should be after.

Whether you opt for an en-suite or decide to create a larger open-plan bathing, dressing and sleeping space, incorporate convertible elements into the design. Sliding doors or panels, track-hung curtains or screens – all will

ABOVE LEFT A curvy screen neatly divides a bedroom from the main living area to create private space when it's needed.

BELOW LEFT Knocking through a bedroom and bathroom can be a good way to bring light to a gloomy interior and provide a luxurious en-suite solution.

ABOVE Here, a section of wall serves as a bedhead and also screens the bedroom from the adjacent space.

OPPOSITE A wooden panel is bedroom 'wall' on one side, shower cubicle on the other.

allow you to enclose space one minute and keep it open the next, giving you maximum flexibility. Alternatively, use the existing architecture. Retain part of a bedroom wall to create a giant bedhead, for example, which can conceal a dressing area or bathroom on the other side.

Combining bed- and bathroom is a luxurious option, but some form of screening is necessary. Conceal the bath behind a half-wall, perhaps, or use a glass screen to define the bathing area without blocking out light. Make sure the space is well ventilated, air bedlinen to prevent mould and – if you are overlooked – don't forget curtains.

■ Don't forget that your furniture can be viewed from all sides in an open-plan space. Invest in shapely pieces that look just as good from the back as from the front.

■ To unify a diverse collection of furniture and furnishings, use a uniform finish for the walls and floor.

■ Be as creative as you dare – a one-off personal look can create a big visual impact in an open-plan area.

■ Use colour carefully. An idiosyncratic collection of bits and pieces can be brought together effectively if they are in harmonious or toning shades.

■ Make sure that whatever pieces you choose work effectively in the space. There is no point including vintage furniture or light fittings if they don't function properly.

■ Keep your clutter under control. Remember: less is more.

An open-plan interior gives you a good dose of creative freedom. Not only can you decide how to configure the space itself, you can also – if you want to – do away with traditional furnishing conventions. Why buy a dining-room table when you don't have a dining room? Why opt for a fitted kitchen when you have no room to fit it in? If you have a more freestyle approach to decorating, an open-plan space can be just the place to indulge it.

What's more, some conventional fixtures and fittings can look out of place in an open-plan arena. Rather than room-specific items, what you want here is more equivocal, go-anywhere furniture that will fit in with the flexibility of the surroundings. Choose pieces that work in the space, whether it's a convertible seating system or some old metal shelving, and don't be afraid to do your own thing.

A quirky collection of bits and pieces can look very effective if the end result expresses a strong personal style. Mix up vintage furniture with modern accessories; industrial elements with soft and comfortable furnishings; an antique sofa with brand-new cushions. Or just use the space to display a diverse collection of things you like.

One drawback of an open-plan interior with its combination of functions and furniture is that it can look disjointed and messy. If you opt for an eclectic scheme, the chances of this happening are all the greater, so it is important to keep control of the space. Try to unify a disparate group of bits and pieces by keeping the background of the space uniform. Stick to plain walls, perhaps, or use the same flooring throughout. And keep your hoarding instincts in check. It is better to put some of your possessions into storage if necessary so that what is left on show has space to breathe.

eclectic

An individual or idiosyncratic look can be the making of an interior, but in an open-plan space you'll need to keep those hoarding instincts under control.

- Keep your colour scheme toning and muted. A neutral palette will always look smart.

- You need clarity of layout for a clean-lined look, so give each part of the space a distinct identity and use half-walls or different flooring to define individual zones.

- Bring in the modernist materials – metal, concrete, glass – for a sleek finish and add the odd natural element to soften up the look.

- Remember that built-in elements – whether a fitted kitchen or a wall of storage units – will always give you a neater end result.

- Choose streamlined, unfussy furniture. If you can't find what you want on the high street (and if your budget is up to it), consider buying bespoke.

- Keep a rectilinear emphasis on the design. Geometrical shapes will create a smart overall look and will also make the most of the space.

An open-plan living space can look chic, modern and sophisticated. Give yours an exclusive flavour with ingenious design, sleek materials and smart colours.

slick & streamlined

The key advantage of an open-plan interior is that it is a structure-less entity but, if you like your home to look streamlined and organized, such freewheeling space can seem dauntingly undisciplined. The solution is to devise a layout for the area that will superimpose a bit of order without creating boundaries.

First, plan the arrangement of space very carefully, employing professional help if necessary. Expertise costs money, but an architect or interior designer can help you achieve a smart and slick result.

To give a streamlined feel to any open-plan interior, the layout should be as unambiguous as possible, so it is important that the role of each part of the space is clearly defined.

Create individual zones – the dining area, sitting area, kitchen – and mark them out with distinctive furniture, flooring or lighting. You might even choose to include the odd half-wall or convertible partition to clarify things further.

For a clean-lined look, keep both the architecture and the furniture of the interior as

rectilinear as possible. Geometrical designs – whether an angular dining table or a set of parallel kitchen units – will create an instant sense of order and work most efficiently within the space. Use simple, good-quality materials – stone, metal, glass, wood – and keep fussy furnishings to a minimum. This doesn't mean you have to compromise on comfort, however; a giant rug or a vast modular sofa would be absolutely in keeping here.

As much storage as possible should be built in to the carcass of the interior so that you can easily keep your clutter under control without the need for extraneous furniture. A seamless wall of kitchen units, for example, will give a much neater finish than a bulky dresser.

outdoor living

taking your living space outside

Increasingly, we view our gardens not as a separate place, but as an extension of our homes, with the outside decoration complementing rather than contrasting with the inside.

TOP LEFT Rugs and throws brighten and soften a wooden bench, injecting sunny colour into this shaded area.

ABOVE LEFT This outdoor space so resembles a room, it even has a roof. This creates shade and protection from the elements, so you can leave furniture outside. Climbers and trailing roses growing up the structure soften its lines and add glorious colour.

ABOVE RIGHT Classic metal garden furniture looks light and stylish, and can be folded for winter storage.

OPPOSITE This covered deck area has a large daybed and lounger, liberally covered with cushions, for outdoor relaxing. Colour comes via the fabrics, rather than the planting.

By selecting key elements from the interior, you can create an outdoor space that can work as a dining room, sitting room, play area – even kitchen. A table and chairs are all you need to create an outside dining room, while a well-positioned barbecue can become your alfresco kitchen.

Plan carefully where you site everything. For instance, don't put a play area next to a dining space, or you may have footballs crashing into your lunch. Create the feel of an extra room by using the same materials inside and out. If a terrace leads directly off your home, lay the same flooring outside as in – ceramic tiles, sandstone and basalt, for example, or decking made of boards the same width as those inside and stained to match. Add splashes of the colours you have used inside, too, on cushions and tablecloths, to blur the divide between in and out. You don't need to buy pieces specifically for the garden, either. Just grab stools, chairs, cushions, candle holders and rugs, and transplant them to the garden when good weather arrives. Finally, even if it's just candles or solar lights on stakes, lighting will let you stay out after dark.

RIGHT **Abundant natural light flooding into this garden room makes it an ideal place to work.**

FAR RIGHT **Keeping external and internal floor heights the same blurs the transition between inside and out; one flows seamlessly into the other.**

BELOW LEFT AND RIGHT **Rather than cutting this tree down to make way for a garden room, it has been left in place so the space extends right up to it.**

OPPOSITE **This handsome garden room has a soaring ceiling and wall of glass, so it feels light and airy. Oversized furniture suits the dimensions of this generous space.**

garden rooms & conservatories

Conservatories have come a long way. Forget the uninspiring half-octagons plonked on the side of many suburban homes; modern conservatories are all about maximum glass, minimum fuss, and enjoying the outside year-round.

BELOW **Detached from the house, this simple wooden shed-like structure gives you somewhere to enjoy the outdoors, even if it's raining. It also creates a focal point in the garden.**

Masses of glass and, on the best examples, well-designed retractable doors create a super-light, flexible space, which brings you closer to the outdoors without leaving your home. With so much glass, regulating heat and glare is an issue. Roller blinds/shades will provide privacy and keep out bright sunshine and some of its heat, but, when pulled down, prevent you enjoying the views. A good alternative is a specialist film for the glass. It can reduce glare, help retain heat in winter and repel excessive heat in summer. There's a big market in furniture for conservatories, but it makes more sense to dress your space as you have the rest of your home; as it flows from the interior, it will be constantly in view, so needs to blend in well. To define the space as a garden room, grow plants here. They will thrive in the light and give an outdoorsy feel distinct from the rest of the house.

OPPOSITE This spacious outdoor dining area is shaded by a thick canopy of vines, trained to grow over it. Its position by a wall gives it some shelter and fuss-free gravel underfoot is a good-looking, low-maintenance base. These director's chairs fold away when not in use and their canvas seats and backs can be removed and machine-washed. Bright green earthenware plates and orange glasses match the lush foliage and dappled sun of this lovely space.

RIGHT There is room to cook and eat on even the smallest of roof terraces. Here, a stool is used instead of a table and, when cleared, becomes a handy seat, too.

FAR RIGHT A large woven basket is useful for carrying utensils and crockery to and from the kitchen.

BELOW RIGHT A long table flanked by simple benches provides generous outdoor dining space. Aged wood can stand to be left outside – just cover it with a bright cloth when you sit down to dine.

outdoor dining

Eating outdoors is one of life's great pleasures. Whether it's a light lunch in the sun or a dinner party lit by twinkling tea lights, even the smallest garden can spare the space for a table and chairs.

It's a good idea to have your dining space close to the house or flowing off it, in the form of a deck or patio. If space is limited, choose extending tables and stacking chairs that can be stored easily and, unless you can store your outside furniture under cover, invest in weatherproof pieces, like those made from sealed or painted wood.

A barbecue is a must-have for every garden. Position it facing the table, so the chef does not feel isolated, but not so close that smoke blows into diners' faces. If you have a large garden, consider building a barbecue from reclaimed bricks. You could even create an alfresco kitchen, with worktop, cupboards and a sink.

Shade is essential for outdoor dining. Put a table under a tree or ask a carpenter to build a wooden structure that you can train a vine or climber over for living shade. Alternatively, hang a shade sail, available from specialists, or a length of sheer fabric that will filter harsh sun without blocking out too much light – ideal in a small garden. Inexpensive silk georgette or dyed organza are ideal.

furniture

From the classic deckchair to the ultra-modern lounger, the choice of furniture for outside is almost as great as it is for inside – and just as beautiful.

Decide whether you want built-in furniture, freestanding pieces or a mix. Built-in garden seats can be super-simple and inexpensive, and make great use of your space. A wooden platform built along a house wall makes a casual bench, but you may decide to create something more solid, with storage beneath for furniture, toys or cushions.

Don't install fixed furniture until you have considered how the sun moves around the garden, and whether you want to sit facing it or away from it. When it comes to freestanding pieces, do you have space to store them, or must they stay outdoors? Classic wooden deckchairs,

ABOVE **Forget back-punishing wooden loungers; contemporary garden furniture aims to be as comfortable as furniture you would have inside. If your living room opens onto a large deck like this, you could also simply pull your sofa outside, for open-air lounging.**

LEFT **A plain wooden bench is a garden stalwart. This one, with its distressed paintwork, suits a casual scheme.**

RIGHT **Woven furniture looks good outside and in, is often available in a range of colours and, because it's quite heavy, won't blow away.**

director's chairs and French café chairs all collapse and are easy to store. Other furniture can be kept outside, but may need help to look its best. Unpainted wooden pieces need feeding with oil annually to keep them watertight and prevent fading. Painted metal furniture may rust, but can be refreshed with wire wool and new paint. If you have a roof space, choose solid materials like wood or iron; lightweight plastic furniture might blow away.

Alternatively, wicker or Lloyd Loom furniture, wooden stools, floor cushions, footstools, rugs and kelims from inside can all feel at home outside.

TOP LEFT Dense polypropylene is waterproof, easy to clean and heavier than plastic, so it's perfect in a garden. Here, polypropylene chairs are teamed with a simple wooden table for an informal look.

ABOVE LEFT This folding chair is a traditional style brought up to date with practical plastic slats instead of wood.

ABOVE RIGHT A matching set of painted metal table and chairs is elegant. The folding chairs are easy to store.

RIGHT Dainty folding café chairs lighten this solid table.

accessories

Have fun with accessories in the garden, just as you would inside, to introduce colour, texture and comfort.

The simple cushion can soften the hardest wooden bench and bring colour to the plainest garden. Choose a robust fabric like thick cotton, which will suit the rougher surfaces of an outdoor space and can be washed easily. For maximum comfort, work in a range of sizes; large floor cushions for low-level lounging, long oblong cushions to soften benches or loungers and simple scatter cushions. At ground level, a hard surface can be improved by throwing down a rug, inexpensive mat or runner in tough woven cotton or natural fibres. Think about incorporating some more unusual accessories: a lazy hammock, strung between a tree or garden walls; a colourful parasol or awning; some pretty bunting to cheer up a drab wall. Mirrors are useful outside, too, creating distance in a small garden, reflecting sunlight into shady areas and making plants look doubly lush. Braziers and firepits create a fantastic focal point and warm up the chilliest of evenings, allowing you to stay outside longer. It's even possible to get outdoor wallpaper. Who says colour in a garden has to come from plants? Finally, for twilight meals, light tapers pushed in among flowerbeds, dot candles on your table and add flowers in jugs or vases.

THIS PICTURE A hammock is a relaxing place from which to enjoy your outdoor space, and practical, too, as it can be taken down and stored away easily. Secure one between house walls or trees.

OPPOSITE, ABOVE LEFT
A kitsch umbrella brings a little fun and frivolity to this outside space. Teamed with patterned cushions and tablecloth, it brings colour even on a cloudy day.

OPPOSITE, ABOVE RIGHT
Tea lights in lanterns are suspended from the trees overhanging this table, leaving the tabletop clear for dinnerware and fresh flowers.

OPPOSITE, BELOW LEFT
Cane tea light holders that can be pushed into the ground are a great way of bringing candlelight to the whole garden, not just your table.

OPPOSITE, BELOW RIGHT
Lanterns filled with twinkling tea lights are an inexpensive way to bring atmosphere to an outside space and allow you to enjoy it into the evening.

In a Mediterranean-inspired garden, creating a place to eat is essential. Outdoor dining is the norm where long evenings and warm summers make it a pleasure.

mediterranean style

Think about creating a decked area or, better still, a paved terrace. Warm terracotta tiles are ideal in a courtyard or terrace garden and create an attractive, rustic look. Natural sandstone paving can be teamed with coloured mosaics inlaid in circular or arcing patterns, reminiscent of ancient Roman floors. Or lay a few Moroccan encaustic tiles to brighten a paved patio.

To furnish your Mediterranean-style garden, choose unfussy folding chairs in wood or metal. The look is traditional and comfortable, so back away from contemporary designs or classic designer pieces in favour of more rustic furniture. Try scouring second-hand shops and fairs for old chairs, tables and loungers, and keep your eyes open for original French or Italian café chairs. Don't let a shabby appearance deter you, either. Both wooden and metal furniture can be sanded down and repainted to freshen it up. On furnishings, choose hot colours like bright oranges, pinks, blues and purples to add drama and a strong Mediterranean flavour. They also reduce the need to create colour in the planting. You can add further year-round colour and effectively warm up a chilly, shady corner by painting walls in bright Mediterranean shades like red, orange, blue and yellow. Exterior masonry paints now come in plenty of enticing colours.

Mediterranean gardens are generally fairly low-maintenance, with the focus on the terrace and dining space. Potted plants are a feature and are easy to look after. Many native plants will thrive in cooler or more humid climates, too. Small olive trees, agave, banana plants, eucalyptus and sculptural ferns all look authentic, while classics like geraniums and lavender bring colour. Find old terracotta pots, or invest in large new ones that can be arranged in rows for a symmetrical look.

■ Dress your table with chunky earthenware decorated with colourful patterns. Coloured glassware looks great, too, and will catch the light.

■ Serve bread and salads from large rustic bowls, wooden platters and baskets lined with colourful napkins for an informal Med look.

■ Think long term and have a simple wooden framework built over your dining area up which you can grow a grapevine or wisteria. Once the foliage has thickened, this will provide shade.

■ Plant different-sized pots, so you always have a small pot of geranium or lavender to use as a table decoration and larger pots to define space.

■ Make your own cushion covers using patterned fabric remnants or old curtains. Get foam cut to size to create soft seating for oddly shaped or large areas, like a long built-in bench.

One of the most iconic examples of a deck is the American front porch. Covered by a roof and with a wooden floor, the porch has been incorporated into millions of American homes and is somewhere to sit, chat to passing neighbours and enjoy the fresh air. In Europe, terraces and decks at the back of the house are more common, but they share many traits with the American porch, many just big enough to house a couple of chairs, but not to dine on. Constructed from hardwood (expensive, but which comes in a range of lovely colours) or specially treated softwood (which is easy to work with and cheaper), decks are good-looking and low-maintenance. The timbers have a warm, easy-on-the-eye appearance and, unless painted with a stain, the original wood colour will fade gradually to a mellow grey.

Wood feels softer and warmer underfoot than paving, so it is ideal in a garden used by children. It can become slippery if not kept clean, but a regular brush with a stiff broom to remove any mildew or fine moss is all that's needed. The mellow wood of a deck or porch can host almost any kind of furniture. A striking designer chair or a chunky old bench will look equally good. If you prefer a rustic look, choose wooden furniture in a similar tone, topped with soft cushions in neutral colours. Lloyd Loom or wicker furniture looks good, too, or go contemporary with clean-lined modern loungers. Decks and porches are often access routes to and from the house, so they need to be kept reasonably clutter-free. Potted plants will add some natural beauty without taking up too much space and can be moved easily. Plain terracotta pots or woven baskets maintain the laid-back, unfussy look. Fill them with geraniums, olive or bay trees for a classic look, or grasses or ferns for a tropical feel.

Whether a modest platform at the back of an urban home or a terrace that wraps around the house, a wooden deck is a great place to enjoy the outdoors.

on the deck

■ To provide privacy and protection from a prevailing wind, consider constructing a wooden screen around part of your deck, using the same wood.

■ Grooved deck boards are often marketed as anti-slip, but perform no better or worse than plain, smooth decking that is kept clean.

■ Many features can share a deck, from built-in storage to a submerged sandpit, pergolas to planters.

■ When buying timber for a new deck, look for wood from a sustainable source.

■ A corner or end of a deck can be fitted with an outside shower, for cooling off after a long day in the sun.

■ Check whether planning or building regulation approval is required before you build a deck. Talk plans through with your neighbours, too. Neighbour objections are the most common reason for planning refusal or enforcement notices after completion.

stockists in the UK

large retailers

The Conran Shop
81 Fulham Road
London SW3 6RD
020 7589 7401
www.conranshop.co.uk
One-stop shopping for tasteful
modern furniture and accessories.

Habitat
196 Tottenham Court Road
London W1T 7PJ
and branches nationwide
08444 991122
www.habitat.net
Accessible contemporary
furnishings.

Heal's
196 Tottenham Court Road
London W1T 7LQ
020 7636 1666
www.heals.co.uk
Stylish contemporary furniture.

IKEA
255 North Circular Road
London NW13 OJQ
0845 3551141
and branches nationwide
www.ikea.co.uk
Inexpensive furniture and
furnishings with a good selection
of kitchen designs.

John Lewis
Oxford Street
London W1A 1EX
08456 049 049
www.johnlewis.com
Everything for the home with a
good selection of bedlinen.

Liberty
Regent Street
London W1B 5AH
020 7734 1234
www.liberty.co.uk
Stylish modern furniture, tableware
and accessories.

Marks & Spencer
458 Oxford Street
London W1N 0AP
020 7935 7954
www.marksandspencer.com
Traditional and contemporary
furniture, plus homewares for
every room.

Selfridges
400 Oxford Street
London W1A 2LR
0800 123400
www.selfridges.com
Classic and cutting-edge design
for the home.

furniture & finishing touches

Antique and flea markets
Check these websites for
information:
www.antiques-atlas.com
www.artefact.co.uk

Baileys
Whitecross Farm
Bridstow
Ross-on-Wye
Herefordshire HR9 6JU
01989 563015
www.baileyshome.com
Everything recycled.

Caravan
11 Lamb Street
Old Spitalfields Market
London E1 6EA
020 7247 6467
www.caravanstyle.com
Ever-changing stock of individual
homewares and accessories; a place
to look at flea-market style.

Classic Modern Vintage Design
www.classic-modern.co.uk
Retro-style lighting and accessories.

The General Trading Company
2–6 Symons Street
London SW3 2GT
020 7730 0411
www.generaltradingcompany.co.uk
Eclectic mix of furniture and
furnishings, plus kitchen
equipment and other small
homewares.

Graham & Green
4 Elgin Crescent
London W11 2HX
020 7243 8908
www.grahamandgreen.co.uk
Glamorous glass, cushions,
tableware and a small range of
furniture including leather pieces.

Josephine Ryan Antiques
63 Abbeville Road
London SW4 9JW
020 8675 3900
www.josephineryanantiques.co.uk
Antiques dealer with an eye for
beautiful French pieces.

LASSCO
30 Wandsworth Road
London SW8 2LG
020 7394 2100
www.lassco.co.uk
Architectural salvage from
fireplaces to floors, plus a very
authentic range of replicas.

Muji
118 Kings Road
London SW3 4TR
020 7823 8688
www.mujionline.co.uk
Modern Japanese storage and
home accessories, plus a limited
range of furniture.

Petersham Nurseries
Off Petersham Road
Richmond
Surrey TW10 7AG
020 8940 5230
www.petershamnurseries.com
Wide selection of plants and
antique garden furniture.

Portobello Road Market
London W11
Friday and Saturday, 8am to 5pm
www.portobelloroad.co.uk
Particularly good for antique
furniture and larger accessories
such as mirrors.

Raw Garden
0870 6092398
www.rawgarden.co.uk
Garden furniture, including
shade sails.

SCP
135–139 Curtain Road
London EC2A 3BX
020 7739 1869
www.scp.co.uk
Contemporary furniture, lighting
and accessories.

Skandium
86 Marylebone High Street
London W1U 4QS
020 7935 2077
www.skandium.com
Modern Scandinavian furniture.

The White Company
0870 9009555
www.thewhitecompany.com
High-quality bed- and bath linen
and other home accessories.

walls & upholstery

Auro Organic Paints
01452 772020
www.auro.co.uk
Natural emulsions, eggshells and
chalk paints in muted colours, also
floor finishes and wood stains.

Bennison Fabrics
16 Holbein Place
London SW1W 8NL
020 7730 8076
www.bennisonfabrics.com
Classic fabrics to suit any scheme.

Designers Guild

020 7351 5775 for stockists

www.designersguild.com

Fresh, pretty, modern designs for curtains and upholstery.

Farrow & Ball

01202 876141 for stockists

www.farrow-ball.com

Subtle paint colours, also papers, varnishes and stains.

Ian Mankin

109 Regents Park Road

London NW1 8UR

020 7722 0997

www.ianmankin.com

Very wide range of natural fabrics, including striped tickings and plain and patterned cottons.

Lewis & Wood

5 The Green, Uley

Gloucestershire GL11 5SN

01453 860080

www.lewisandwood.co.uk

Interesting and eccentric range of fabrics and wallpapers.

Osborne & Little

304 Kings Road

London SW3 5UH

020 7352 1456

www.osborneandlittle.com

Stylish fabrics, wallpapers and trimmings.

The Paint Library

5 Elystan Street

London SW3 3NT

020 7823 7755

www.paintlibrary.co.uk

Paint and wallpaper, including many shades of off-white.

kitchens

Aga Rayburn

08457 125207

www.aga-rayburn.co.uk

Classic cast-iron range cookers, essential for the country kitchen, even in town.

Alno

Visit the website to find a stockist.

www.alnokitchens.co.uk

Contemporary and elegant kitchen designs from Germany.

Bulthaup

37 Wigmore Street

London W1U 1PP

020 7495 3663 for stockists

www.bulthaup.com

High-quality contemporary and high-tech kitchens, including clever design features.

Crabtree Kitchens

17 Station Road

London SW13 0LF

020 8392 6955

www.crabtreekitchens.co.uk

Traditional kitchen designs.

Divertimenti

227–229 Brompton Road

London SW3 2EP

020 7581 8065

www.divertimenti.co.uk

Complete range of cookware and kitchen accessories.

Summerill & Bishop

100 Portland Road

London W11 4LN

020 7221 4566

www.summerillandbishop.com

Inspirational collection of tableware, utensils and accessories.

bathrooms

Aston Matthews

141–147a Essex Road

London N1 2SN

020 7226 7220

www.astonmatthews.co.uk

Modern and traditional bathroom fittings, including washbasins in china, glass and stainless steel.

Bathstore.com

08000 232323

www.bathstore.com

Sanitary ware in all styles.

C P Hart

Newnham Terrace

Hercules Road

London SE1 7DR

020 7902 5250 and branches

www.cphart.co.uk

Bathroom designs by Philippe Starck among others.

Ideal Standard

The Bathroom Works

National Avenue

Hull HU5 4HS

01482 346461 for stockists

www.ideal-standard.co.uk

Wide range of sanitary ware.

Stiffkey Bathrooms

89 Upper St Giles Street

Norwich NR2 1AB

01603 627850

www.stiffkeybathrooms.com

Antique sanitary ware and their own range.

lighting

Artemide

106 Great Russell Street

London WC1B 3NB

020 7291 3853

www.artemide.com

Contemporary designer lighting.

John Cullen

585 Kings Road

London SW6 2EH

020 7371 5400

www.johncullenlighting.co.uk

Extensive range of contemporary light fittings and bespoke lighting design service.

The London Lighting Company

135 Fulham Road

London SW3 6RT

020 7589 3612

www.londonlighting.co.uk

Contemporary lighting.

Mathmos

01202 644600

www.mathmos.com

The original lava lamps.

flooring

Alternative Flooring Company

01264 335111

www.alternativeflooring.com

Coir, seagrass, sisal, jute and wool floor coverings.

Crucial Trading

01562 743747

www.crucial-trading.com

All types of natural floorings.

Junckers

01376 517512 for stockists

www.junckershardwood.com

Solid hardwood flooring.

Limestone Gallery

Arch 47, South Lambeth Road

London SW8 1SS

020 7735 8555

www.limestonegallery.com

A wide selection of limestone flooring, also French ceramic tiles and terracotta tiles.

Sinclair Till Flooring

791–793 Wandsworth Road

London SW8 3JQ

020 7720 0031

www.sinclairtill.co.uk

All kinds of flooring including range of linoleums.

stockists in the US

large retailers

ABC Carpet & Home

888 Broadway
New York, NY 10003
212 473 3000
Visit www.abchome.com for a retail
outlet near you.
An eclectic collection of accessories
for the home.

Anthropologie

Rittenhouse Square
1801 Walnut Street
Philadelphia, PA 19103
215 568 2114
www.anthropologie.com
Select mix of often vintage-
inspired home accessories
and decorative details.

Barneys New York

660 Madison Avenue
New York, NY 10021
212 826 8900
www.barneys.com
High-quality home furnishings.

Conran Shop

407 East 59th Street
New York, NY 10022
212 755 7249
www.conranusa.com
Well-designed contemporary
furniture and accessories.

Crate & Barrel

800 996 9960
www.crateandbarrel.com
Home accessories for
contemporary living.

Ethan Allen

Call 888 EAHELP1 for a retail
outlet near you or visit
www.ethanallen.com
Fine furniture for every room.

IKEA

1800 East McConnor Parkway
Schaumburg, IL 60173
Call 800 434 IKEA or visit
www.ikea.com for a store near you.
Simple but well-designed flat-pack
furniture, plus inexpensive storage
and kitchenware.

Pier 1 Imports

71 Fifth Avenue
New York, NY 10003
Call 212 206 1911 or visit
www.pier1.com to find a store
near you.
Affordable home accessories and
furniture from all over the world.

Pottery Barn

Call 888 779 5176 or visit
www.potterybarn.com for a retail
outlet near you.
Contemporary furniture and home
accessories with a world beat.

R 20th Century Design

82 Franklin Street
New York, NY 10013
212 343 7979
www.r20thcentury.com
Mid-century modern furniture,
lighting, and accessories.

Restoration Hardware

935 Broadway
New York, NY 10010
212 260 9479
www.restorationhardware.com
Fine hardware, including flooring,
curtains, and lighting, but also
furniture and accessories for
the home.

furniture & finishing touches

20CDesign.com

214 821 0262
www.20cdesign.com
Specializes in Italian and
Scandinavian modern designs.

Bombay

Call 800 956 1782 or visit
www.bombaycompany.com to find
a store near you.
Reproductions of classic, often
British colonial-style home
furnishings and accessories.

California Closets

800 274 6754
www.californiaclosets.com
Customized storage solutions,
not just for home offices but
every room.

Charles P. Rogers

55 West 17th Street
New York, NY 10011
212 675 4400
www.charlesprogers.com
Brass, iron, and wood bed frames,
from classic to contemporary.

Country Farm Furniture

148 Front Street
Bath, ME 04530
207 443 2367
www.qualityfurniture.com
Finely designed and crafted
country-style furniture.

Georgetown Flea Market

Arlington County Court House
Washington, D.C.
202 775 FLEA
www.georgetownfleamarket.com
If you visit the nation's capital,
this is a stop worth making. Open
Sundays, March through December.

Gump's

135 Post Street
San Francisco, CA 94108
800 882 8055
www.gumps.com
Luxury home furnishings for every
room of the house.

Pierre Deux

625 Madison Avenue
New York, NY 10022
212 521 8012
www.pierredeux.com
Fine French country wallpaper,
fabric, upholstery and antiques.

Shaker Style

292 Chesham Road
Harrisville, NH 03450
888 824 3340
www.shakerstyle.com
Custom-built Shaker-style furniture.

Swartzendruber Hardwood Creations

1100 Chicago Avenue
Goshen, IN 46528
800 531 2502
www.swartzendruber.com
French-country, Shaker, and Prairie-
style quality reproductions.

Takashimaya

693 Fifth Avenue
New York, NY 10022
212 350 0100
This Japanese department store
features luxury bedlinens and
tabletop accessories.

Urban Outfitters

Call 800 282 2200 to find a retail
outlet near you or visit
www.urbanoutfitters.com.
Playful, affordable home details
and furnishings that follow
interior trends.

West Elm

888 922 4119
www.westelm.com
Contemporary furniture and
accessories featuring clean design.

Williams-Sonoma

121 East 59th Street
New York, NY 10022
917 369 1131
www.williams-sonomainc.com
Specializes in utensils and
tableware.

walls & upholstery

Benjamin Moore Paints

Visit the website for stockists.
www.benjaminmoore.com
Fine paints.

Calico Corners

203 Gale Lane
Kennett Square, PA 19348
800 213 6366
www.calicocorners.com
Vast range of furnishing fabrics.

Clarence House Fabrics, Ltd.

979 Third Avenue, Suite 205
New York, NY 10022
800 211 4704
www.clarencehouse.com
Natural-fiber fabrics with prints
based on 15th- to 20th-century
documents.

Farrow & Ball

D&D Building, Suite 1519
979 Third Avenue
New York, NY 10022
212 752 5544
www.farrow-ball.com
Subtle paint colors, also papers
and varnishes.

Garnet Hill

231 Main Street
Franconia, NH 03580
800 870 3513
www.garnethill.com
An online retailer of natural-fiber
duvets, pillows, and linens.

Gracious Home

1220 Third Avenue
New York, NY 10021
212 517 6300
www.gracioushome.com
Bedding, linens, and fine fixtures.

Hancock Fabrics

Visit the website for a retailer
near you.
877 FABRICS
www.hancockfabrics.com
America's largest fabric store.

The Old Fashioned Milk Paint Co.

436 Main Street, P.O. Box 222
Groton, MA 01450
978 448 6336
www.milkpaint.com
These paints replicate the
color and finish of Colonial
and Shaker antiques.

kitchens

Bosch

5551 McFadden Avenue
Huntington Beach, CA 92649
800 944 2904
www.boschappliances.com
Kitchen appliances and fixtures.

Bulthaup

578 Broadway, Suite 306
New York, NY 10012
212 966 7183
800 808 2923 for other stockists
www.bulthaup.com
High-quality contemporary and
high-tech kitchens, including clever
design features.

Fishs Eddy

869 Broadway
New York, NY 10003
212 420 2090
www.fishseddy.com
Overstock supplies of simple mugs,
plates, bowls, and other tableware.

Poggenpohl

350 Passaic Avenue
Fairfield, NJ 07004
973 812 8900
www.poggenpohl-usa.com
Custom kitchen designs.

bathrooms

Bed Bath & Beyond

620 Sixth Avenue
New York, NY 10011
212 255 3550
www.bedbathandbeyond.com
Everything for bed- and bathroom,
plus kitchen utensils and storage.

Clawfoot Supply

at Signature Hardware
2700 Crescent Springs Pike
Erlanger, KY 41017
877 682 4192
www.clawfootsupply.com
Complete supply of authentic
reproduction clawfoot tubs,
pedestal and console sinks, copper
soaking tubs, and more.

The Company Store

800 323 8000
www.thecompanystore.com
Online retailer of accessories
for bedroom and bath.

Waterworks

23 West Putnam Avenue
Greenwich, CT 06830
800 899 6757 for other stockists.
www.waterworks.com
Bathroom fixtures, furniture,
and lights.

lighting

Boyd Lighting

944 Folsom Street
San Francisco, CA 94107
415 778 4300
www.boydlighting.com
Classic and elegant lighting designs
from uplighters to table lamps.

Brass Light Gallery

131 South First Street
Milwaukee, WI 53204
800 243 9595
www.brasslight.com
Wide range of designs with many
traditional styles.

Flos Inc.

200 McKay Road
Huntington Station, NY 11746
631 549 2745
www.flos.com
Cutting-edge lighting style
including many designs by
Philippe Starck.

Lighting Collaborative

333 Park Avenue South, Suite B
New York, NY 10010
212 253 7220
www.lightingcollaborative.com
Electro Track lighting supplier.

flooring

Anderson Hardwood Flooring

P.O. Box 1155
Clinton, SC 29325
864 833 6250
www.andersonfloors.com
Large selection of hardwood flooring.

Country Floors

15 East 16th Street
New York, NY 10003
212 627 8300
www.countryfloors.com
American and imported ceramics
and terra-cotta.

Linoleum City

5657 Santa Monica Boulevard
Hollywood, CA 90038
323 469 0063
www.linoleumcity.com
Every kind of linoleum, from
period to modern to high-tech.

Native Tiles and Ceramics

2317 Border Avenue
Torrance, CA 90501
310 533 8684
www.nativetile.com
Reproduction tiles.

Patina Old World Flooring

3820 North Ventura Avenue
Ventura, CA 93001
800 501 1113
www.patinawoodfloors.com
Reproduction parquet and wide-
plank flooring.

architects, designers & businesses featured in this book

KEY: **a**=above, **b**=below, **r**=right, **l**=left, **c**=centre

A

Alex Michaelis and Tim Boyd
Michaelis Boyd Associates
9B Ladbroke Grove
London W11 3BD
020 7221 1237
info@michaelisboyd.com
www.michaelisboyd.com
Pages 135r, 194

A.L.M. Interior Design
Andy L. Marcus
935 Westbourne Drive, # 201
West Hollywood, CA 90069
213 716 9797
alminteriordesign@earthlink.net
Page 42br

Amanda Martocchio, Architect
189 Brushy Ridge Road
New Canaan, CT 06840
Pages 48l, 58b

An Angel At My Table
www.angelatmytable.co.uk
Page 5al

Andrew Hair
Tapis Vert
020 8678 1408 (UK)
tapis.vert@virgin.net
Page 184al

Ann Louise Roswald Ltd
The Toy Factory
11–13 Corsham Street
London N1 6DP
020 7250 1583
info@annlouiseroswald.com
www.annlouiseroswald.com
Page 10

Annabel Grey
07860 500356 (UK)
annabel.grey@btinternet.com
www.annabelgrey.com
Pages 38, 135l, 208l

Anthropologie
800 309 2500 (US)
www.anthropologie.com
Pages 65bl, 113, 209br

Asfour Guzy Architects
594 Broadway
New York, NY 10012
212 334 9350
easfour@asfourguzy.com
and

Cutting Edge Construction
71 Hudson Avenue
Brooklyn, NY 11201
718 965 3027
Pages 49ar, 59

Ash Sakula Architects
24 Rosebery Avenue
London EC1R 4SX
020 7837 9735
www.ashsak.com
Pages 49al, 49ac

Atelier Abigail Ahern
137 Upper Street
Islington
London N1 1QP
020 7354 8181
contact@atelierbypost.com
www.atelierabigailahern.com
Pages 8–9, 111, 213r, 223cr

B

Baileys
Whitecross Farm
Bridstow
Herefordshire HR9 6JU
01989 561931
www.baileys-home-garden.co.uk
Pages 41cl, 64bl, 65r, 69br, 140, 201, 208r

Beach Studios
01797 344077 (UK)
office@beachstudios.co.uk
www.beachstudios.co.uk
Pages 13r, 46br, 47b, 57b, 80br, 86bc, 94l, 104r, 115all, 145, 149cr, 204, 209al, 209ar

Belmont Freeman Architects
110 West 40th Street
New York, NY 10018
212 382 3311
www.belmontfreeman.com
Page 209cr

Ben de Lisi
40 Elizabeth Street
London SW1 9NZ
020 7730 2994
Pages 16bl, 64br, 87c
Kitchen: Abacus Direct Ltd
0845 8505040
www.abacusdirectltd.com
Page 16bl

Ben Johns CEO Scout Ltd
(bags and floor coverings)
1055 Thomas Jefferson Street, NW
Washington DC 20007
202 944 9590
ben@bungalowco.com
and

Deb Waterman Johns
Get Dressed Wardrobe and Home and Fifi
1633 29th Street, NW
Washington DC 20007
202 625 6425
deb@dogbunny.com
Pages 22–23, 92b, 157r, 159, 169ar, 174b, 176, 184bc, 184br, 185b, 187al, 187br

Bennison Fabrics Ltd
16 Holbein Place
London SW1W 8NL
020 7730 6781
www.bennisonfabrics.com
Pages 29a, 98ar, 98b, 116al, 116bl, 116ar, 116bc, 146bc

Briffa Phillips
19–21 Holywell Hill
St Albans AL1 1EZ
01727 840567
www.briffaphillips.com
Pages 219bl, 219r

Brissi Contemporary Living
196 Westbourne Grove
London W11 2RH
020 7727 2159
info@brissi.co.uk
www.brissi.co.uk
Pages 47a, 69ar, 71a, 86cl, 86br, 118al, 149ar

Brookes Stacey Randall
www.bsr-architects.com
Page 130l

Bruce Mink
Los Angeles
213 591 1110
brucemink@thehouseofmink.com
Pages 42al, 121ac, 121b, 238bl, 239cr

Buildburo Ltd
346 Fulham Road
London SW10 9UH
020 7352 1092
www.buildburo.co.uk
Page 205r

C

Castles in the Sand
+212 (0)679 65 386 (Morocco)
07768 352190 (UK)
emma@castlesinthesand.com
www.castlesinthesand.com
Pages 224–225, 235, 236bl

Catherine Malandrino
www.catherinemalandrino.com
Pages 42bl, 62al

Cecilia Proserpio
cecilia.proserpio@fastwebnet.it
Page 45bl

Century Design
68 Marylebone High Street
London W1M 3AQ
modern@centuryd.com
www.centuryd.com
Pages 34, 120bl, 141, 214b, 218–219a

Chambre d'amis
www.chambredamis.com
Pages 220c, 220cr, 236cl, 236ar, 237b

Charmaine and Paul Jack
Interior architecture and design
LESUD Design
lesudchar@wanadoo.fr
Pages 35a, 80acr

Christopher Coleman Interior Design
55 Washington Street, Suite 707
Brooklyn, NY 11021
718 222 8984
www.ccinteriordesign.com
Pages 74ar, 89al, 89cr, 89bl, 97al

Circus Architects
7 Brooks Court
Kirtling Street
London SW8 5BP
020 7627 6080
www.circus-architects.com
Page 180 all

Cooper/Taggart Designs
323 254 3048 (US)
coopertaggart@earthlink.net
Page 227bl

Cote Jardin (boutique)
Place du Marche
17590 Ars En Re
France
Pages 17, 24br, 150bl

D

Daniela Micol Wajskol
Interior Designer
Via Vincenzo Monti 42
20123 Milano
danielaw@tiscalinet.it
Page 196

David Jimenez
www.djimenez.com
Pages 120br, 121ar, 121cr

De Brinkhof Garden and Nursery
Dorpsstrat 46
6616 AJ Hernen Holland
+31 487 531 486
Page 229br

DIVE Architects Ltd
A009 The Jam Factory
19 Rothsay Street
London SE1 4UF
020 7407 0955
www.divearchitects.com
Pages 61ar, 178r

dMFK (de Metz Forbes Knight Architects)
formerly de Metz Architects
The Old Library
119 Cholmley Gardens
London NW6 1AA
www.dmfk.co.uk
Page 218a

Davy Hezemans, Spice PR
Leidsegracht 38-40
1016 CM – Amsterdam
+31 65 530 0375
Steven Pooters
Ganbaroo
Haarlemmerweg 317 L
1051 LG Amsterdam
+31 20 688 5818
Page 49bl

Drake Design Associates
315 East 62nd Street
New York, NY 10021
212 754 3099
www.drakedesignassociates.com
Page 3c

E

Eger Architects
Architects and Landscape Architects
2 D'Eynsford Road
London SE5 7EB
020 7701 6771
www.egerarchitects.com
Page 229ar

Emily Chalmers
Author and stylist
emily@emilychalmers.com
and

Caravan
11 Lamb Street
Spitalfields
London E1 6EA
020 7247 6467
www.caravanstyle.com
Pages 220al, 220br

Emma Bridgewater
739 Fulham Road
London SW6 5UL
020 7371 5489
www.emmabridgewater.co.uk
Page 96br

Emma Cassi
Lace jewellery designer
020 8487 2836 (UK)
www.emmacassi.com
Page 163ac

Enrica Stabile
Antiques dealer, interior
decorator, photographic stylist
L'Utile e il Dilettevole (shop)
Via Carlo Maria Maggi 6
20154 Milano
+39 0234 53 60 86
www.enricastabile.com
Pages 233br, 234ar

Etienne Mery
johngo@club-internet.fr
Pages 165bl, 172b, 182a, 183ac,
183bcr

Eva Johnson
www.evajohnson.com
Page 150ar

Fil de Fer
St. Kongensgade 83 A
1264 Copenhagen K
Denmark
+45 33 32 32 46
fildefer@fildefer.dk
www.fildefer.dk
Pages 153, 217b

Gabriella Abbado
Designer
+39 333 90 30 809 (Italy)
Pages 133, 237a

Gavin Jackson Architects
50 Holland Park Road
London W11 3RS
020 7243 9000
www.gavinjacksonarchitects.com
Page 19al, 19ar

Gert Wingardh, Architect
Wingårdhs
Kungsgatan 10A
SE411 19 Göteborg
Sweden
+46 31 743 7000
NOD (nature-oriented design) –
landscape architecture
Pages 30, 112bc

Granath
Pile Alle 53
2000 Frederiksberg
Copenhagen
Denmark
info@granath.com
www.granath.com
Page 86c, 86bl, 97bl, 110acl

Grosfeld Architecten
Pascal Grosfeld
Minervum 7489
4817 ZP Breda
The Netherlands
+31 76 522 18 11
www.grosfeld-architecten.nl
Page 174a

Gus Alexander Architects
46–47 Britton Street
London EC1M 5UJ
020 7336 7227
gusalex@btinternet.com
www.gusalexanderarchitects.com
Pages 57a, 112c, 126br

Gustavo Martinez Design
206 Fifth Avenue
4th Floor
New York, NY 10010
212 686 3102
gmdecor@aol.com
Pages 48l, 58b

Haberfield Hall
available for hire as a
photographic location via:
Shootspaces
020 7912 9989
www.shootspaces.com
Pages 53bl, 69al, 82br, 103br,
226, 234al, 236al, 236br

Han Feng
50 West 29th Street, Suite 6E
New York, NY 10001
www.hanfeng.com
Page 221 both

Henri Fitzwilliam-Lay Ltd
07968 948053 (UK)
hfitz@hotmail.com
Pages 163ar, 182b

Hilary Robertson
No. Eight
8 East Parade
Hastings TN34 3AL
01424 443521
www.noeight.co.uk
and
Alistair McGowan
West Matravers
07770 765106
al@westmatravers.com
Pages 86ac, 117al, 126l, 148l

Hogarth Architects Ltd
020 7565 8366 (UK)
info@hogartharchitects.co.uk
www.hogartharchitects.co.uk
Pages 134, 181 both, 193, 202a

Hotel Endsleigh
Milton Abbot
Tavistock
Devon
01822 870000
www.hotelendsleigh.com
Page 65al

Hôtel Le Sénéchal
6, rue Gambetta
17590 Ars en Ré
France
+33 (0)5 46 29 40 42
www.hotel-le-senechal.com
and
**Christophe Ducharme
Architecte**
15 rue Hégésippe Moreau
75018 Paris
France
+33 (0)1 45 22 07 75
Pages 72ar, 80bl, 95, 239bl

Hotel Tresanton
St Mawes, Cornwall
01326 270055
www.tresanton.com
Page 101

Household Hardware
www.householdhardware.nl
Page 220bl

Ilaria Miani
Shop
Via Monserrato 35
00186 Roma
+39 0668 33160
ilariamiani@tin.it
Podere Casellaccia and Podere
Buon Riposo in Val d'Orcia are
available to rent.
Pages 24bl, 40

Imogen Chappel
07803 156081 (UK)
Page 48r

Ingegerd Raman
Bergsgafan 53
SE-11231 Stockholm
Sweden
+46 8 6502824
Ingegerd.raman@orrefors.se
and
**Claesson Koivisto Rune
Arkitektkontor**
Sankt Paulsgatan 25
SE-118 48 Stockholm
Sweden
+46 8 644 5863
Arkitektkontor@claesson-koivisto-
rune.se
Page 223bl

Inner Sanctum Interiors
32 Charlotte Road
London EC2A 3PB
020 7613 3706
www.innersanctum.co.uk
Pages 32a, 92al, 92ar, 143,
152al

Jacques Azagury
50 Knightsbridge
London SW1X 7JN
020 7245 1216
www.jacquesazagury.com
Pages 27br, 84bc, 89cl, 107r

Jamb Limited
Antique chimneypieces
Core One, The Gas Works
Gate D, Michael Road
London SW6 2AN
020 7736 3006
sales@jamblimited.com
Pages 37bl, 64bl

James Gorst Architects
The House of Detention
Clerkenwell Close
London EC1R 0AS
020 7336 7140
info@jamesgorstarchitects.com
www.jamesgorstarchitects.co.uk
Page 53al

James Slade
Slade Architecture
150 Broadway, No. 807
New York, NY 10038
212 677 6380
info@sladearch.com
www.sladearch.com
Pages 60, 186l

Jan Constantine
01270 821194 (UK)
www.janconstantine.com
Page 130r

Jane Packer
London-Tokyo-New York
www.janepacker.com
Page 39b

Jestico +Whiles Architects
1 Cobourg Street
London NW1 2HP
020 7380 0382
www.jesticowhiles.com
Page 229al

Joanne Cleasby
At Snoopers Paradise
7–8 Kensington Gardens
Brighton BN1 4AL
01273 602558
Pages 42ar, 73, 83ar, 83cr,
144br

John Barman Inc.
Interior design and decoration
500 Park Avenue
New York, NY 10022
212 838 9443
www.johnbarman.com
Page 27ar

John Nicolson
House available to hire as
a location
johnnynicolson@aol.com
Pages 41ar, 52

John Pearse
6 Meard Street
London W1F OEG
020 7434 0738
jp@johnpearse.co.uk
www.johnpearse.co.uk
Pages 5b, 44b, 45ar, 77b

Johnson Naylor
13 Britton Street
London EC1M 5SX
020 7490 8885
www.johnsonnaylor.co.uk
Page 223al, 223br

Jon Pellicoro
jpellicoro@earthlink.net
Pages 156–157

Jonathan Adler
212 645 2802 (US)
www.jonathanadler.com
Page 111

Jonathan Bell
11 Sinclair Gardens
London W14 0AU
020 7371 3455
jb@jbell.demon.co.uk
Page 229cl, 229c

Jonathan Woolf
Woolf Architects
39–51 Highgate Road
London NW5 1RT
Page 222 both

Josephine Macrander
Interior decorator
+31 6 43053062
(The Netherlands)
Page 200al

Josephine Ryan Antiques
63 Abbeville Road
London SW4 9JW
020 8675 3900
www.josephineryanantiques.co.uk
Page 162

JPLT
2 rue Jean-Baptiste Clément
93170 Bagnolet
France
+33 1 43 60 01 10
jplt@jplt.net
www.jplt.net
Pages 45al, 45cr, 152bl, 223ar

Judd Street Gallery
www.juddstreetgallery.com
Page 146bl

Julia Clancey
www.juliaclancey.com
Page 110cb

Kaffe Fassett
www.kaffefassett.com
and
Brandon Mably
www.brandonmably.com
Pages 68a, 117br

Katrin Arens
info@katrinarens.it
www.katrinarens.it
Pages 41cr, 41bc

Kenyon Kramer and Jean-Louis Raynaud
Décoration et Jardins
3 Place des Trois Ormeaux
13100 Aix-en-Provence
France
+33 44 2 23 52 32
Page 136br

Kjaerholm's
Rungstedvej 86
DK-2960 Rungsted Kyst
Denmark
+45 45 76 56 56
info@kjaerholms.dk
www.kjaerholms.dk
Page 206br

KRD–Kitchen Rogers Design
www.krd-uk.com
Page 179ar

Kristiina Ratia Designs
203 852 0027 (US)
Pages 128, 149br

'La Maison'
Place de L'Eglise
30700 Blauzac, France
+33 4 66 81 25 15
lamaisondeblauzac@wanadoo.fr
www.chambres-provence.com
Pages 98al, 110ca

Le Mas de Flore
Pierre and Sandrine Degrugillier
Lagnes 84800, France
+33 4 90 20 37 96
Page 227r

Les Sardines aux Yeux Bleus
+33 4 66 03 10 04 (France)
contact@les-sardines.com
www.les-sardines.com
Page 96bl

Lisa Jackson Ltd
212 593 0117 (US)
LCJPeace@aol.com
Pages 171r, 184bcc

L'oro dei Farlocchi
Via Madonnina fronte No 5
Milano
+39 02 860589
www.lorodeifarlocchi.com
Page 41bl

LOT-EK
55 Little West 12th Street
New York, NY 10014
212 255 9326
www.lot-ek.com
Page 220ar

Louise Robbins
Insideout House and Garden Agency and
Malt House Bed and Breakfast
Malt House, Almeley
Herefordshire HR3 6PY
01544 340681
lulawrence1@aol.com
www.insideout-house&garden.co.uk
Pages 78a, 93

Lovelylovely
020 7482 6365 (UK)
info@lovelylovely.co.uk
www.lovelylovely.co.uk
Page 16ar

Lucille Lewin
Chiltern Street Studio
78a Chiltern Street
London W1U 5AB
020 7486 4800
www.chilternstreetstudio.com
Pages 1, 46ar, 54b, 62br, 79

M2 A/S
+45 70 23 24 23 (Denmark)
info@m2.dk
and
Århus Office
Sibirien, Centralværkstedet
Værkmestergade 13
8000 Århus C
Copenhagen Office
Kanonbådsvej 2, Holmen
1437 Copenhagen K
Page 216bl

Maisonette
79 Chamberlayne Road
London NW10 3ND
020 8964 8444
maisonetteuk@aol.com
www.maisonette.uk.com
Pages 69bl, 74cl, 83bc, 94br, 108ar, 112cl, 112ar

Malin Iovino Design
43 St Saviour's Wharf
Mill Street
London SE1 2BE
020 7252 3542
iovino@btconnect.com
Page 160ar

Marianne Cotterill
Shop
4a–5a Perrins Court
London NW3 1QR
020 7435 2151
Pages 13l, 50-51, 83ac, 83bl, 118bl

Marianne Pascal
Architecte D.P.L.G.
85, rue Albert
75013 Paris
+33 1 45 86 60 01
www.mariannepascal.com
Pages 18, 74bl, 105br

Marino + Giolito, Inc.
Architecture/interior design
161 West 16th Street
New York, NY 10011
212 260 8142
marino.giolito@rcn.com
Pages 191r, 199bc

Mark Smith
Smithcreative
15 St George's Road
London W4 1AU
020 8747 3909
info@smithcreative.net
Page 199ar

matali crasset productions
26 rue du Buisson Saint Louis
75010 Paris
France
+33 1 42 40 99 89
matali.crasset@wanadoo.fr
www.matalicrasset.com
Pages 129, 132r, 136al, 170br, 184cr, 185a

Matthew Patrick Smyth, Inc.
12 West 57th Street
New York, NY 10019
212 333 5353
www.matthewsmyth.com
Pages 2, 75l, 118ar

McLean Quinlan Architects
1 Milliners
Eastfields Avenue
London SW18 1LP
020 8870 8600
info@mcleanquinlan.com
www.mcleanquinlan.com
Page 218b

Melin Tregwynt
Castlemorris
Haverfordwest
Pembrokeshire SA62 5UX
01348 891644
info@melintregwynt.co.uk
www.melintregwynt.co.uk
Pages 67a, 72al, 80acl, 90–91, 205l

Mibo
08700 119620
info@mibo.co.uk
www.mibo.co.uk
Page 82a, 82bl

Michael Bains and Catherine Woram
020 8672 3680 (UK)
Michael@mbains.demon.co.uk
Catherine@cworam.demon.co.uk
www.catherineworam.co.uk
Pages 46al, 46cr, 114, 142, 144al

Michael Leva
P.O. Box 100
Roxbury, CT 06783
860 355 2225
Pages 78b, 84al, 107l, 110al, 112al, 152br

Michael Nathenson
Uniquenvironments
Design and Architecture
33 Florence Street
London N1 2FW
020 7226 3006
www.uniquenvironments.co.uk
Page 29bl

Mlinaric, Henry and Zervudachi
020 7730 9072 (London)
+33 1 42 96 08 62 (Paris)
www.mlinaric-henry-zervudachi.com
and
Laurent Bourgois Architecte
6 rue Basfroi
75011 Paris
Pages 46bl, 54a, 104l, 127, 138, 139bl, 152ar, 213l

MMM Architects
The Banking Hall
26 Maida Vale
London W9 1RS
020 7286 9499
post@mmmarchitects.com
www.mmmarchitects.com
Pages 86ar, 195, 207

Modern Homes Design Showroom
760 320 8422 (US)
sales@psmodhome.com
www.shopmodernhomes.com
Pages 120al, 179al

Modernway
745 North Palm Canyon Drive
Palm Springs, CA 92262
760 320 5455
greco@earthlink.net
www.modernway.com
Page 43a

Moneo Brock Studio
Francisco de Asis Mendez
Casariego 7, Bajo
28002 Madrid
+34 91 563 8056
www.moneobrock.com
Pages 28a, 36

Mullman Seidman Architects
443 Greenwich Street
New York, NY 10013
212 431 0770
www.mullmanseidman.com
Pages 19b, 168–169, 172a

Naja Lauf A/S
Strandvejen 340
DK-2930 Klampenborg
Denmark
+45 7025 1325
nl@najalauf.dk
www.najalauf.dk
Page 239cl, 239br

Nancy Braithwaite Interiors
2300 Peachtree Road, Suite C101
Atlanta, GA 30309
404 355 1740
Page 151l

Nico Rensch ARCHITEAM
Campfield House
Powdermill Lane
Battle TN33 0SY
01424 775211
nr@architeam.co.uk
www.architeam.co.uk
Page 177c

Ole Lynggaard Copenhagen
Hellerupvej 15B
DK – 2900 Hellerup
+45 39 46 03 00
www.olelynggaard.dk
Pages 6,132l, 238al, 239al, 239ar

Osborne & Little Ltd
Showroom
304 Kings Road
London SW3 5UH
020 7352 1456
www.osborneandlittle.com
Pages 39a, 67bl, 118cl, 119l, 215a

Pamplemousse Design, Inc.
212 980 2033 (US)
Pages 158al, 165br

Pennington Robson
Tea Warehouse
10A Lant Street
London SE1 1QR
020 7378 0671
www.penningtonrobson.co.uk
Page 89ar

Peri Wolfman
Wolfman Gold
peri@charlesgold.com
and
Upholstered Furniture
Mitchell Gold and Bob Williams
www.mgandbw.com
Pages 20al, 21, 31cl, 80ar, 81

Philip Mould Fine Paintings
29 Dover Street
London W1S 4NA
020 7499 6818
www.philipmould.com
Pages 11r, 151r

Philippe Guilmin
philippe.guilmin@skynet.be
Pages 37ar, 200cr

Philippe Menager and Nicolas Hug
'Immobilier de Collection'
31 rue de Tournon
75006 Paris
+33 1 53 10 22 60
Architecte: Christophe Murail
Murail Architectures
MA – agence de Paris
christophe.murail@m-a.fr
www.m-a.fr
Sculptures: Sébàstien Kito
+33 6 11 51 31 32
Page 197r

Rachel van der Brug
Interior Design Consultant
Ineke Schierenberg & Rachel
van der Brug Vof
Leidsegracht 42
1016 CM Amsterdam
+31 (0)20 6390881
www.inekeschierenberg.nl
Page 68b

Raffaella Barker
raffaella.barker@btinternet.com
For location work, see property
number HC601 at
www.locationpartnership.com
Page 136–137 main

Reinhard Weiss
3s Architects LLP
47 High Street
Kingston upon Thames
Surrey KT1 1LQ
020 8549 2000
reinhard.weiss@3architects.com
www.3sarchitects.com
Pages 31cr, 56

**Roeline Faber Interior
Styling and Design**
Tweede Molenweg 22
1261 HC Blaricum
The Netherlands
+31 35 6668411
faber.styling@wxs.nl
Pages 23, 165a
Kitchen: Paul van de Kooi
Heliumweg 40A
3812 RE Amersfoort
+31 33 465 1111
www.heuhenopmaat.nl
Page 23

ROLLO Contemporary Art
17 Compton Terrace
London N1 2UN
020 7493 8383
www.rolloart.com
Pages 20b, 70

Rose Uniacke Interiors
8 Holbein Place
London SW1W 8NL
020 7730 7050
www.roseuniacke.com
Pages 170a, 187bl

Royal Scandinavia A/S
Smallegade 45
2000 Frederiksberg
Denmark
+45 38144848
and
**Designer and architect MAA
Grethe Meyer**
Page 206bl

Rützou A/S
+45 35 24 06 16 (Denmark)
www.rutzou.com
cph@rutzou.com
Page 69cr

Sanctuary Garden Offices
Devon
www.sanctuarygardenoffices.com
01363 772061 (UK)
Pages 146al, 192b

Sanne Hjermind
Artist
+45 26 91 01 97 (Denmark)

Claes Bech-Poulsen
Photographer
+45 40 19 93 99 (Denmark)
claes@claesbp.com
www.claesbp.dk
Pages 87r, 103bl

**Sasha Waddell Interior
Design and Lectures**
www.sashawawaddelldesign.com
Pages 16al, 41al, 76, 105a

Schmidt Hammer Lassen
Vester Farimagsgade 3
1606 Copenhagen v
Denmark
+45 70 20 19 00
info@shl.dk
Pages 19cl, 19cr, 214a

Sera Loftus-Hersham
www.seraoflondon.com
Pages 170bl, 183ar

Shamir Shah Design
10 Greene Street
New York, NY 10013
212 274 7476
www.shamirshahdesign.com
Pages 74al, 89ac, 125l, 126ar

Sidsel Zachariassen
Stenderupgade 1 1tv
1738 Copenhagen V
www.sidselz.dk
Pages 83br, 97ar

Sieff Interiors
020 7978 2422 (UK)
sieff@sieff.co.uk
www.sieff.co.uk
Page 33

Sigmar
263 Kings Road
London SW3 5EL
020 7751 5802
www.sigmarlondon.com
Pages 37al, 63 inset

Sixty 6
66 Marylebone High Street
London W1M 3AH
020 7224 6066
Pages 49br, 89ccl, 89br, 166l

**Space Architecture
and Design**
+45 35 24 84 84 (Denmark)
sh@spacecph.dk
www.spacecph.dk
Page 216br

Stella Nova ApS
Hauser Plads 32, 1st Floor
DK-1128 Copenahgen K
Denmark
+45 33 30 89 89
info@stella-nova.dk
www.stella-nova.dk
Pages 12, 32b, 89ccr, 217a

Stelle Architects
48 Foster Avenue
P.O. Box 3002
Bridgehampton NY 11932
631 537 0019
info@stelleco.com
www.stelleco.com
Page 45c

Stephen Blatt Architects
207 761 5911 (US)
www.sbarchitects.com
Page 150ac

Steven Learner Studio
307 7th Avenue, Room 2201
New York, NY 10001
212 741 8583
mstevens@stevenlearnerstudio.com
www.stevenlearnerstudio.com
Pages 61al, 64a, 84c, 131, 216a

Steven Shailer
917 518 8001 (US)
Page 197l

**Studio Architettura
Benaim**
Via Giotto, 37
50121 Florence
Italy
+39 055 6632 84
benaim@tin.it
Page 144ar

Susan Chalom
Options
480 Park Avenue
New York, NY 10022
212 486 9207
212 486 8682
susan@susanchalom.com
www.susanchalom.com
Pages 71c, 74br

Susie Atkinson Design
07468 814137 (UK)
Page 169br

Swan House
1 Hill Street
Hastings TN34 3HU
01424 430014
res@swanhousehastings.co.uk
www.swanhousehastings.co.uk
and
No. Eight
www.noeight.co.uk
and
Melissa White
www.fairlyte.co.uk
Pages 109, 112br

Teresa Ginori
Teresa.ginori@aliceposta.it
Pages 136bl, 147r, 202b

**The Children's Cottage
Company**
Devon
01363 772061 (UK)
www.play-houses.com
Pages 146al, 192b

The Cross
141 Portland Road
London W11 4LR
020 7727 6760
Pages 71b, 110cc, 124, 236c,
236bc

The Dodo
www.thedodo.co.uk
Pages 150al, 158ar, 232l

**The New England Shutter
Company**
16 Jaggard Way
London SW12 8UB
020 8675 1099
www.tnesc.co.uk
Pages 148r, 149bc

Theis & Khan Architects
22a Bateman's Row
London EC2A 3HH
020 7729 9329
mail@theisandkhan.com
www.theisandkhan.com
Page 177a

Tore Lindholm
Tore.lindholm@nchr.uio.no
and
Lund & Hagem Arkitektur AS
Filipstadun 5
0250 Oslo
Norway
+47 23 33 31 50
mail@lundhagem.no
www.lundhagem.no
Pages 3r, 5ar, 31a, 239bc

Touch Interior Design
020 7498 6409
Page 256

Tsé &Tsé associeés
Catherine Lévy & Sigolène
Prébois
www.tse-tse.com
Pages 161, 186r

Tyler London Ltd
22a Ives Street
London SW3 2ND
020 7581 3677
www.tylerlondon.com
Page 206a

Urban Salon Ltd
Unit D
Flat Iron Yard
Ayres Street
London SE1 1ES
020 7357 8800
www.urbansalonarchitects.com
Page 199bl

Vicente Wolf Associates
333 West 39th Street
New York, NY 10018
212 465 0590
www.vicentewolfassociates.com
Pages 14r, 24a, 45br, 99

Voon Wong & Benson Saw
(formerly Voon Wong Architects)
Unit 3D, Burbage House
83 Curtain Road
London EC2A 3BS
020 7033 8763
www.voon-benson.com
Page 4

**Weston-Pardy Design
Consultancy**
020 7587 0221 (UK)
weston.pardy@mac.com
Page 28b

White Rabbit England
01625 419 622 (UK)
718 852 7442 (US)
www.whiterabbitengland.com
Pages 158br, 163b

Wild at Heart
The Turquoise Island
222 Westbourne Grove
London W11 2RJ
020 7727 3095
flowers@wildatheart.com
www.wildatheart.com
Pages 3l, 67br, 84bl

William W. Stubbs, IIDA
William W. Stubbs and
Associates
2100 Tanglewilde, Suite 17
Houston, TX 77063
stubbsww1@aol.com
Page 206a

Wim Depuydt
+32 495 777 217 (Belgium)
Depuydt.architect@pandora.be
Page 173

Yancey Richardson Gallery
535 West 22nd Street
New York, NY 10011
www.yancaeyrichardson.com
Pages 61al, 64a, 84c, 131, 216a

Yves-Claude Design
Architectural/industrial design
199 Layfayette Street
New York, NY 10012
www.kanso.com
Pages 31bl, 44a

picture credits

KEY: *ph*=photographer, **a**=above, **b**=below, **r**=right, **l**=left, **c**=centre

Page 1 *ph* Debi Treloar/Lucille and Richard Lewin's London house; **2** *ph* Chris Everard/Manhattan home of designer Matthew Patrick Smyth; **3l** *ph* Debi Treloar/Nikki Tibbles' London home, owner of Wild at Heart – flowers and interiors; **3c** *ph* Chris Everard/Jamie Drake's Manhattan apartment; **3r** *ph* Paul Ryan/summer house at Hvasser, of Astir Eidsbo and Tore Lindholm; **4** *ph* Christopher Drake/Florence Lim's house in London – architecture by Voon Wong Architects, interior design by Florence Lim Design; **5al** *ph* Debi Treloar/the home of Patty Collister in London, owner of An Angel At My Table; **5ar** *ph* Paul Ryan/summer house at Hvasser, of Astir Eidsbo and Tore Lindholm; **5b** *ph* Winfried Heinze/Florence and John Pearse's apartment in London; **6** *ph* Paul Massey/the home in Denmark of Charlotte Lynggaard, designer of Ole Lynggaard Copenhagen; **8–9** *ph* Polly Wreford/Abigail Ahern's home in London; **10** *ph* Claire Richardson/fashion and textile designer Ann Louise Roswald's London home; **11l** *ph* Andrew Wood/the New York home of Jonathan Adler and Simon Doonan; **11r** *ph* Chris Tubbs/Philip and Catherine Mould's house in Oxfordshire; **12** *ph* Winfried Heinze/the home of Christian Permin and Kamilla Byriel of Stella Nova, in Copenhagen; **13l** *ph* Claire Richardson/Marianne Cotterill's house in London; **13r** *ph* Polly Wreford/Foster House at www.beachstudios.co.uk; **14l** *ph* Paul Massey/Michael Giannelli and Greg Shano's home in East Hampton; **14r** *ph* Winfried Heinze/Jodi and Scott Markoff; **15** *ph* Polly Wreford/Charlotte-Anne Fidler's home in London; **16al** *ph* Polly Wreford/Sasha Waddell's home available from www.beachstudios.co.uk; **16ar** *ph* Debi Treloar/the London home of Louise Scott-Smith of www.lovelylovely.co.uk; **16bl** *ph* Polly Wreford/Ben de Lisi's home in London; **17** *ph* Paul Massey/all items from Cote Jardin boutique; **18** *ph* Winfried Heinze/a Parisian pied-a-terre designed by Marianne Pascal for an Anglo-French couple; **19al&ar** *ph* Chris Everard/a London apartment designed by architect Gavin Jackson; **19cl&cr** *ph* Sus Rosenquist/house designed by Schmidt Hammer Larssen, developer: Birkeengen Aps, Denmark – www.birkeengen.dk; **19b** *ph* Chris Everard/John Kifner's apartment in New York, designed by Mullman Seidman Architects; **20al** *ph* Polly Wreford/Peri Wolfman and Charles Gold's New York loft; **20ar** *ph* Winfried Heinze/Trine and William Miller's home in London; **20b** *ph* Chris Everard/Simon and Coline Gillespie's home in North London; **21** *ph* Polly Wreford/Peri Wolfman and Charles Gold's New York loft; **22–23** *ph* Winfried Heinze/the home of Ben Johns and Deb Waterman Johns; **23** *ph* Debi Treloar/Roeline Faber, interior designer; **24a** *ph* Winfried Heinze/Jodi and Scott Markoff; **24bl** *ph* Chris Tubbs/Giorgio and Ilaria Miani's Podere Casellaccia in Val d'Orcia **24br** *ph* Paul Massey/all items from Cote Jardin boutique; **25** *ph* Paul Ryan/the home of Nils Tunebjer in Sweden; **26** *ph* Andrew Wood/the home of Gwen Aldridge and Bruce McLucas; **27bl** *ph* Chris Tubbs/Matthew and Miranda Eden's home in Wiltshire; **27ar** *ph* Chris Everard/John Barman's Park Avenue apartment; **27br** *ph* Winfried Heinze/the apartment of Jacques Azagury in London; **28a** *ph* Chris Everard/Hudson Street loft designed by Moneo Brock Studio; **28b** *ph* Christopher Drake/designer Stephen Pardy's Georgian house in London; **29a** *ph* Chris Tubbs/the Norfolk home of Geoff and Gilly Newberry of Bennison Fabrics; **29bl** *ph* Chris Everard/Michael Nathenson's house in London; **29br** *ph* Andrew Wood/Curtice Booth's house in Pasadena, California; **30** *ph* Paul Ryan/the summer house of Peter Morgan at the Bjäte peninsula (in the north-west of Scania); **31a** *ph* Paul Ryan/summer house at Hvasser, of Astir Eidsbo and Tore Lindholm; **31cl** *ph* Polly Wreford/Peri Wolfman and Charles Gold's New York loft; **31cr** *ph* Polly Wreford/home of architect Reinhard Weiss and Bele Weiss in London; **31b** *ph* Chris Everard/Vicson Guevara's apartment in New York designed by Yves-Claude; **31br** *ph* Debi Treloar/ Vine Cottage; **32a** *ph* Chris Everard/home of David Walsh, Creative Director of Inner Sanctum, London; **32b** *ph* Winfried Heinze/the home of Christian Permin and Kamilla Byriel of Stella Nova, in Copenhagen; **33** *ph* Chris Tubbs/Diana Sieff's home in Devon; **34** *ph* Andrew Wood/an original Florida home restored by Andrew Weaving of Century, www.centuryd.com; **35a** *ph* Claire Richardson/the home of Charmaine and Paul Jack – Belvezet, France; **35b** *ph* Claire Richardson/Tania Bennett and Adrian Townsend's home in London; **36 both** *ph* Chris Everard/Hudson Street loft designed by Moneo Brock Studio; **37al** *ph* Winfried Heinze/the Notting Hill flat of Ebba Thott from 'Sigmar' in London; **37ar** *ph* Debi Treloar/the guesthouse of the interior designer and artist Phílippe Guilmin, Brussels; **37bl** *ph* Christopher Drake/antique dealer and co-owner of Jamb Ltd /antique chimneypieces; **37br** *ph* Claire Richardson/the home of writer Meredith Daneman in London; **38** *ph* Chris Tubbs/Annabel Grey's Norfolk cottage;

39a *ph* Claire Richardson/Graham Noakes of Osborne and Little's home in London; **39b** *ph* Paul Massey/Jane Packer's home in Suffolk; **40** *ph* Chris Tubbs/Giorgio and Ilaria Miani's Podere Buon Riposo in Val d'Orcia; **41al** *ph* Polly Wreford/Sasha Waddell's home available from www.beachstudios.co.uk; **41ac** *ph* Chris Tubbs/Marina Ferrara Pignatelli's home in Val d'Orcia, Tuscany; **41ar** *ph* Chris Everard/John Nicolson's house in Spitalfields, London; **41cl** *ph* Debi Treloar/Mark and Sally Bailey's home in Herefordshire; **41cr&bc** *ph* Debi Treloar/Katrin Arens; **41bl** *ph* Christopher Drake/Maurizio Epifani, owner of L'oro dei Farlocchi; **41br** *ph* Chris Tubbs/Vanni and Nicoletta Calamai's home near Siena; **42al** *ph* Andrew Wood/the Alexander home of Bruce Mink in Palm Springs; **42ar** *ph* Debi Treloar/the home of Joanne Cleasby, Hove: **42bl** *ph* Chris Everard/fashion designer Catherine Malandrino's Manhattan apartment; **42br** *ph* Andrew Wood/the home of Andy Marcus and Ron Diliberto in Palm Springs, CA; **43a** *ph* Andrew Wood/the home of Joy and Courtney Newman, owners of Modernway, vintage furniture store, Palm Springs; **43b** *ph* Andrew Wood/the home of Sean and Tricia Brunson in Orlando; **44a** *ph* Chris Everard/Vicson Guevara's apartment in New York designed by Yves-Claude; **44b** *ph* Winfried Heinze/Florence and John Pearse's apartment in London; **45al&cr** *ph* Andrew Wood/the Paris apartment of art director, stage designer and designer Jean-Pascal Levy-Trumet; **45ar** *ph* Winfried Heinze/Florence and John Pearse's apartment in London; **45c** *ph* Paul Massey/Stelle Architects: Surfside: **45bl** *ph* Debi Treloar/design: Cecilia Proserpio; **45br** *ph* Winfried Heinze/Jodi and Scott Markoff; **46al&cr** *ph* Polly Wreford/London home of Michael Bains and Catherine Woram; **46ar** *ph* Debi Treloar/Lucille and Richard Lewin's London house; **46bl** *ph* Winfried Heinze/a Parisian apartment designed by Tino Zervudachi and Antoine de Sigy; **46br & 47b** *ph* Polly Wreford/Foster House at www.beachstudios.co.uk; **47a** *ph* Polly Wreford/Siobhán McKeating's home in London: **48l** *ph* Debi Treloar/a family home in Manhattan, designed by architect Amanda Martocchio and Gustavo Martinez Design; **48r** *ph* Debi Treloar/Imogen Chappel's home in Suffolk; **49al&ac** *ph* Debi Treloar/designed by Ash Sakula Architects; **49ar** *ph* Debi Treloar/Catherine Chermayeff and Jonathan David's family home in New York, designed by Asfour Guzy Architects; **49cr** *ph* Polly Wreford/Alex White; **49bl** *ph* Chris Everard/Davy Hezeman and Steven Pooters' home in Amsterdam; **49br** *ph* Andrew Wood/the London home of Steven and Jane Collins, owner of Sixty 6 boutique – painting by their daughter Juliet; **50–51** *ph* Claire Richardson/Marianne Cotterill's house in London; **52** *ph* Chris Everard/John Nicolson's house in Spitalfields, London; **53al** *ph* Debi Treloar/a country house rebuilt and extended by James Gorst Architects; **53bl** *ph* Debi Treloar/the home of Isobel Trenouth, her husband and their four children; **53r** *ph* Chris Everard/Jeremy Hackett's house in London; **54a** *ph* Winfried Heinze/a Parisian apartment designed by Tino Zervudachi and Antoine de Sigy; **54b** *ph* Debi Treloar/Lucille and Richard Lewin's London house; **55** *ph* Winfried Heinze/Trine and William Miller's home in London; **56** *ph* Polly Wreford/home of architect Reinhard Weiss and Bele Weiss in London; **57a** *ph* Christopher Drake/the home of Adrian and Belinda Hull in London, designed by architect Gus Alexander; **57b** *ph* Polly Wreford/Foster House at www.beachstudios.co.uk; **58al&ar** *ph* Winfried Heinze/Isabel and Ricardo Ernst's family home; **58ac** *ph* Winfried Heinze/the Fried family home in London; **58b** *ph* Debi Treloar/a family home in Manhattan, designed by architect Amanda Martocchio and Gustavo Martinez Design; **59** *ph* Debi Treloar/Catherine Chermayeff and Jonathan David's family home in New York, designed by Asfour Guzy Architects; **60** *ph* Winfried Heinze/Glasserman/Gilsanz residence, architect James Slade at Cho Slade Architecture, www.sladearch.com; **61al** *ph* Winfried Heinze/the apartment of Yancey and Mark Richardson in New York, architecture and interior design by Steven Learner Studio (picture on left by Vic Muniz, picture on right by Adam Fuss); **61ar** *ph* Chris Everard/Tim and Celia Holman's house in London, designed by DIVE Architects Ltd; **61b** *ph* Debi Treloar/private residence in Washington, Connecticut; **62al** *ph* Chris Everard/fashion designer Catherine Malandrino's Manhattan apartment; **62bl** *ph* Claire Richardson; **62bc** *ph* Debi Treloar/Marcus Hewitt and Susan Hopper's home in Litchfield County, Connecticut; **62br** *ph* Debi Treloar/Lucille and Richard Lewin's London house; **63 main** *ph* Winfried Heinze/the home of Hernando and Gigi Pérez in New York City; **63 inset** *ph* Winfried Heinze/the Notting Hill flat of Ebba Thott from 'Sigmar' in London; **64a** *ph* Winfried Heinze/the apartment of Yancey and Mark Richardson in New York, architecture and interior design by Steven Learner Studio

248

(photographs by Vic Muniz); **64bl** *ph* Debi Treloar/Mark and Sally Bailey's home in Herefordshire; **64br** *ph* Polly Wreford/Ben de Lisi's home in London; **65al** *ph* Chris Tubbs/Hotel Endsleigh; **65bl** *ph* Debi Treloar/the Philadelphia home of Glen Senk and Keith Johnson of Anthropologie; **65r** *ph* Debi Treloar/Mark and Sally Bailey's former home in Herefordshire; **66** *ph* Chris Everard/writer Rita Konig's house in London; **67a** *ph* Claire Richardson/Eifion and Amanda Griffiths of Melin Tregwynt's house in Wales; **67bl** *ph* Claire Richardson/Graham Noakes of Osborne and Little's home in London; **67br** *ph* Debi Treloar/Nikki Tibbles' London home, owner of Wild at Heart – flowers and interiors; **68a** *ph* Claire Richardson/Brandon Mably and Kaffe Fassett's family home in Hastings, www.kaffefassett.com; **68b** *ph* Claire Richardson/interior design consultant Rachel van der Brug's home in Amsterdam; **69al** *ph* Debi Treloar/the home of Isobel Trenouth, her husband and their four children; **69bl** *ph* Debi Treloar/available for photographic location at www.inspacelocations.com; **69ar** *ph* Polly Wreford/Siobhán McKeating's home in London; **69cr** *ph* Debi Treloar/designer Susanne Rutzou's home in Copenhagen; **69br** *ph* Debi Treloar/Mark and Sally Bailey's former home in Herefordshire; **70** *ph* Chris Everard/Simon and Coline Gillespie's home in North London; **71a** *ph* Polly Wreford/Siobhán McKeating's home in London; **71c** *ph* Polly Wreford/www.susanchalom.com; **71b** *ph* Debi Treloar/the London home of Sam Robinson, co-owner of 'The Cross' and 'Cross the Road'; **72al** *ph* Claire Richardson/Eifion and Amanda Griffiths of Melin Tregwynt's house in Wales; **72ar** *ph* Paul Massey/Hôtel Le Sénéchal, Ars en Ré, designed by Christophe Ducharme Architecte; **72bl** *ph* Debi Treloar/Christina and Allan Thaulow's home in Denmark; **72br** *ph* Polly Wreford/Alex White; **73** *ph* Debi Treloar/the home of Joanne Cleasby, Hove; **74al** *ph* Chris Everard/New York family home designed by Shamir Shah; **74cl** *ph* Debi Treloar/available for photographic location at www.inspacelocations.com; **74bl** *ph* Winfried Heinze/a Parisian pied-a-terre designed by Marianne Pascal for an Anglo-French couple, photograph by Erasmus Schröter; **74ar** *ph* Chris Everard/Christopher Coleman's New York apartment; **74br** *ph* Polly Wreford/www.susanchalom.com; **75l** *ph* Chris Everard/Manhattan home of designer Matthew Patrick Smyth; **75r** *ph* Claire Richardson/the London apartment of author and journalist Bradley Quinn; **76** *ph* Polly Wreford/Sasha Waddell's home available from www.beachstudios.co.uk; **77a** *ph* Chris Tubbs/Justin and Eliza Meath Baker's house in the West Country; **77c** *ph* Polly Wreford/Charlotte-Anne Fidler's home in London; **77b** *ph* Winfried Heinze/Florence and John Pearse's apartment in London; **78a** *ph* Alan Williams/Louise Robbins' house in north-west Herefordshire; **78b** *ph* Debi Treloar/Michael Leva's home in Litchfield County, Connecticut; **79** *ph* Debi Treloar/Lucille and Richard Lewin's London house; **80al&bc** *ph* Debi Treloar/Vine Cottage and 'Moogi' the dog; **80acl** *ph* Claire Richardson/Eifion and Amanda Griffiths of Melin Tregwynt's house in Wales; **80acr** *ph* Claire Richardson/the home of Charmaine and Paul Jack – Belvezet, France; **80ar** *ph* Polly Wreford/Peri Wolfman and Charles Gold's New York loft; **80cl** *ph* Paul Ryan/the home of Nils Tunebjer in Sweden; **80cr** *ph* Debi Treloar/private residence in Washington, Connecticut; **80bl** *ph* Paul Massey/Hôtel Le Sénéchal, Ars en Ré, designed by Christophe Ducharme Architecte; **80br** *ph* Polly Wreford/Foster House at www.beachstudios.co.uk; **81** *ph* Polly Wreford/Peri Wolfman and Charles Gold's New York loft; **82a&bl** *ph* Debi Treloar/Madeleine Rogers of Mibo; **82br** *ph* Debi Treloar/the home of Isobel Trenouth, her husband and their four children; **83al** *ph* Claire Richardson; **83ac&bl** *ph* Claire Richardson/Marianne Cotterill's house in London; **83ar&cr** *ph* Debi Treloar/the home of Joanne Cleasby, Hove; **83bc** *ph* Claire Richardson/available for photographic location at www.inspacelocations.com; **83br** *ph* Winfried Heinze/interior stylist Sidsel Zachariassen; **84al** *ph* Debi Treloar/Michael Leva's home in Litchfield County, Connecticut; **84ac,ar&br** *ph* Winfried Heinze/the home of Hernando and Gigi Pérez in New York City; **84cl** *ph* Claire Richardson/Nick and Flora Phillips' home in Gascony; **84c** *ph* Winfried Heinze/the apartment of Yancey and Mark Richardson in New York, architecture and interior design by Steven Learner Studio; **84cr** *ph* Claire Richardson/Tania Bennett and Adrian Townsend's home in London; **84bl** *ph* Debi Treloar/Nikki Tibbles' London home, owner of Wild at Heart – flowers and interiors; **84bc** *ph* Winfried Heinze/the apartment of Jacques Azagury in London (painting on chest by Howard Hodgkin, painting on right wall by Tim Woolcock); **85** Winfried Heinze/the home of Hernando and Gigi Pérez in New York City; **86al&cr** *ph* Polly Wreford/Charlotte-Anne Fidler's home in London: **86ac** *ph* Polly Wreford/Hilary Robertson and Alistair McGowan, Hastings; **86ar** *ph* Polly Wreford/Ingrid and Avinash Persaud's home in London; **86cl&br** *ph* Polly Wreford/Siobhán McKeating's home in London; **86c&bl** *ph* Polly Wreford/Cecilia and Peter Granath's home in Copenhagen; **86bc** *ph* Polly Wreford/Foster House at www.beachstudios.co.uk; **87l** *ph* Polly Wreford/Charlotte-Anne Fidler's home in London: **87c** *ph* Polly Wreford/Ben de Lisi's home in London; **87r** *ph* Debi Treloar/Sanne Hjermind and Claes Bech-Poulsen; **88** *ph* Paul Ryan/Aki Wahlman's summer home in Finland; **89al,cr&bl** *ph* Chris Everard/Christopher Coleman's New York apartment; **89ac** *ph* Chris Everard/New York family home designed by Shamir Shah; **89ar** *ph* Chris Everard/Tony Loizou of Pennington Robson – the Loizou's house in North London; **89cl** *ph* Winfried Heinze/the apartment of Jacques Azagury in London; **89ccl&br** *ph* Andrew Wood/the London home of Steven and Jane Collins, owner of Sixty 6 boutique; **89ccr** *ph* Winfried Heinze/the home of Kamilla Bryiel and Christian Permin in Copenhagen; **90–91** *ph* Claire Richardson/Eifion and Amanda Griffiths of Melin Tregwynt's house in Wales; **92al&ar** *ph* Chris Everard/home of David Walsh, Creative Director of Inner Sanctum, London; **92b** *ph* Winfried Heinze/the home of Ben Johns and Deb Waterman Johns; **93** *ph* Alan Williams/Louise Robbins' house in north-west Herefordshire; **94l** *ph* Polly Wreford/Foster House at www.beachstudios.co.uk; **94ar** *ph* Debi Treloar/private residence in Washington, Connecticut; **94br** *ph* Claire Richardson/available for photographic location at www.inspacelocations.com; **95** *ph* Paul Massey/Hôtel Le Sénéchal, Ars en Ré, designed by Christophe Ducharme Architecte; **96a** *ph* Claire Richardson/a family home in Blackheath, South London; **96bl** *ph* Claire Richardson/www.les-sardines.com; **96br** *ph* Chris Everard/a family home in Norfolk; **97al** *ph* Chris Everard/Christopher Coleman's New York apartment; **97ar** *ph* Winfried Heinze/interior stylist Sidsel Zachariassen; **97bl** *ph* Polly Wreford/Cecilia and Peter Granath's home in Copenhagen; **97br** *ph* Claire Richardson; **98al** *ph* Claire Richardson/www.chambres-provence.com; **98ar** *ph* Alan Williams/the Norfolk home of Geoff and Gilly Newberry of Bennison Fabrics – all fabrics and wallpapers by Bennison; **98b** *ph* Claire Richardson/the London townhouse belonging to Louise Laycock of Bennison; **99** *ph* Winfried Heinze/Jodi and Scott Markoff; **100al** *ph* Debi Treloar/Christina and Allan Thaulow's home in Denmark; **100ar** *ph* Claire Richardson/Tania Bennett and Adrian Townsend's home in London; **100br** *ph* Paul Massey/the Spreitzer residence, Southampton, New York; **101** *ph* Paul Massey/Hotel Tresanton, St Mawes, Cornwall, owned and designed by Olga Polizzi; **102** *ph* Winfried Heinze/the home of Hernando and Gigi Pérez in New York City; **103bl** *ph* Debi Treloar/Sanne Hjermind and Claes Bech-Poulsen; **103ar** *ph* Claire Richardson; **103br** *ph* Debi Treloar/the home of Isobel Trenouth, her husband and their four children; **104l** *ph* Winfried Heinze/a Parisian apartment designed by Tino Zervudachi and Antoine de Sigy; **104r** *ph* Polly Wreford/Foster House at www.beachstudios.co.uk; **105a** *ph* Polly Wreford/Sasha Waddell's home available from www.beachstudios.co.uk; **105bl** *ph* Polly Wreford/the Shelter Island home of Lois Draegin and David Cohen; **105br** *ph* Winfried Heinze/Parisian pied-a-terre designed by Marianne Pascal for an Anglo-French couple; **106** *ph* Paul Massey/a house in Île de Ré; **107l** *ph* Debi Treloar/Michael Leva's home in Litchfield County, Connecticut; **107r** *ph* Winfried Heinze/the apartment of Jacques Azagury in London – furniture: Catherine Memmi; **108l** *ph* Winfried Heinze/Trine and William Miller's home in London; **108ar** *ph* Debi Treloar/owners of Maisonette, Martin Barrell and Amanda Sellers' home in London – available for photographic location at www.inspacelocations.com; **108br** *ph* Winfried Heinze/the Éclair-Powell home in London; **109** *ph* Claire Richardson/Swan House bed and breakfast in Hastings; **110al** *ph* Debi Treloar/Michael Leva's home in Litchfield County, Connecticut; **110acl** *ph* Polly Wreford/Cecilia and Peter Granath's home in Copenhagen; **110acr** *ph* Polly Wreford/Charlotte-Anne Fidler's home in London; **110ar** *ph* Polly Wreford/Alex White; **110ca** *ph* Claire Richardson/www.chambres-provence.com; **110cc** *ph* Debi Treloar/the London home of Sam Robinson, co-owner of 'The Cross' and 'Cross the Road', **110cb** *ph* Debi Treloar/www.juliaclancey.com; **111** *ph* Polly Wreford/Abigail Ahern's home in London; **112al** *ph* Debi Treloar/Michael Leva's home in Litchfield County, Connecticut; **112cl&ar** *ph* Debi Treloar/available for photographic location at www.inspacelocations.com; **112bl** *ph* Chris Everard/Jeremy Hackett's house in London; **112c** *ph* Christopher Drake/the home of Adrian and Belinda Hull in London, designed by architect Gus Alexander; **112bc** *ph* Paul Ryan/the summer house of Peter Morgan at the Bjäte peninsula (in the north-west of Scania); **112br** *ph* Claire Richardson/Swan House bed and breakfast in Hastings; **113** *ph* Debi Treloar/the Philadelphia home of Glen Senk and Keith Johnson of Anthropologie; **114** *ph* Polly Wreford/London home of Michael Bains and Catherine Woram; **115 all** *ph* Polly Wreford/Foster House at www.beachstudios.co.uk; **116al&bl** *ph* Claire Richardson/the London townhouse belonging to Louise Laycock of Bennison; **116ar&bc** *ph* Alan Williams/the Norfolk home of Geoff and Gilly Newberry of Bennison Fabrics – all fabrics and wallpapers by Bennison; **116br & 117bl** *ph* Claire Richardson; **117al** *ph* Polly Wreford/Hilary Robertson and Alistair McGowan, Hastings; **117ar** *ph* Debi Treloar/the home of Netty Nauta in Amsterdam; **117br** *ph* Claire Richardson/

Brandon Mably and Kaffe Fassett's family home in Hastings, www.kaffefassett.com; **118al** *ph* Polly Wreford/Siobhán McKeating's home in London; **118ar** *ph* Chris Everard/Manhattan home of designer Matthew Patrick Smyth; **118cl** *ph* Claire Richardson/Graham Noakes of Osborne and Little's home in London; **118bl** *ph* Claire Richardson/Marianne Cotterill's house in London; **118c** *ph* Claire Richardson/a family home in Blackheath, South London; **118br** *ph* Winfried Heinze/the home of Hernando and Gigi Pérez in New York City; **119l** *ph* Claire Richardson/Graham Noakes of Osborne and Little's home in London; **119r** *ph* Claire Richardson/a family home in Blackheath, South London; **120al** *ph* Andrew Wood/home of Mark and Kristine Davis, Palm Springs, CA; **120ar** *ph* Andrew Wood/the home of Sean and Tricia Brunson in Orlando; **120bl** *ph* Andrew Wood/an original Florida home restored by Andrew Weaving of Century, www.centuryd.com; **120br,121ar&cr** *ph* Andrew Wood/the home of David Jimenez in Palm Springs; **121al** *ph* Andrew Wood/the home of Sean and Tricia Brunson in Orlando; **121ac&b** *ph* Andrew Wood/the Alexander home of Bruce Mink in Palm Springs; **122–123** *ph* Winfried Heinze/the Éclair-Powell home in London; **124** *ph* Debi Treloar/the home of Sarah O'Keefe, co-owner of 'The Cross' in West London; **125l** *ph* Chris Everard/New York family home designed by Shamir Shah; **125r** *ph* Paul Massey/a house in Denmark (summer house in the south of France to rent, www.villalagachon.com); **126l** *ph* Polly Wreford/Hilary Robertson and Alistair McGowan, Hastings; **126ar** *ph* Chris Everard/New York family home designed by Shamir Shah; **126br** *ph* Christopher Drake/the home of Adrian and Belinda Hull in London, designed by architect Gus Alexander; **127** *ph* Winfried Heinze/a Parisian apartment designed by Tino Zervudachi and Antoine de Sigy; **128** *ph* Debi Treloar/Kristiina Ratia and Jeff Gocke's family home in Norwalk, Connecticut; **129** *ph* Winfried Heinze/interior architecture: matali crasset; **130l** *ph* Chris Everard/Freddie Daniells' apartment in London designed by Brookes Stacey Randall; **130r** *ph* Paul Massey/Jan Constantine – www.janconstantine.com; **131** *ph* Winfried Heinze/the apartment of Yancey and Mark Richardson in New York: architecture and interior Design by Steven Learner Studio; **132l** *ph* Paul Massey/the home in Denmark of Charlotte Lynggaard, designer of Ole Lynggaard Copenhagen; **132r** *ph* Winfried Heinze/interior architecture: matali crasset; **133** *ph* Chris Tubbs/Gabriella Cantaluppi Abbado's home in Monticchiello; **134** *ph* Debi Treloar/Ian Hogarth of Hogarth Architects' family home in London; **135l** *ph* Chris Tubbs/Annabel Grey's Norfolk cottage; **135r** *ph* Winfried Heinze/the O'Connor Bandeen family home in London; **136al** *ph* Winfried Heinze/interior architecture: matali crasset; **136ar** *ph* Winfried Heinze/the Éclair-Powell home in London; **136bl** *ph* Chris Tubbs/Teresa Ginori's home near Varese; **136br** *ph* Christopher Drake/Pavillion de Levant, gate house on the property of the Pavillion de Victoire, Verneques, France, designed by Kenyon Kramer and Jean-Louis Raynaud; **136–137** *ph* Chris Tubbs/Raffaella Barker's house in Norfolk; **138 & 139bl** *ph* Winfried Heinze/a Parisian apartment designed by Tino Zervudachi and Antoine de Sigy; **139ar** *ph* Claire Richardson/the home of writer Meredith Daneman in London; **139br** *ph* Polly Wreford/the Shelter Island home of Lois Draegin and David Cohen; **140** *ph* Debi Treloar/Mark and Sally Bailey's home in Herefordshire; **141** *ph* Andrew Wood/an original Florida home restored by Andrew Weaving of Century, www.centuryd.com; **142** *ph* Polly Wreford/London home of Michael Bains and Catherine Woram; **143** *ph* Chris Everard/home of David Walsh, Creative Director of Inner Sanctum, London; **144al** *ph* Polly Wreford/London home of Michael Bains and Catherine Woram; **144ar** *ph* Chris Tubbs/Podere Sala, Lori De Mori's home in Tuscany restored by architect André Benaim; **144br** *ph* Debi Treloar/the home of Joanne Cleasby, Hove; **145** *ph* Polly Wreford/Foster House at www.beachstudios.co.uk; **146al** *ph* Chris Tubbs; **146cl** *ph* Chris Tubbs/Matthew and Miranda Eden's home in Wiltshire; **146bl** *ph* Chris Tubbs/Powers house, London; **146ar** *ph* Claire Richardson/the home of writer Meredith Daneman in London; **146bc** *ph* Alan Williams/the Norfolk home of Geoff and Gilly Newberry of Bennison Fabrics – all fabrics and wallpapers by Bennison; **146br** *ph* Christopher Drake/Tim Whittaker's Georgian house in East London; **147l** *ph* Claire Richardson/Nick and Flora Phillips' home in Gascony; **147r** *ph* Chris Tubbs/Teresa Ginori's home near Varese; **148l** *ph* Polly Wreford/Hilary Robertson and Alistair McGowan, Hastings; **148r** *ph* Jan Baldwin/Sophie Eadie's family home in London – The New England Shutter Company; **149al** *ph* Claire Richardson/Tania Bennett and Adrian Townsend's home in London; **149bl** *ph* Polly Wreford/Alex White; **149ar** *ph* Polly Wreford/Siobhán McKeating's home in London; **149cr** *ph* Polly Wreford/Foster House at www.beachstudios.co.uk; **149bc** *ph* Jan Baldwin/Sophie Eadie's family home in London – The New England Shutter Company; **149br** *ph* Debi Treloar/Kristiina Ratia and Jeff Gocke's family home in Norwalk, Connecticut; **150al** *ph* Paul Massey/the Barton's seaside home in West

Sussex: www.thedodo.co.uk; **150bl** *ph* Paul Massey/Cote Jardin boutique; **150ac** *ph* Jan Baldwin/a house in Maine designed by Stephen Blatt Architects; **150ar** *ph* Christopher Drake/Eva Johnson's house in Suffolk, interiors designed by Eva Johnson; **150br** *ph* Paul Massey/Michael Giannelli and Greg Shano's home in East Hampton; **151l** *ph* Simon Upton/Nancy Braithwaite; **151r** *ph* Chris Tubbs/Philip and Catherine Mould's house in Oxfordshire; **152al** *ph* Chris Everard/home of David Walsh, Creative Director of Inner Sanctum, London; **152bl** *ph* Andrew Wood/the Paris apartment of art director, stage designer and designer Jean-Pascal Levy-Trumet; **152ar** *ph* Winfried Heinze/a Parisian apartment designed by Tino Zervudachi and Antoine de Sigy; **152br** *ph* Debi Treloar/Michael Leva's home in Litchfield County, Connecticut; **153** *ph* Winfried Heinze/the apartment of Lars Kristensen, owner of Fil de Fer, Copenhagen: **154–155** *ph* Debi Treloar/Victoria Andreae's house in London; **156–157** *ph* Winfried Heinze/Jon Pellicoro, artist and designer; **157r** *ph* Debi Treloar/Ben Johns and Deb Waterman Johns' house in Georgetown; **158al** *ph* Winfried Heinze/a family home in Southampton; **158ar** *ph* Paul Massey/the Bartons' seaside home in West Sussex: www.thedodo.co.uk; **158br** *ph* Winfried Heinze/the Sullivan's home in New York – mushroom lighting designed by White Rabbit England; **159** *ph* Debi Treloar/Ben Johns and Deb Waterman Johns' house in Georgetown; **160al** *ph* Debi Treloar/Victoria Andreae's house in London; **160ar** *ph* Debi Treloar/an apartment in London by Malin Iovino Design; **160b** *ph* Winfried Heinze; **161** *ph* Debi Treloar/Sigolène Prébois of Tsé andTsé associeés' home in Paris; **162** *ph* Winfried Heinze/Josephine Ryan's house in London; **163al** *ph* Winfried Heinze/Elle and Aarron's rooms on Riverbank, Hampton Court; **163ac** *ph* Winfried Heinze/Emma Cassi's home in London; **163ar** *ph* Winfried Heinze/a family house designed by Henri Fitzwilliam-Lay; **163b** *ph* Winfried Heinze/the Sullivans' home in New York – mushroom lighting designed by White Rabbit England; **164** *ph* Debi Treloar/Debi Treloar's home in London; **165a** *ph* Debi Treloar/Roeline Faber, interior designer; **165bl** *ph* Winfried Heinze/the designer Etienne Mery's home in Paris; **165br** *ph* Winfried Heinze/a family home in Manhattan; **166l** *ph* Andrew Wood/the London home of Steven and Jane Collins, owner of Sixty 6 boutique; **166r** *ph* Debi Treloar/Victoria Andreae's house in London; **166–167** *ph* Debi Treloar/Sudi Pigott's house in London; **168–169** *ph* Winfried Heinze/Dr Alex Sherman and Ms Ivy Baer Sherman's residence in New York City; Mullman Seidman Architects; **169l** *ph* Winfried Heinze/Trine and William Miller's home in London; **169ar** *ph* Winfried Heinze/the home of Ben Johns and Deb Waterman Johns; **169br** *ph* Debi Treloar/Sue and Lars-Christian Brask's house in London designed by Susie Atkinson Design; **170a** *ph* Winfried Heinze/Rose Uniacke's home in London; **170bl** *ph* Winfried Heinze/Madame Sera Hersham-Loftus's home; **170br** *ph* Winfried Heinze/interior architecture: matali crasset; **171l** *ph* Winfried Heinze/the Fried family home in London; **171r** *ph* Winfried Heinze/interior designer Lisa Jackson's home in New York; **172a** *ph* Winfried Heinze/Dr Alex Sherman and Ms Ivy Baer Sherman's residence in New York City; Mullman Seidman Architects; **172b** *ph* Winfried Heinze/the designer Etienne Mery's home in Paris; **173** *ph* Winfried Heinze/Val, Wim, Kamilla, Juliette and Joseph's home in Ghent; designed and built by Wim Depuydt, architect; **174a** *ph* Winfried Heinze/the Collettes' home in Holland designed by architect Pascal Grosfeld; **174c** *ph* Debi Treloar; **174b** *ph* Debi Treloar/Ben Johns and Deb Waterman Johns' house in Georgetown; **175** *ph* Debi Treloar/Eben and Nica Cooper's bedroom, the Cooper family playroom; **176** *ph* Debi Treloar/Ben Johns and Deb Waterman Johns' house in Georgetown; **177a** *ph* Dan Duchars/architects Patrick Theis and Soraya Khan's home in London; **177c** *ph* Winfried Heinze/architect and interiors: Nico Rensch, Architeam; **177b** *ph* Debi Treloar/Debi Treloar's home in London; **178l** *ph* Debi Treloar/Eben and Nica Cooper's bedroom, the Cooper family playroom; **178r** *ph* Chris Everard/Tim and Celia Holman's house in London, designed by DIVE Architects Ltd; **179al** *ph* Andrew Wood/home of Mark and Kristine Davis, Palm Springs, CA; **179ar** *ph* Debi Treloar/Ab Rogers and Sophie Braimbridge's house, London, designed by Richard Rogers for his mother. Furniture design by KRD – Kitchen Rogers Design; **179cl&br** *ph* Debi Treloar/Eben and Nica Cooper's bedroom, the Cooper family playroom; **179bl** *ph* Debi Treloar/Sudi Pigott's house in London; **179bc** *ph* Debi Treloar/Rudi, Melissa and Archie Thackray's house in London; **180 all** *ph* Debi Treloar/the Boyes' home in London designed by Circus Architects; **181 both** *ph* Debi Treloar/Ian Hogarth of Hogarth Architects' family home in London; **182a** *ph* Winfried Heinze/the designer Etienne Mery's home in Paris; **182b** *ph* Winfried Heinze/a family house designed by Henri Fitzwilliam-Lay; **183al,acr&bl** *ph* Winfried Heinze/Stella's room in NYC; **183ac&bcr** *ph* Winfried Heinze/the designer Etienne Mery's home in Paris; **183ar** *ph* Winfried Heinze/Madame Sera Hersham-Loftus's home; **183br** *ph* Winfried Heinze/the Éclair-Powell home in London; **184al** *ph* Winfried Heinze/Freddie Hair's room in London;

184ar&bl *ph* Winfried Heinze/the Fried family home in London; 184ccr *ph* Winfried Heinze/Isabel and Ricardo Ernst's family home; 184cr *ph* Winfried Heinze/interior architecture: matali crasset; 184bcc *ph* Winfried Heinze/interior designer Lisa Jackson's home in New York; 184bc&br, 185b *ph* Winfried Heinze/the home of Ben Johns and Deb Waterman Johns; 185a *ph* Winfried Heinze/interior architecture: matali crasset; 186l *ph* Winfried Heinze/Glasserman/Gilsanz residence – architect: James Slade at Cho Slade Architecture, www.sladearch.com; 186r *ph* Debi Treloar/Sigolène Prébois of Tsé andTsé associeés' home in Paris; 187al&br *ph* Winfried Heinze/the home of Ben Johns and Deb Waterman Johns; 187ar *ph* Winfried Heinze/the Éclair-Powell home in London; 187bl *ph* Winfried Heinze/Rose Uniacke's home in London; 188–189 *ph* Andrew Wood; 190 *ph* Andrew Wood/the home of Sean and Tricia Brunson in Orlando; 191l *ph* Andrew Wood/a house in Stockholm, Sweden; 191r *ph* Andrew Wood/Chelsea Studio New York City, designed by Marino + Giolito, Inc.; 192a *ph* Andrew Wood; 192b *ph* Chris Tubbs/Sanctuary Garden offices; 193 *ph* Dan Duchars/Ian Hogarth of Hogarth Architects' home office in London; 194 *ph* Winfried Heinze/the O'Connor Bandeen family home in London; 195 *ph* Polly Wreford/Ingrid and Avinash Persaud's home in London; 196 *ph* Christopher Drake/an apartment in Milan designed by Daniela Micol Wajskol, interior designer; 197l *ph* Debi Treloar/designer Steven Shailer's apartment in New York City; 197r *ph* Andrew Wood/the Paris apartment of Nicolas Hug; 198 *ph* Andrew Wood/Ian Bartlett and Christine Walsh's house in London; 199ar *ph* Dan Duchars/designer Mark Smith's home in London; 199bl *ph* Andrew Wood/Rosa Dean and Ed Baden-Powell's apartment in London, designed by Urban Salon 020 7357 8800; 199bc *ph* Andrew Wood/Chelsea Studio New York City, designed by Marino + Giolito, Inc.; 200al *ph* Debi Treloar/Wim and Josephine's apartment in Amsterdam; 200cr *ph* Debi Treloar/the guesthouse of the interior designer and artist Philippe Guilmin, Brussels; 200br *ph* Debi Treloar/Clare and David Mannix-Andrews' house, Hove, East Sussex; 201 *ph* Debi Treloar/Mark and Sally Bailey's home in Herefordshire; 202a *ph* Dan Duchars/Ian Hogarth of Hogarth Architects' home office in London; 202b *ph* Chris Tubbs/Teresa Ginori's home near Varese; 203 *ph* Polly Wreford/Charlotte-Anne Fidler's home in London; 204 *ph* Polly Wreford/Foster House at www.beachstudios.co.uk; 205l *ph* Claire Richardson/Eifion and Amanda Griffiths of Melin Tregwynt's house in Wales; 205r *ph* Debi Treloar/North London flat of presentation skills trainer/actress and her teacher husband, designed by Gordana Mandic of Buildburo; 206a *ph* Christopher Drake/a house in London, architectural design and procurement by Tyler London Ltd, interior design by William W. Stubbs, IIDA; 206bl *ph* Andrew Wood/architect Grethe Meyer's house, Hørsholm, Denmark, built by architects Moldenhawer, Hammer and Frederiksen,1963; 206bc *ph* Andrew Wood/Kurt Bredenbeck's apartment at the Barbican, London; 206br *ph* Andrew Wood/the Kjaerholms' family home in Rungsted, Denmark; 207 *ph* Polly Wreford/Ingrid and Avinash Persaud's home in London; 208l *ph* Chris Tubbs/Annabel Grey's Norfolk cottage – *Nuclear Horse* by Jennifer Binney; 208r *ph* Debi Treloar/Mark and Sally Bailey's former home in Herefordshire; 209al&ar *ph* Polly Wreford/Foster House at www.beachstudios.co.uk; 209cr *ph* Polly Wreford/an apartment in New York designed by Belmont Freeman Architects; 209bl *ph* Debi Treloar/the home of Netty Nauta in Amsterdam; 209br *ph* Debi Treloar/the Philadelphia home of Glen Senk and Keith Johnson of Anthropologie; 210–211 *ph* Claire Richardson; 212 *ph* Debi Treloar/Christina and Allan Thaulow's home in Denmark; 213l *ph* Winfried Heinze/a Parisian apartment designed by Tino Zervudachi and Antoine de Sigy; 213r *ph* Polly Wreford/Abigail Ahern's home in London; 214a *ph* Sus Rosenquist/a house designed by Schmidt Hammer Larssen, developer: Birkeengen Aps, Denmark – www.birkeengen.dk; 214b *ph* Andrew Wood/an original Florida home restored by Andrew Weaving of Century, www.centuryd.com; 215a *ph* Claire Richardson/Graham Noakes of Osborne and Little's home in London; 215b *ph* Paul Ryan/the home of Nils Tunebjer in Sweden; 216a *ph* Winfried Heinze/the apartment of Yancey and Mark Richardson in New York, architecture and interior design by Steven Learner Studio – painting on centre wall by Vic Muniz, three nudes on desk by Alvin Booth and work on far right wall by Adam Fuss; 216bl *ph* Sus Rosenquist/M2; 216br *ph* Winfried Heinze/Signe Bindslev Henriksen of Space Architecture and Design; 217a *ph* Winfried Heinze/the home of Kamilla Bryiel and Christian Permin in Copenhagen; 217b *ph* Winfried Heinze/the apartment of Lars Kristensen, owner of Fil de Fer, Copenhagen; 218a *ph* Andrew Wood/Nicki De Metz's flat in London designed by De Metz architects; 218b *ph* Christopher Drake/designed by McLean Quinlan Architects; 218–219a *ph* Andrew Wood/an original Florida home restored by Andrew Weaving of Century, www.centuryd.com; 219bl&r *ph* Andrew Wood/an apartment in Bath designed by Briffa Phillips Architects; 220al&br *ph* Debi Treloar/author, stylist and Caravan (shop)

owner Emily Chalmers and director Chris Richmond's home in London; 220ar *ph* Andrew Wood/Jones Miller studio in New York designed by Giuseppe Lignano and Ada Tolla of LOT/EK Architecture; 220bl *ph* Debi Treloar/private house in Amsterdam owner, Ank de la Plume; 220c&cr *ph* Debi Treloar/Riad 'Chambres d'amis' in Marrakech (B&B), designed and owned by Ank de la Plume, decorated in co-production with Household Hardware and Rutger Jan de Lange; 221 both *ph* Andrew Wood/Han Feng's apartment in New York designed by Han Feng; 222 both *ph* Andrew Wood/Patricia Ijaz's house in London designed by Jonathan Woolf of Woolf Architects; 223al&br *ph* Andrew Wood/Brian Johnson's apartment in London designed by Johnson Naylor; 223ar *ph* Andrew Wood/the Paris apartment of art director, stage designer and designer Jean-Pascal Levy-Trumet; 223cr *ph* Polly Wreford/Abigail Ahern's home in London; 223bl *ph* Paul Ryan/the home of Ingegerd Raman and Claes Söderquist's home in Sweden; 224–225 *ph* Debi Treloar/Dar Beida and Dar Emma, available to rent at www.castlesinthesand.com, interior designers Emma Wilson and Graham Carter, for commissions email emma@castlesinthesand.com; 226 *ph* Debi Treloar/the home of Isobel Trenouth, her husband and their four children; 227al *ph* Christopher Drake/Giorgio Irene Silvagni's house in Provence; 227bl *ph* Melanie Eclare/Laura Cooper and Nick Taggart's Los Angeles garden designed by Cooper/Taggart Designs; 227r *ph* Christopher Drake/Mr and Mrs Degrugillier, Le Mas de Flore, Antiquite et Creation, Lagnes, Isle sur Sorgue, Provence; 228 *ph* Chris Everard/Jeremy Hackett's house in London; 229al *ph* James Morris/Tom Jestico and Vivien Fowler's house in London, design team Tom Jestico and Vivien Fowler; 229ar *ph* Chris Everard/garden room, London for David and Anne Harriss designed by Eger Architects; 229cl&c *ph* Melanie Eclare/a garden in London designed by Jonathan Bell; 229br *ph* Melanie Eclare/the garden and nursery De Brinkhof of Riet Brinkhof and Joop Van Den Berk; 230 *ph* Chris Tubbs/Vanni and Nicoletta Calamai's home near Siena; 231al *ph* Christopher Drake/garden designer Mary Z. Jenkins's house in New York; 231ar *ph* Christopher Drake; 231b *ph* Chris Tubbs/Toia Saibene and Giuliana Magnifico's home in Lucignano, Tuscany; 232l *ph* Paul Massey/the Bartons' seaside home in West Sussex: www.thedodo.co.uk; 232ar *ph* Paul Massey/a house in Denmark (summer house in the south of France to rent, www.villalagachon.com); 232br *ph* Christopher Drake/garden designer Mary Z. Jenkins's house in New York; 233al *ph* Paul Ryan/the home of Nils Tunebjer in Sweden; 233bl *ph* Christopher Drake/La Bastide Rose, Nicole and Pierre Salinger's house, Le Thor, Provence; 233ar *ph* Paul Massey/a house in Île de Ré; 233br *ph* Christopher Drake/Enrica Stabile's house in Provence; 234al *ph* Debi Treloar/the home of Isobel Trenouth, her husband and their four children; 234bl *ph* Christopher Drake; 234br *ph* Melanie Eclare/Elspeth Thompson's garden in London; 234ar *ph* Christopher Drake/Enrica Stabile's house in Provence; 235 & 236bl *ph* Debi Treloar/Dar Beida and Dar Emma, available to rent at www.castlesinthesand.com, interior designers Emma Wilson and Graham Carter, for commissions email emma@castlesinthesand.com; 236al&br *ph* Debi Treloar/the home of Isobel Trenouth, her husband and their four children; 236cl&ar *ph* Debi Treloar/Riad 'Chambres d'amis' in Marrakech (B&B), designed and owned by Ank de la Plume, decorated in co-production with Household Hardware and Rutger Jan de Lange; 236c&bc *ph* Debi Treloar/the London home of Sam Robinson, co-owner of 'The Cross' and 'Cross the Road'; 237a *ph* Chris Tubbs/Gabriella Cantaluppi Abbado's home in Monticchiello; 237b *ph* Debi Treloar/Riad 'Chambres d'amis' in Marrakech (B&B), designed and owned by Ank de la Plume, decorated in co-production with Household Hardware and Rutger Jan de Lange; 238al *ph* Paul Massey/the home in Denmark of Charlotte Lynggaard, designer of Ole Lynggaard Copenhagen; 238bl *ph* Andrew Wood/the Alexander home of Bruce Mink in Palm Springs; 238br&ar *ph* Paul Massey/the Spreitzer residence, Southampton, New York; 239al&ar *ph* Paul Massey/the home in Denmark of Charlotte Lynggaard, designer of Ole Lynggaard Copenhagen; 239cl&br *ph* Paul Massey/Naja Lauf; 239c *ph* Paul Massey/Michael Giannelli and Greg Shano's home in East Hampton; 239bl *ph* Paul Massey/Hôtel Le Sénéchal, Ars en Ré, designed by Christophe Ducharme Architecte; 239bc *ph* Paul Ryan/summer house at Hvasser, of Astir Eidsbo and Tore Lindholm; 239cr *ph* Andrew Wood/the Alexander home of Bruce Mink in Palm Springs; 256 *ph* Alan Williams/Katie Bassford King's house in London designed by Touch Interior Design.

index

Page numbers in *italic* refer to the illustrations

A

accessories
  bathrooms 147, 151
  children's rooms 178, 182
  home offices 205
  kitchens 16, 43
  living rooms 81, 85, 87
  outdoor living space 234, 235
  pink 182
Aga cookers 27, 32, 39
Anglepoise lights 104, 104, 172, 202
appliances, kitchen 11, 27, 27, 40
  brushed steel 16, 31
architectural salvage companies 75,
  147
armchairs
  babies' rooms 160, 163, 163
  bathrooms 128, 147, 151
  bedrooms 98, 98, 119, 120
  kitchens 23, 48
  living rooms 53, 57
  open-plan living 215
  rattan 151
armoires 20, 40, 77, 109, 119
artwork
  architectural reliefs 79
  arranging 65, 78, 79
  bathrooms 144, 147
  bedrooms 96, 110, 111
  children's rooms 158, 171, 185
  hanging in groups 65, 110
  home offices 205
  kitchens 11
  living rooms 65, 67, 78, 79, 85
  Perspex 144
awnings 234

B

babies' rooms 158, 160–3, 160, 163
bamboo flooring 140
bar stools 23, 24
barbecues 231
basketball hoop 58
baskets 48, 77, 231
bathmats 151
bathrooms
  accessories 147, 151
  blinds/shades 151
  coastal style 151
  colour 136, 136, 147, 148, 151, 153
  design and decoration 125, 125
  displaying objects 135, 143, 144, 147,
    151
  distressed furniture 151
  en-suite 93, 126, 218, 218
  family 128, 129
  finishing touches 144, 144
  flooring 125, 128, 129, 135, 136, 140,
    140, 147, 148, 151
  grouting 140
  hotel glamour 153
  lighting 139, 139, 148

  mirrored cabinets 139
  mixing old and new 144
  nonslip flooring 129, 132
  open plan with bedrooms 94,
    218–19, 218
  planning 126, 126
  sealing 132
  seating in 128, 129, 147, 151
  small 126, 130, 135, 135, 139, 143
  storage 126, 126, 128, 129, 135, 135,
    139, 143, 143
  taps/faucets 129, 130, 147
  Thirties 144
  traditional style 147
  walls 135, 136, 136, 147, 148, 151
  white 136, 139, 148
baths 130
  copper 147
  decorating side panels 144, 153
  infinity 153
  re-enamelling 147
  renovating 136, 147
  sculptural white 136
  side-by-side 129
  stone freestanding 125
  sunken 153
  traditional roll-top 130, 136
bay windows 53, 71
bedding 93, 97, 100, 101, 113, 114, 120,
  166
  bedspreads 96, 114, 119
  children's 158, 158, 165, 171, 178
  floral 117
  patchwork quilts 100
bedrooms
  black and white 97
  colour 93, 96, 97, 97, 113, 117, 119,
    120
  cushions 111, 113, 114, 117, 119,
    120
  design and decoration 93, 93
  finishing touches 110, 111
  flooring 107, 107, 113, 114, 114, 119,
    120
  furniture 98, 98, 99, 108, 109, 113,
    114, 117, 119, 120
  grown-up glamour 119
  lighting 97, 104, 104, 113, 114, 119,
    120
  modern country 113
  modern retro 120
  multi-tasking space 99
  open-plan with bathrooms 94,
    218–19, 218
  planning 94, 94
  romantic floral 117
  seating 98, 98, 119, 120
  storage 94, 94, 98, 98, 108, 108, 109,
    110, 120
  wallpaper 103, 108, 114, 117, 119,
    120
  white 97, 103, 111, 114
  window treatments 103, 103, 113,
    117, 119

beds, adult 94, 98, 98, 100, 113, 117,
  119
beds, children's 158, 166, 169, 169
  bespoke 181
  bunk 158, 169, 169
  canopies 165, 165, 178
  cot beds 163, 163
  mezzanine level 171, 177
  safe positioning 157, 160
bedside lamps 104, 120
bedside tables 96, 98, 98, 99, 111, 113,
  119
bedspreads 96, 114, 119
benches 232
Bertoia, Harry 120
blackboard paint 158
blanket boxes 98
blankets 100, 100, 101, 113, 120
blinds/shades
  bathrooms 151
  bedrooms 103, 103, 113, 117, 119
  blackout 160
  bottom-up 103
  children's rooms 178, 182
  garden rooms 229
  kitchens 32
  living rooms 57, 71, 71
  to make windows appear smaller or
    taller 57
books
  children's 163, 166
  kitchens 39, 48
  living rooms 61, 63, 77, 77
bookshelves
  adjustable 58, 177
  children's 166, 177
  floating 77
  mesh covered 77
  as room dividers 58
  understair 57
boxes recycled as display units 65
boys' rooms 166, 166, 185
braziers 234
breakfast bar 18
brushed steel
  appliances 16, 31
  kitchen units 19, 31, 31, 44
bunting 165, 234
bureaux 197, 207
butcher's block 13
butcher's rail 36

C

candles
  bathrooms 139, 144, 144
  bedrooms 104, 110
  living rooms 78
  outdoor living space 227, 234
  scented 110, 144
candlesticks 79, 148
canopies 165, 165, 178
carpets
  abstract design 75
  bedrooms 107, 107, 114, 120
  children's rooms 160, 174, 178
  living rooms 75, 75
Castiglioni, Achille 120
CD storage 58, 58, 185

ceiling rose 72
ceilings, decorating 181
ceramics 11, 82
chairs
  20th-century design 62, 82, 120
  on bold carpets 75
  café 233, 233, 237
  dining 23, 24, 47, 213
  director's 231, 233
  elegant living rooms 85
  foldaway 237
  garden 231, 231, 232–3, 232, 233, 237
  Le Corbusier 62
  living rooms 62, 62, 75, 82, 85, 88
  Louis XV style 197
  masculine living rooms 88
  office 186, 194, 194
  oversized chair 229
  pink 67
  polypropylene 233
  stacking 231
  see also armchairs
chaise longues 98
chandeliers 72, 104, 104, 114, 119
changing tables 160, 163, 163
Cherner, Norman 120
chests
  bedrooms 98
  living rooms 57, 62, 77
children's rooms
  accessories 178, 182
  action stations 186
  babies' rooms 158, 160–3, 160, 163
  boys' rooms 166, 166, 185
  colour 160, 165, 165, 166, 166, 174,
    178
  customized 181
  design and decoration 156, 157, 157
  desks 156, 158, 166, 171, 171, 172,
    185, 186, 197
  displaying objects 160, 177
  flooring 158, 160, 166, 174, 174, 178,
    186
  furniture 157, 158, 163, 163, 166,
    166, 177, 177, 178, 182
  girls' rooms 157, 165, 165, 182
  lighting 160, 169, 171, 172, 172, 185,
    186
  multi-task storage unit 177
  pink 182
  planning 158, 158
  rugs 158, 158, 160, 166, 171, 174, 178
  shared 158, 169, 169, 177
  storage 158, 165, 166, 169, 177, 177,
    185
  storage for babies 160, 163, 163
  storage for teenagers 171, 171, 186
  teenagers 156, 166, 171, 171, 185,
    186
  themed 174, 176, 181
  Tintin 174, 176
  walls 158, 165, 166, 171, 178, 181, 182
  window treatments 160, 178, 182
chimneybreasts 53
coastal-style bathrooms 151
collage of images 171
collections
  displaying in the living room 65, 65,
    79

green-glazed pots 79
kitchens 40, 43
of mirrors *144*

colour
of the 20th century 82
accents of 39, *67*, 78, 87, 97, 113, 148, *205*, 227
for babies' rooms 160
bathrooms 136, *136*, 147, 148, 151, 153
bedrooms *93*, *96*, 97, *97*, 113, 117, 119, 120
boys' rooms 166, *166*
children's rooms 160, 165, *165*, 166, *166*, *174*, 178, 182
girls' rooms 165, *165*, 182
kitchens *11*, 14, *14*, 39, *39*, 40
living rooms 63, 67, *67*, *71*, 78, 81, 82, 84, 87, 88
modern country bedrooms 113
modern country living rooms 81
modern retro bedrooms 120
in monochrome living rooms 88
neutral palette *63*, *67*, 71, 85, 214, 217
open-plan living 213, 214, 217, 221, 222
outdoor living space 227, *227*, 235, 237
ultra-brights 178
concrete flooring 35, *75*, 151
conservatories 229
cooker hoods 19
cookers *13*, 27
cork flooring 35, 140, 151
cork noticeboard 158, 186, *191*
corner offices 197, *197*, 207
cot beds 163, *163*
cots 163
country kitchens *11*, *24*, *28*, *31*, 40, 47
curtains
babies' rooms 160
bathrooms 147
bedrooms *93*, 103, *103*, 117, 119
blackout 103
home offices 202
kitchens *13*, 32
living rooms 57, 71, *71*, 81
to make windows appear smaller or taller 57
as screens 197, 218
cushions
as an accent of colour 87
bedrooms *111*, 113, 114, 117, 119, 120
contrasting 68
floral *67*
in girls' rooms *165*, 182
gros-point 68
living rooms *53*, 67, *68*, 87
making 237
outdoor 227, 234, *235*, 237, 238
patterned *53*, *67*
rejuvenating a room 68
sequinned *68*
textured *68*

D

Danish lye 114
daybeds *53*, *62*, *67*, 227
decking *28*, 227, *227*, *232*, 237, 238
desk tidies 200
desks
bedrooms 99
children's rooms *156*, *158*, 166, 171, *171*, *172*, 185, 186, *197*
customizing 205
fold-down *191*
with integral storage 199
dimmer switches 32, 72, 160, 172, 202
dining areas
combined with kitchens *13*, *16*, *20*, *23*, *24*, *24*, 35, 47, 48
open-plan living 213, 214, 215, 217
outdoors 231, *231*, *233*, 237
dishwasher drawers *28*, *28*
dishwashers 24, 28
displaying objects
babies' clothes *160*
bathrooms *135*, *143*, *144*, 147, 151
bedrooms *108*, *111*
children's rooms *160*, 177
in groups 78, *79*
kitchens *11*, 32, *36*, *39*, 40, 43
living rooms 57, 65, *65*, 78, *79*, 87
open-plan living 221
overscaled items 205
shoes and handbags *108*
tablescapes 78
against a white background 87
doors *23*, 57
downlighters 32, 104, *139*
dressers *39*, 40
dressing tables 119
duvets 100

E

Eames 120
eclectic open-plan living 221
elegant living rooms 85

F

fabrics
20th-century design 82
bathrooms 147
bedrooms *103*, 113, 117, 119
to filter sunlight 202, 231
floral *103*, 113, 117, 147
luxury 119
mixing and matching *53*, *68*
old 68, 182
outdoor furniture 227
pink gingham 182
pink ticking 182
scale of the pattern 68
study areas *205*
using less expensive 68, 71
vintage *103*, 119
fairy lights 165, 172, 182
faucets *see* taps
filing cabinets *191*, 199, *199*
filing systems *199*, 200, 205
firepits 234

fireplaces 54, *54*, 57
floor lamps 72, *104*, 120, *217*
flooring
bamboo 140
bathrooms 125, *128*, 129, *135*, 136, 140, *140*, 147, 148, 151
bedrooms 107, *107*, 113, 114, 119, 120
children's rooms 158, 160, 166, 174, *174*, 178, 186
concrete 35, *75*, 151
cork 35, 140, 151
correcting uneven 75
defining work space 205
demarcating zones in open-plan living 215, 222
external and internal heights *229*
from indoors to outdoors 227, *229*
kitchens *34*, 35
linoleum 35, 140
living rooms 58, *67*, 75, *75*, 81, 85, 87, 88
mosaic *125*, *135*, 140
nonslip 129, *132*
open-plan living 215, *217*, 221, 222
outdoor terraces 227, 237
pebble 151
rubber 35, *174*, 186
seagrass/sisal 35, 75, *75*, 107, 151
slate *132*, 140
stencilling 166
stone *34*, 35, 140, 151
terracotta 35, *75*, 227
terrazzo *34*, *140*
tiled 81, 140
vinyl 35, 140, *174*, 186
visual tricks 107
wet rooms *132*, *133*
in white living rooms 87
wooden *217*
see also wooden flooring
flowers
bathrooms 144, *144*
bedrooms 110, *111*, 114
dried *79*
home offices 205
kitchens 39
living rooms 78, *79*, 85, 87
football table *58*
freeform offices 208
front porches 238
full-spectrum bulbs 202
furniture
20th-century design *63*, 82, 88, 120
antique shop counter *20*
armoires *20*, 40, 77, *109*, 119
arrangements in long thin rooms 57, *57*
bedrooms 98, *98*, *99*, 108, *109*, 113, 114, 117, 119, 120
chests 57, *62*, 77, *98*
children's rooms 157, *158*, 163, *163*, 166, *166*, 177, *177*, 178, 182
contemporary 87
distressed *177*
distressed bathroom 151
dressers *39*, 40
flat-pack 192
foldaway *191*

freeform home offices 208
garden rooms 229, *229*
glass-fronted cupboards *36*
home offices *191*, 192, *205*, 208
kitchens 20, 24, 32, *36*, 39, 40, 77
living rooms 54, 57, *57*, *61*, 62, *62*, 63, 77, *79*, 82, 87, 88
Lloyd Loom 233, 238
mixing styles and periods 81, 82, 208, *217*, 221
open-plan living *213*, 215, *217*, 221, 222
oversized country cupboard *24*
painted 87, 108, 114, 177, *177*, 186
painting pine 108
pink 182
purpose-designed television unit *61*
scale and proportion 54, 62, *62*, 229
vintage 221
vintage locker unit *177*
wardrobes *94*, 108, *108*, 120, 177
washstand, painted *79*

G

garden furniture 227, 231, *231*, 232–3, *232*, *233*, 238
in the living room *62*
maintenance 233, 237
metal 233, *233*, 237
garden rooms 229, *229*
garden sheds 192, 229
girls' rooms *157*, 165, *165*, 182
glass
20th-century design 82
specialist film for 229
worktops *31*
glass-fronted cupboard *36*
glasses, coloured *231*, 237
globes, illuminated 172
green-glazed pot collection 79
grout 140
grown-up glamour bedrooms 119
guitars *171*

H

halls 79
hammocks *171*, 234, *235*
handbags *108*
handles *94*
headboards 97, 98, 104, 117, 119
as room dividers *94*, 219, *219*
heating
bathrooms 126, 129, *132*, 140
kitchens 35
living rooms 57, 75, 77, 81
open-plan areas 215
outdoor 234
radiators 77, 81
Hicks, David 78
hobs 20, *20*, 27, 36
home offices
accessories *205*
corner 197, *197*, 207
design and decoration 191, *191*
display space 208
filing systems/cabinets *191*, 199, *199*, 200, 205

finishing touches 205, *205*
foldaway features *191*
freeform 208
on the landing *205*
lighting 202, *202*
in living rooms *63*
one-wall 207
planning 192, *192*
purpose-built 207
storage *194*, 199, *199*, 200, *200*, 208
window treatments 202
workstations *191*, 194, *194*, *197*, 199, *205*
hotel glamour bathrooms 153

I

industrial steel fittings 44
internet 27, 43, 75, 147
island units 13, 20, *23*, *24*, *32*, *34*, 48, *217*

J

jewellery 110, 119, *135*
jigsaw, foam *174*

K

kitchens
accessories *16*, 43
adapting an existing 14, *14*
Aga cookers 27, 32, 39
alfresco 231
appliances 11, *16*, 27, *27*, *31*, 40
brushed steel units 16, 19, 31, *31*, 44
on a budget 47
colour 11, 14, *14*, 39, *39*, 40
combined with dining areas 13, *16*, *20*, *23*, 24, *24*, *34*, 35, 47, 48
comfortable seating in 23, 48
cooker hoods 19
cookers 13, 27
country 11, *24*, 28, *31*, 40, 47
dark 32, *34*, 44, 47, 67
design and decoration 11, *11*
displaying objects 11, *32*, *36*, *39*, 40, 43
family 23, *23*, 48
finishing touches 39, *39*
fitted 16, *16*, 43, 47
fitted versus unfitted 16, *16*
flooring *34*, 35
furniture 20, *24*, 32, *36*, *39*, 40, 77
galley 19, *19*
hobs 20, *20*, 27, 36
iconic equipment 39
island units 13, 20, *23*, *24*, *32*, *34*, 48, *217*
L-shaped *16*, 19
large 20, *20*, 23
leading into a dining area 31, *34*, 47
lighting 23, 32, *32*
materials 31, *31*
narrow 14, 39
in open-plan living 217, *217*
ovens 20, 27, *27*, 36
as part of a living area 11, *11*, 16, 18, *19*, 20, 47

planning 13, *13*
plumbing 18, 28, *28*
ranges 11, 27, 40
replacing unit doors 14, 47
retro-style *13*, 43
small 18, 19, *19*, 23, 24, 28, 47
stainless-steel 27, 31, 44
storage *13*, 19, *20*, 24, 27, 36, *36*, 40, 48
tables 13, *16*, 20, *23*, 24, *24*, 47, 48
wall-hung cupboards 32
white *13*, *16*, *31*, 47
wooden 14, *16*, *31*, *34*, 40, 44
knife rack *36*

L

lace, vintage 119
lamps, clip-on *172*
lamps, freestanding 72
lamps, vintage *217*, 221
lampshades *97*, 117, 120, *205*
lanterns *235*
laundry baskets 147
Le Corbusier 62
lighting
Anglepoise lights 104, *104*, 172, 202
babies' rooms 160
bathrooms 139, *139*, 148
bedrooms *97*, 104, *104*, 113, 114, 119, 120
bedside lamps 104, 120
Castiglioni 120
children's rooms 160, 169, 171, 172, *172*, 185, 186
clip-on *172*
dimmer switches 32, 72, 160, 172, 202
displays 23, 32, *32*
downlighters *32*, 104, *139*
fairy lights 165, 172, 182
floor lamps 72, *104*, 120, *217*
full-spectrum bulbs 202
home offices 202, *202*
kitchens 23, 32, *32*
living rooms 72, *72*, *73*, 85, 87, 88
outdoor living space 227, 234, *235*
pendant lights 32, *32*, 72, 202
rope lights 104
table lamps 72, 85
tablescapes 78
uplighters 72, 104
vintage lamps *217*, 221
wall lights 32, 104, *104*, 139, 172, *172*
in wardrobes *108*
linoleum flooring 35, 140
living rooms
accessories 81, 85, 87
adapting an existing 57, *57*
books *61*, *63*, 77, *77*
collections and display 65, *65*
colour scheme *63*, 67, *67*, *71*, 78, 81, 82, 85, 87, 88
combined with work space *63*
cushions *53*, *67*, 68, *68*, 87
design and decoration 52, *52*, *53*
elegant 85
family 58, *58*, *59*
finishing touches 78, *78*, *79*

flooring *58*, *67*, 75, *75*, 81, 85, 87, 88
focal points 54, *54*
furniture 54, *54*, 57, *57*, *61*, 62, *62*, *63*, 77, *79*, 82, 87, 88
lighting 72, *72*, *73*, 85, 87, 88
long, narrow 57, *57*
masculine monochrome 88
modern country 77, 81
open-plan *213*, *214*, *215*, 217, *217*
planning 54, *54*
scale and proportion in 54, *54*, 62, *62*
soft furnishings 68, *68*, 81, 85
storage *57*, 58, *58*, 61, 77, *77*, 88
tables 62, *62*, *63*
technology in 61, *61*, 88
vintage-inspired 82
walls *67*, 82
white *75*, 87
window treatments 57, 71, *71*, 81
Lloyd Loom furniture 233, 238
locker unit *177*

M

magnetic boards 186
magnetic paint 158
mantelpieces 65
masculine living rooms 88
mattresses 100, 163
metal tables 233
mirrored cabinets *139*
mirrors
bathrooms 135, *144*
bedrooms *108*, *111*, 114, 119
collection *144*
gilded *79*
living rooms 77, *79*
outdoors 234
modern country bedrooms 113
modern country living rooms 77, 81
modern retro bedrooms 120
monochrome living rooms 88
mood boards 181
Moroccan tiles 237
mosaic
flooring *125*, *135*, 140
outdoor 237
walls *135*, *136*
murals 181

N

narrow rooms 57, *57*
night lights 172
noise 215
noticeboard 158, 186, *191*, 200, 208

O

open-plan living 213, *213*, *217*
colour *213*, *214*, 217, 221, 222
cooking, living and eating 213, *213*, *214*, *215*, 217, *217*
eclectic 221
flooring *215*, 217, 221, 222
furniture *213*, *215*, 217, 221, 222
materials *214*, 222
partitioning rooms *94*, *214*, *215*, 218–19, *219*, 222

pros and cons 214–15, *214*, *215*
sleeping, dressing and bathing *94*, 218–19, *218*
slick and streamlined 222
ornaments 110
ottomans 77
outdoor living space 23, 227, *227*
accessories 234, *235*
colour 227, *227*, *235*, 237
on the deck 238
dining 231, *231*, *233*, 237
garden rooms and conservatories 229, *229*
lighting 227, 234, *235*
Mediterranean style 237
see also garden furniture
ovens 20, 36
built-in 27, *27*
overscaled objects 24, 205, *229*

P

paint
in bathrooms 148, 151
exterior masonry 237
floor 75, 107
in kitchens 14
in modern country living rooms 81
in white living rooms 87
parasols 234, *235*
pebble flooring 151
pendant lights 32, *32*, 72, *202*
pergolas 237, 238
photographs 48, 110
blown-up 205
plants *79*, 114
outdoor *227*, 229, 237, 238
plumbing 28, *28*, 126

Q

quilts, patchwork *100*

R

radiators 77, 81
ranges 11, 27, 40
refrigerator drawers 27
refrigerators 27, 40
retro-style kitchens *13*, 43
Rohe, Mies van der 62
roller blinds/shades 178, 182
garden rooms 229
Roman blinds/shades
bedrooms 103, *103*, 113, 117
living rooms *71*
romantic floral bedrooms 117
roof terraces *231*, 233
room dividers *58*, *65*, 169, *169*, 192, 197
headboards as *94*, 219, *219*
open-plan living *94*, *214*, *215*, 218–19, *219*, 222
room temperature 160
rope lights 104
rubber flooring 35, 174, 186
rugs 205
bathrooms 151
bedrooms 107, 113, 114

bespoke 107
children's rooms 158, *158*, 160, *166*, 171, *174*, 178
demarcating zones in open-plan living *215*, 222
in dining areas *24*, 35
living rooms 75, *75*, 81, 85
outdoors 227
sheepskin 107, 113, 114, *158*, *166*

S

scale
of furniture in living rooms 54, *54*, 62, *62*
of patterns 68, 117
in small rooms 77
screens 110, *111*, 117, 192, 197
curtains as 197, 218
in open-plan living *214*, 218, *218*
outdoor 238
seagrass floor covering 35, 75, *75*, 107, 151
seating units *62*, 75
shade, outdoor 231
shade sail 231
shades *see* blinds
sheepskin 107, 113, 114, *158*, 166
sheets 100
shelves 36, *143*, *194*, *199*
adjustable *199*
coiled *160*
display 65, *65*, *108*, *135*
floating *77*, 98
metal *31*
see also bookshelves
shoe tidies 200
shoeboxes *200*
shoes and handbags *108*
shop counter, antique *20*
shower curtains 147, 148
shower mixers 147
shower rooms 135, *135*, *218*
showers
feature 153
outdoor 238
power 132
screens *125*
walk-in *126*, *130*
shutters *57*, *71*, 103, 148, 160
sinks 20, *24*, 28
butler's *28*, 147
copper *28*
enamelled *31*
stainless-steel *28*
sisal floor covering 35, 75, *75*, 107
skateboards *171*, 185
slate flooring 132, 140
slick and streamlined open-plan living 222
small rooms
flooring 107
mirrors *108*
scaling up 77
sofas
antique *62*, 68
covered with throws 57
elegant living rooms 85
kitchens 23, 48

masculine living rooms 88
mixing and matching fabrics on *53*, 68
modern country living rooms 81
open-plan living 222
scale and proportion 62
seating units *62*, 75
teen bedrooms 171
soft furnishings
bathrooms *128*
living rooms 68, *68*, 81, 85
loose covers/slipcovers 81, 85
sports equipment *58*, *171*, 185
stainless-steel
kitchen appliances 27
kitchen units 27, 31, 44
stairs, using space underneath *19*, *57*
steel fittings, industrial 44
stone
flooring *34*, 35, 140, 151
kitchens 40
outdoor paving 237
walls *16*, 72
storage
babies' rooms *160*, 163, *163*
bathrooms 126, *126*, *128*, 129, 135, *135*, *139*, 143, *143*
bedrooms 94, *94*, 98, *98*, 108, *108*, *109*, 110, 120
built-in wall of 27, *36*, *61*, *108*, *143*, *160*, *177*, *199*
built-in wardrobes *94*, 108, *108*, 120
children's rooms 158, 165, *166*, 169, 177, *177*, 185
DVDs and CDs 58, *58*
filing cabinets/systems 191, 199, *199*, 200, 205
home office storage containers *200*
home offices *194*, 199, *199*, 200, *200*, 208
kitchens *13*, 19, *20*, 24, 27, 36, *36*, 40, 48
living rooms 57, 58, *58*, *61*, 77, *77*, 88
teen rooms 171, *171*, 186
wall of open *36*, *194*, *199*
storage containers *200*
storage unit, multi-tasking *177*
stoves *57*

T

table lamps 72, 85
tablecloths 227, *231*
tables
bathrooms *144*
bedside *96*, 98, *98*, *99*, *111*, 113, 119
children's 186
kitchen/dining *13*, *16*, *20*, *23*, 24, *24*, 47, 48, *215*, *217*
living rooms 62, *62*, *63*
outdoor 231, *231*, *233*
refectory *23*
tablescapes 78
tailor's dummy *111*
taps/faucets
bathrooms 129, 130, 147
kitchens 28, *28*, 47
tea lights *235*

technology 61, *61*, 88
bathrooms 153
teen rooms *156*, *166*, 171, *171*, 185, 186
televisions 54, 61, *61*
terraces, outdoor 227, 237, 238
terracotta flooring 35, *75*
outdoor living space 227
terrazzo flooring *34*, *140*
texture
bathrooms 148
bedrooms 93, 114
living rooms 67, *68*, 85, 87
in tablescapes 78
themed children's bedrooms *174*, *176*, 181
throws *53*, *57*, 81, 113, 120, 227
tiled floors 81, 140
Tintin themed room *174*, *176*
toilets 130
tongue and groove *31*, 151
toys, rotating 177
traditional style bathrooms 147
trees 229
trimmings 68, *68*
twig arrangement *79*

U

underfloor heating
bathrooms 126, 129, *132*, 140
kitchens 35
living rooms 75, 81
uplighters 72, 104
upstands *14*, 24

V

vegetable crates *200*
vegetable drainers 28
vintage
definition 82
fabric *103*, 119
furniture 221
lamps *217*, 221
vintage-inspired living rooms 82
vinyl flooring 35, 140, 174, 186

W

wall hangings 117, *217*
wall lights 32, 104, *104*, *139*, 172, *172*
wall stickers 166, 181
wallpaper
bathrooms *136*, 147
bedrooms *103*, *108*, 114, 117, 119, 120
children's rooms *165*, 178
home offices 205
kitchens 43
living rooms 67
outdoor 234
walls
bathrooms *135*, 136, *136*, 148, 151
children's rooms 158, 165, 166, *171*, 178, 181, 182
cleaning white paintwork 114
collage of images *171*
display space *171*, 208
feature 43, 136, 158, 178

hand-decorated *109*
knocking down 213
living rooms 67, 82
mosaic *135*, *136*
open-plan living 221, 222
painted pink 182
painting one 43, 82, 165, 182
stone *16*, 72
striped 67
trompe l'oeil painting 181
wardrobes *94*, 108, *108*, 120
children's 177
washbasins
built-in *126*
butler's sink 147
double 129
fabric skirts 147
glass *130*
wall-hung *130*, 135
washstand, painted *79*
wet rooms 132, *132*, *133*, 135
white
bathrooms 136, *139*, 148
bedrooms 97, *103*, *111*, 114
kitchens *13*, *16*, *31*, 47
living rooms 75, 87
wicker hamper *11*
windows
bay *53*, *71*
frosted film 103, 144, 202
tricks to appear smaller or taller 57
wood
kitchens *14*, *16*, *31*, *34*, 40, 44
tongue and groove *31*, 151
worktops *14*, 28, *28*
wooden flooring 67, 227
advantages 75
bathrooms *128*, 140, *140*, 148, 151
bedrooms 107, *107*, 114
children's rooms 166, 174, 178
complementing white rooms 75
Danish lye 114
kitchens *34*
limed 148
living rooms 58, *67*, 75, *75*, 81, 85, 88
open-plan living *217*
painted 75, 107, 114, *128*, 174, *217*
polished *75*
reclaimed 75
renovating 75
reproduction 75
stencilling 166
whitewashed 148
workstations *191*, 194, *194*
in a cupboard 199
on landings *205*
quirky *197*
worktops, kitchen *13*
additional features 20
granite *28*
marble *31*
toughened glass *31*
wooden *14*, 28, *28*